NEW ZEALAND ARMY INVOLVEMENT,
SPECIAL OPERATIONS AUSTRALIA

VNZ 422668 Sgt F.A. Wigzell, 'Z' Special Unit. AKS 173, S.O.A.

New Zealand Army Involvement

Special Operations Australia
South-West Pacific World War II

Francis Alexander Wigzell – AKS 173

The Pentland Press
Edinburgh – Cambridge – Durham – USA

First published in 2001 by
The Pentland Press Ltd
1 Hutton Close
South Church
Bishop Auckland
Durham
manuscripts@pentlandpress.co.uk
sales@pentlandpress.co.uk
www.pentlandpress.co.uk

ISBN 1-85821-815-2

Typeset in Bell 11 on 13
by Carnegie Publishing
Carnegie House
Chatsworth Road
Lancaster
www.carnegiepub.co.uk

Printed and bound by
Antony Rowe Ltd
Chippenham

Special Operations Australia
Allied Intelligence Bureau
'Z' Special Unit
(Cover name for S.O.A.)

This book is dedicated to the 22 members of the 2 NZEF personnel seconded to 'Z' Special Unit SOA (AIF), and their missions into Japanese occupied Borneo by the following methods.

Parachute
B–24 Liberator (USA) – 200 Flight RAAF

Submarine
USS Tantalus, USS Tuna USS Perch

Snake-boat
40-ft Aust-built copy of Jap fishing boat

Workboat
US PT Boat

Auster
US single-engine aircraft

Flying-Boat
US Catalina (PBY)

Folboats
Similar to two-man kayaks.

Contents

Foreword

Special Operations Australia

It is true that history tends to repeat itself and there would seem today to be many similarities between the present state of Special Warfare planning in Australia and that pertaining in the early 1940s. There are, of course, obvious differences in that perception of the potential enemy has changed, a major war is not envisaged, and low-level operations at short notice the most probable type of action that will be required.

Major General C.H. Finlay CB, CBE who was commander of Z Special Unit for a period in 1944 and early 1945 and later Director of Military Intelligence, has written of those early days:

> Prior to the entry of Japan into World War II the extent to which that country had the capacity to overrun and occupy territory in the South East Asia was very greatly under-estimated, and as a result, plans for 'left behind parties' and nuclei of resistance groups in such eventuality were not prepared. Further, before the war very little intelligence material on the territories occupied had been collected and collated, much less disseminated with the result that we had little knowledge of possible landing areas, the composition of gradients of beaches, the 'going' nature of beach hinterlands and so on, all vital information should we be required to land and recapture those areas as future planning could possibly have dictated. The situation in occupied South East Asia had some similarity with occupied Europe but also some very major differences particularly in the wealth of intelligence available to the Allies in Europe as against our lack of it, and the racial homogeneity of all combatants and occupied nations in Europe against our position, with the occupying enemy and the occupying nations all Asiatic in origin as against the Allies being almost completely European Caucasian in racial origin.

The basic objectives of special operations were, however, the same in both theatres, namely:

(a) to foster and support the spirit of resistance in the occupied nations.

(b) to discourage collaboration with the occupying forces.

(c) to establish and maintain intelligence networks in the occupied territories.

(d) where the opportunity offered, to damage and disrupt the enemy's war effort.

In pursuit of these broad objectives the Services Reconnaissance Department (SRD), of which Z Special Unit was the administrative core, inserted some 81 parties into Japanese occupied countries during World War II. These missions covered a broad spectrum of unconventional warfare, from small specialised one night reconnaissance and sabotage raids of the Special Boat Service (SBS) type, to the larger inland fighting and intelligence patrols of which the British Special Air Service (SAS) were the originators in Europe and the Middle East which could be in the field for several weeks or months. Finally, and of greater value to the regular forces, SRD undertook the formation and training of guerrilla bands in occupied territories to provide pre-invasion intelligence for the A.I.F. and close tactical support during and after the assault phase. After this was added the maintenance of civil and administration order in the interior until a civilian government could take over. As the Australian offshoot of the British Special Operations Executive (SOE) this para-military organising of local resistance was the role of which SRD has been preparing throughout the previous years of bitter frustration and of employment on tasks for which we were not really intended. It was the final justification for our troubled existence, so often the target of attacks.

However we in SRD had one great advantage denied to our fellow practitioners of Special Warfare in the United Kingdom and the Middle East. There the British genius (or aberration if you prefer it) for eccentricity coupled with one-upmanship had resulted in the formation of private armies, often created and commanded by romantic individualists. These competed with each other for men, stores, and operational transport and their obsession with secrecy and inter-unit jealousies often resulted in duplication of effort and wastage of scarce resources. We in SRD were organised to carry out the roles of SBS and SAS, and the para-military tasks of SOE under one Commanding Officer and staff directly responsible to the C-in-C AMF and for operational policy to GHQ South West Pacific Area (SWPA) through the Allied Intelligence Bureau.

It is interesting to learn that the tasks of the modern SASR are similar to those which we were faced with fifty odd years ago and as diverse. It is encouraging to know that the planning and execution of these tasks are also centralised under one headquarters as were ours, and it is to be hoped that this concentration of command can be applied throughout Special Forces, with consequent economy of effort and efficient co-ordination of operations.

While equipment has changed in the interim period the basics of special operations have remained much the same, subject as always to laws of the wind, water, topography, and human limitation. It is valuable to examine the tasks laid down for the modern SAS in light of the experiences of its fore-runner SRD, and the lessons that may be learned from them. The gathering of intelligence through reconnaissance on land was rarely satisfactory in the SWPA as SRD parties were generally composed of white faces among a brown population and, in mainly agricultural societies, they were easily and quickly detected. Where the population was not actively hostile it often had been cowed by enemy brutality and hastened to give our operations away to the Japanese. Even if they were able to exist unbetrayed our general lack of fluency in the local language and reliance on native English speakers, possibly of doubtful loyalty and competence, made the acquisition of accurate and useful information extremely difficult. Intensive language courses during pre-operational training were better than nothing but the re-cruitment of Malay pearl divers from Broome in the latter stages of the war provided the best answer. They not only generally made good soldiers but could usefully be sent into native villages to gather information and not be easily detected by the enemy.

Surveillance was effective only where the existence of the party could remain undetected by local inhabitants. This was easier to accomplish for a standing patrol observing from afar movement on an airfield or in a port or on a shipping lane than for a reconnaissance patrol on the move. The difficulty here was the limited period that they could remain in a place without re-supply by submarine or aircraft, both of which could reveal their presence in the area. It was a fallacy to believe that soldiers could live off the land and remain efficient.

SRD also provided canoe (folboats similar to modern-day kayaks) pairs to travel in U.S. submarines to attack Japanese merchant shipping at anchor, for island reconnaissance in the South China Sea, and for sabotage on coastal railways in French Indo-China (now Vietnam). Successful or not these activities would have caused the enemy to divert men and materials as a safeguard against future attacks. Best known among seaborne raids was the successful attack on Japanese shipping in Singapore harbour in September 1943 by an SRD party from Australia, which sailed there and back in an old Japanese fish-storage ship renamed HMAS Krait, proving thereby that a vessel suitably adapted or constructed to blend with the local scene could operate successfully deep inside enemy controlled waters: a conclusion that was later developed for SRD in the form of 'country craft'.

In March and April 1945 three intelligence parties were dropped by parachute from RAAF Liberators into tribal country in the interior of

Sarawak. They were commanded by British Officers who had served or spent time in the country in various civilian capacities before the Japanese invasion and were familiar with the language and customs of the people. They were received with enthusiasm by the tribes of the interior, who were bitterly opposed to the Japanese after three years of shortage and oppression, and proceeded to penetrate down the river valleys towards the coast, training and arming the already warlike natives in preparation for full-scale attacks against the enemy in support of the eventual invasion by Australian forces. They were able to provide much pre-invasion tactical intelligence for 1 Australian Corps by whom, unfortunately, their potential use was not always appreciated. However, the assault on Labuan and Brunei Bay by the 9th Australian Division on 10 June 1945 was the signal for an all-out guerrilla offensive against the Japanese forces concentrated near the coast, and this unexpected threat from the rear had the effect of discouraging the Japanese from their usual reaction, which was to counter-attack invading troops before they could become established.

We were fortunate in Sarawak and British North Borneo (now Sabah) in that we had no indigenous local government, as there was in Vietnam, to complicate matters with vested interest, corruption, and political intrigue. We were also fortunate that the local population was mainly friendly, and their friendship was cemented by a policy of bringing medial treatment to all communities with which SRD operatives were involved. However simple this treatment was from the hands of non-medical personnel it was greatly appreciated by people who had been deprived of any for three years. Each operative carried a basic medical pack which was essential also for his own needs in a land where malaria, dysentery, and tropical sores were endemic.

During the early days SRD faced an uphill task in recruiting and training personnel from a reluctant military establishment which had no conception of special operations and little sympathy for such an unconventional mode of warfare. There was much prejudice from the regular forces, mostly because of ignorance about what we were supposed to be doing. This was partly our own fault as we tended to be mysterious and indulge in too much secrecy. This was unfortunate as there was an inclination by Australian staffs to undervalue our contribution and for American GHQ to regard us with suspicion and seek to control our activities as irrelevant to their long-term interests. Luckily we possessed a 'Big Daddy' in the person of General Blamey who time and again saved us from extinction, or absorption by the Americans.

Finally, I am quite convinced that the planning and execution of special operations in war is best carried out at all stages by officers experienced, or at least fully trained, in the peculiar rules which govern unconventional warfare, not the least of which is the realisation that nothing in it ever goes by the book. Special operations are different, and special operatives are different, being mostly self-sufficient individuals with a well developed critical faculty and a poacher's mentality. General Lord Slim, one-time Governor General of Australia, has written, 'There is one kind of special unit which should be retained, that designed to employ in small parties, usually behind the enemy, on tasks beyond the normal scope of warfare in the field.' He would have been a good 'Big Daddy'.

G.B. Courtney Lt/Colonel (RL)

The reader may be curious about my competency for the task of writing this Foreword. I was a Regular Officer in the British Army serving with the Special Boat Section of the Army Commandos on pre-invasion amphibious operations in the western Mediterranean in 1942 and 1943. In early 1944 I was transferred to SOE Ceylon and, in July, joined SRD in Melbourne as a G2 (Plans). In March 1945 I joined Advanced HQ of SRD in Morotai and became Officer Commanding Group A of SRD with HQ 9th Division in Labuan with responsibility for the control of SRD parties in Sarawak and British North Borneo. I returned to England in 1946 and emigrated to Australia ten years later. Since 1981 I have been carrying out research into these little known operations in London, Washington, Canberra, and Melbourne and have also been able to record many of my reminiscences with my old comrades in SRD. I published in 1993 *Silent Fleet* as a contribution towards Australia's military history of SOA.

New Zealanders Seconded to 'Z'

Services Reconnaissance Department & 'Z' Special Unit – cover names in the South-West Pacific for 'Special Operations Australia' during the Second World War – allocated all their operatives with special security numbers at the end of the war. The following is an identification of the alphabetical letters used, plus the codes of members of the 2 NZEF who were selected and seconded to the above units.

AK	Operatives – Army and Civilian
AKN	Navy Personnel including Operatives
AKO	Ordinance
AKQ	Female Staff
AKR	Air Force Personnel including Operatives
AKS	Signals including Operatives
AKV	Instructional and Camp Staff
AKX	Headquarters Staff – Army and Civilian

AK	198	VNZ549709	Sgt	P.J. Boyle
AKS	174	VNZ271450	Sgt	W.J. Butt
AKS	177	VNZ441420	Sgmn	A.J. Campbell
AKS	172	VNZ233068	Cpl	G.R. Edlin
AKS	175	VNZ45794	Sgmn	N. Flemming
AKS	179	VNZ452668	S/Sgt	G. Greenwood MID.
AK	260	VNZ275480	Cpl	J.K. Harris
AKS	181	VNZ76162	Sgt	W. Horricks
AKS	182	VNZ444165	WOII	R.G. Houghton
AK	256	VNZ66570	Lt	F.J. Leckie
AK	258	VNZ64785	Capt	L.T. McMillan
AK	259 (SOE)	VNZ22884	Lt	R.M. Morton MC, DCM
AKS	176	VNZ616204	Sgmn	E.H. Myers
AK	153	VNZ636815	Sgt	R.J. Newdick
AKO	447 (SOE)	VNZ31763	WOII	L.N. Northover MM
AKS	178 (SOE)	VNZ412556	Sgt	R.B. Shakes(RNZAF)
AKS	180	VNZ446826	Sgt	V.E. Sharp
AK	257 (SOE)	VNZ20681	Maj	D.J. Stott DSO/Bar
AK	253	VNZ280669	Lt	R. Tapper
AKS	173	VNZ422668	Sgt	F.A. Wigzell

On searching the records of the unit code numbers on 6 December 1991 the following two members names appeared on the document.

| AKX | 102 | VNZ635600 | Maj | J.K.L. Brown |
| AK | 223 | VNZ325731 | Lt | A.G. Palmer |

Summary Composition of the Special Operations Personnel in 'Z' Special Unit at the End of the War

Total Personnel at the end of the War   1704

Operatives trained   550

Operatives who saw action   380

Total number who parachuted into operational areas (2 NZers)   78

Australians in force (incl 59 female members, W/T & Cipher in Aust)   1251

UK, New Zealand and South African   353

F.A.N.Y.   35

British Civilians   29

Dutch, Portuguese, Timorese, Indonesians   36

Operatives in the Field on 31 August 1945

Australians (185 Army, 68 Navy, 5 RAAF)   258

British (33 Army, 18 Navy)   51

New Zealanders   12

Canadian   2

Netherlands (NEI), East Indies   3

Civilians (Portuguese & Timorese)   6

'Z' Special Casualties

KIA (Executed or Missing)   112

POW (Recovered)   8

Total: 120

Enemy Battle Casualties

Japanese Killed   1846

Japanese POW   249

Total: 2095

HONOUR ROLL on reverse side of memorial at Garden Island.

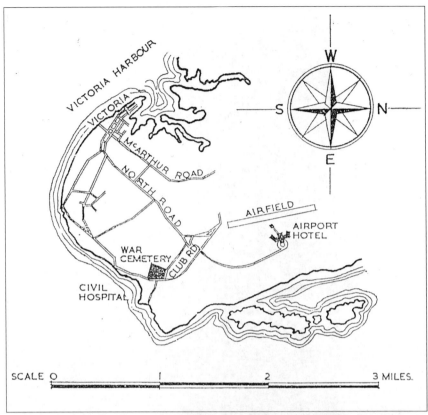

Labuan War Cemetery, Labuan Island – North Borneo, Location Plan.

SURRENDER POINT, LABUAN ISLAND CEMETERY
Unknown Soldier's grave, probably from the Sandakan-Ranau death march.
1,800 AIF & 600 British POWs were involved, <u>5 SURVIVED</u>

Left: ROCKINGHAM
CHURCH W.A.
Stained-Glass window in
honour of Services
Reconnaissance
Department.

Below: PLATYPUS 7.
Balikpapan-Semoi-Mt
Mentawir area – 30 June
1945.

Introduction to 'Z' Special Unit SOA

In July 1940, after the fall of France and the evacuation of the British Army, the Special Operations Executive (SOE) was formed in Great Britain – in the words of Winston Churchill: 'to set Europe ablaze'. Its broad objective was to foster passive and active resistance to enemy occupation forces by the inhabitants of countries which were overrun. The method to be used ranged from non-cooperation, industrial sabotage, ambushes, and guerrilla warfare, to the training of secret armies. It had been under study since 1938 but SOE virtually started from scratch and had to learn from bitter experience, and against much prejudice, as it went along. Throughout the war it increased in effectiveness as the shock of defeat began to wear off in the occupied countries, and as the will to resist therein became stronger. Its period of greatest vindication came during the Allied landings in France in June 1944.

Meanwhile, with the British war effort concentrated in Europe and North Africa little preparation for SOE activities was undertaken in South-East Asia, and none at all in the South-West Pacific Area. A training school was established near Singapore in July 1941 but the organisation of stay-behind parties was actively discouraged by the civil and military authorities, so as not to alarm the local inhabitants by implying that Singapore was not impregnable and Malayan forests impenetrable.

Both these illusions were rapidly and ruthlessly dispelled by the speed and penetration of the Japanese advance through South-East Asia in July 1942, and in March of that year, the formation of an offshoot of SOE in Australia was proposed by General Blamey, C-in-C Australian Military Forces, and approved by General MacArthur as the Allied Theatre Commander. At SOE Headquarters in London this organisation was known as SOA (Special Operations Australia) but for reasons of security was given the cover name of IASD (Inter Allied Services Department) known as ISD for short. All Australian service personnel in it were to be administered by a holding unit, specially created in June 1942, called 'Z Special Unit', by which name it is more commonly known in Australia and New Zealand. A few SOE-trained British officers who had escaped from Singapore became the nucleus of ISD, with headquarters in Melbourne. They faced an uphill task in recruiting and training officers and men from a reluctant military establishment which had no concept of the nature of special operations, and little sympathy for such an unconventional mode of warfare. This attitude was echoed in GHQ SWPA (South-West Pacific Area) among senior American operational and intelligence staff who, in addition, did not intend to allow independent action by any foreign intelligence organisation in an area which they now regarded as a solely American sphere of interest. In order to control and coordinate the sometimes maverick tendencies of the British and Dutch intelligence agencies then operating in Australia, GHQ SWPA formed the Allied Intelligence Bureau (AIB) in June 1942, with a senior Australian army officer as Controller and an American army officer as his Deputy or Finance Officer. GHQ suspected, not unreasonably, that the British and Dutch were more interested in regaining their colonial territories, of which they had been deprived by the Japanese, than in furthering MacArthur's plans for the recapture of the Philippines and for eventual hegemony in the Western Pacific. In a post-war history of the AIB, written by the American Finance Officer concerned, it was frankly admitted that: 'With an American Finance Officer, GHQ still had indirect but vital control, without his approval any proposed operation would die from financial anaemia.'

As a fledgling organisation, hampered by the lack of trained men, stores, and long-range transport, ISD was able to mount one intelligence operation of any significance during 1942 – that into Portuguese Timor in support of the Australian Independent Companies. In addition eight intelligence parties were sent into Dutch-Indonesian territory in Australia's Near North using a majority of Dutch and Dutch-Indonesian personnel. These had little or no success as six of the parties were betrayed to the Japanese and captured – a foretaste of the disasters to come. However, by December 1942 AIB had become fully operational and itself assumed direct control of the Netherlands-East Indies sub-section.

By March 1943 relations with AIB had become so bad that the British Commanding Officer of ISD was replaced by GHQ SWPA with another SOE officer from London, and the unit itself was reformed as the 'Services Reconnaissance Department' (SRD). Intelligence parties were inserted during the year into New Guinea and Portuguese Timor, but operations further afield were prevented by the lack of long-range transport. The only exception was made by GHQ in the case of an intelligence party sent in October by US submarine to a point on the coast of north-east Borneo to report on Japanese shipping using the Sibutu Passage, and to maintain contact with US supported guerrilla parties in the Southern Philippines.

The year 1943 was one of frustration, trial and much error. Conditions governing special operations in the SWPA were found to be very different from those experienced in Europe and many pre-conceived ideas had to be modified or abandoned. Sabotage targets were few and far between and anyway of no interest to GHQ. To foster local resistance in enemy-occupied territories it is essential to have the goodwill and cooperation of the inhabitants. This was notably absent in the Dutch colonies, and elsewhere by 1943 the population had generally become too cowed by Japanese brutality to assist SRD parties in any way, and often were actively hostile.

To expect a small party of white soldiers in uniform, speaking few or any words of the local language, to collect accurate and useful tactical intelligence, was to expect the impossible. A static observation post overlooking an anchorage, strait, or aerodrome, and concealed in the jungle, was sometimes productive of useful information, but only when all contact with natives could be avoided – not easy for a party of white men among a brown population. SOE forgot that their operatives in the European theatres of operation could hide behind the colour of skin of the population domiciled in that area. We in the South-West Pacific could not even hide behind a blade of grass.

However, there was one bright spot during the year. In August 1942 Major Ivan Lyon of the Gordon Highlanders, a keen small-boat sailor with an intimate knowledge of the waters to the south of Singapore, had arrived in Australia with a plan for attack against Japanese shipping in Singapore harbour, to be known as Operation Jaywick. This area was within the operational responsibility of the C-in-C India and outside that of GHQ SWPA so the latter, though kept informed, was not involved in the planning and execution of the project. Because of poor security in India and the Japanese vigilance in the western approaches to Singapore, SOE's India Mission asked ISD, and later SRD, to undertake the training, manning, equipment and despatch of the expedition to its target. An old Japanese motor vessel previously based on Singapore and employed as a fish carrier, which had lately been used to rescue evacuees from Sumatra, was shipped to Australia from India as deck cargo to carry Jaywick to the area. It was aptly renamed the 'Krait' after a small but highly venomous Asian snake. 'Krait' was a wooden vessel about 70 feet long with a maximum speed of about 6½ knots and a range of 8,000 miles.

Serious engine trouble delayed the departure of the 'Krait' from Australia and it was not until 2 September of the following year that she sailed from Exmouth Gulf, bound for the South China Sea through the Lombok Strait. Jaywick was led by Ivan Lyon in person and consisted of four Britons and eleven Australians, most of the latter being naval ratings.

Souvenir photograph of Historic Vessel 'Krait'. Manned by Australian 'Z' Special Unit Troops sank 38,000 tons of Japanese shipping in a wartime raid on Singapore Harbour, September 1943.

To cut a long and fascinating story sadly short, 'Krait' lumbered along unobtrusively through the Java Sea towards the Rhio Archipelago just South of Singapore and during the night of 26/27 September three officers and three ratings paddled three frail rubber and canvas canoes (folboats) and sank or damaged some 38,000 tons of Japanese merchant shipping lying at anchor in the Roads by attaching limpet mines to their hulls. Lyons was observed in his folboat by a member of one boat and questioned as to what he was about. His immediate reply in Malay that he was a fisherman collecting bait apparently satisfied that person. Lingering in the harbour only long enough to observe the resultant explosions and furious reactions of the Japanese air and sea patrols, the six men paddled some 50 miles south to their rendezvous with the 'Krait' on 2 October. The whole party then sailed silently back the way they had come, arriving back at Exmouth Gulf on 19 October. They had a close shave in the Lombok Strait, but audacity must have brought its own luck because they were approached by a Japanese destroyer but inexplicably were unchallenged.

This necessarily summarised account of what was an epic among small-scale raids in the tradition of Drake and Hawkins cannot convey

4

Singapore, Straits Settlements, 1943. Members of Operation Jaywick, 'Z' Special Unit, Australian Services Reconnaissance Department, on board the MV 'Krait' en route for Japanese occupied Singapore where a successful raid was carried out on shipping in the harbour by means of limpit mines being attached to the underside of vessels by daring two-men crews in folboats. Here the men can be seen staining their bodies in preperation for the raid. Seen are: Lieutenant H.E. Carse, Royal Australian Volunteer Reserve (1); Able Seaman M. Berryman, Royal Australian Navy (2); NX19158 Lieutenant R.C. Page, Australian Imperial Force (3); 66175 Major I. Lyon, MBE, The Gordon Highlanders, Officer Commanding (4); Corporal A.A. Crilly, Australian Imperial Force (5); Able Seaman F.W. Marsh, Royal Australian Navy (6); Leading Telegraphist H.S. Young, Royal Australian Navy (7); Able Seaman A.W. Huston, Royal Australian Navy (8); Able Seaman W.G. Falls, Royal Australian Navy (9).

to the reader the anxieties experienced by these men in constant fear of challenge by Japanese patrols, or of betrayal by local natives met by chance. Nor can it describe the exhaustion of the canoe pairs battling against headwinds, rainstorms, and the adverse tides to drive their heavily laden canoes for hour after hour through choppy seas. Although the damage inflicted on the Japanese merchant shipping was small compared with that by US submarines, Jaywick was a tonic for Allied morale in the dark days, a loss of face for the Japanese, and a badly needed success for SOE in India and Australia.

A Close Call. Near midnight on 11 October 1943, 'Krait', returning with 'Z' Special Unit men of Operation Jaywick, the successful attack on enemy shipping in Singapore Harbour, sinking 38,000 tons, encounters, but is not challenged, by a Japanese Destroyer in Lombok Straight

For SRD 1944 was to be the year of greater activity but with mixed results, marred by continued frustration, and by strained relations with AIB and GHQ. In the latter part of the year, in support of the Allied plan to occupy Morotai in the Halmaheras as a stepping stone on the way to the Philippines, GHQ ordered SRD to establish an observation post to watch Japanese air and shipping movements from an island off the northern tip of Dutch New Guinea, as well as a fighting patrol to watch enemy movements on the mainland further to the east. Both were eventually safely withdrawn after carrying out their tasks successfully.

The intelligence party which had been sent to the coast of north-east Borneo in October 1943 had established a successful coast-watching network but came under increasing Japanese pressure in the New Year and, after great hardship and some casualties, was withdrawn in June 1944 by a US submarine following three abortive attempts at evacuation. However, this experience did not persuade the American commanding the US submarines based at Fremantle of the value of carrying SRD pairs of canoeists in his submarines for missions against targets of opportunity. Six pairs were to operate usefully from various US submarines as part of the crew till May 1945 when the fleet base had moved to Subic Bay in the Philippines.

In addition to these encouraging and constructive activities SRD was asked by SOE India (Force 136) to help with the insertion in October 1944 from a submarine, of an intelligence party into south-east Malaya and to provide training, some stores, and a ferry party to take it ashore. Owing to aggressive enemy action offshore, the ferry party was marooned unhappily for four and a half months, but was later evacuated to Ceylon.

In warfare, as in every form of human activity, you win some and you lose some – 1944 was to see a series of operations in Portuguese Timor which demonstrated what can only be described as criminal inefficiency on the part of SRD headquarters in Melbourne. Voltaire, famous French philosopher of the eighteenth century, has written: '**We owe respect to the living; to the dead we owe only truth**', a sentiment which a historian should follow, but these days with due regard to the laws of libel.

In July 1943 an intelligence party consisting of Portuguese and Timorese was landed on the south-east coast of Portuguese Timor and was joined a month later by an Australian Sergeant from SRD to act as wireless operator. In the five months that had elapsed since the departure of the last ISD party, Japanese reprisals against local natives who had helped the Australians had reversed their previous friendly reception of Europeans. Most tribesmen and the party were betrayed and hunted down. Captured at the end of September 1943 they were subjected to prolonged brutality and torture until the Australian signaller had been finally beaten into operating his radio set, reopening communications to SRD HQ with messages from the Japanese, in his own cipher. Although uneasy at certain inconsistencies and delays, SRD HQ gave the matter the benefit of the doubt, arranging with them to meet a second party when it landed on the coast at the end of January. This party was duly captured intact shortly after arriving in a naval motor launch, and the leader was subjected to the same treatment as his predecessor, being forced to communicate and transmit messages in cipher to SRD HQ. Despite his deliberate omissions of his authenticator word SRD did not apparently detect anything wrong, and continued to drop stores to both parties by parachute and conduct a lively exchange of signals. In August 1944 a third party was intercepted, captured and killed after its intended area of operations was disclosed in a signal some months previously. Local native scouts had been alerted by the Japanese to watch for its arrival.

In March 1944 the crowning folly was committed by SRD HQ when signals were sent to both parties, now for some time under Japanese control, revealing that an intercepted and deciphered signal from Timor to Tokyo had been received announcing that one of them had been captured, and congratulating the party leader on having escaped. This erroneous assumption derived from a reply to a challenge in a signal sent to SRD HQ, which reply contained the right authenticator word, in any case already known to the Japanese. The attitude of the latter towards these signals was one of plain disbelief. They told one captured party leader that their cipher could not possibly be cracked, and even if it could, Australia would not be stupid enough to send such information to the field.

SRD's relations with AIB had been steadily deteriorating for some time and one must assume that these flagrant breaches of enormously important Sigint secrecy would have provided GHQ with sufficient grounds, those of SRD's dangerous irresponsibility, to bring the organisation under complete and strict control of the AIB, possibly with the elimination of the British element. In the delicate state of inter-Allied relations in the Far East at that period of the war, it can be appreciated that the British and Australian interests would have been ill-served by revealing those serious breaches of security to AIB and GHQ to hush the matter up at all costs, even to the extent of holding the relevant records incommunicado until after the war. SRD continued to drop stores by parachute to both parties on a regular basis and appeared to give both of them the benefit of the doubt whenever their replies to signals gave rise to unease through the omission of an authenticator word when challenged, or when Japanese intercept gave cause for alarm. However, by April 1945 doubts about the two parties had become so strong that it was decided that the officers and signallers who were standing by to relieve them should be dropped in 'blind', one day earlier than announced so as to see whether or not they were under Japanese control. At the beginning of July one relief mission was dropped in, betrayed to the Japanese and captured. But the other officer was able to observe the party leader he was to relieve, waiting for him on the dropping zone surrounded by Japanese soldiers concealed in the scrub. After four days he was able to get a short report to Melbourne by radio, but he and his men were on the run for a further five weeks before he could be evacuated from the south-east coast by RAN motor launch.

Any speculation regarding the fate of SRD parties in Portuguese Timor over the last two years was to cease abruptly and finally on 12 August 1945 when signals were received from both of the original parties thanking SRD for their assistance and wishing them the best of health – signed 'Nippon Army'. There was one more signal, unofficial and not on file, to 'The SRD cipher lovelies' from the 'Sons of Nippon'.

The Rimau Mission into Singapore

It is said to be always darkest in the hour before the dawn and one final tragedy was to depress the spirits of SRD in the autumn of 1944, with the complete disappearance of the 23 officers and men of Operation Rimau. The success of Jaywick the previous year had suggested to SOE in London that native craft could be based within the perimeter of Japanese occupied islands for the purpose of carrying out sabotage raids, and inserting SO parties into the Malayan Peninsular, Siam and French Indo-China in support of Lord Louis Mountbatten's South-East Asia Command's (SEAC's) plans for invasion in 1945. To this end, it was planned to reconnoitre the Natuna Islands north of Singapore in the South China Sea, and carry out a repeat of Jaywick on Japanese shipping in Singapore Harbour. Four 66-ft trawlers under construction in Australian ports were requisitioned and preparations made to alter their appearance to that of a craft similar in outline to the native junk used extensively in Singapore waters. They were referred to as 'Country Craft' and were to be powered by a 225 HP marine diesel engine and armed with a concealed 20-millimetre Oerlikon gun. The plan to establish a base in the Natuna Islands was abandoned early in 1944 because of the build-up in resources in England before the invasion of Europe, but it was decided to go ahead with the attack on Singapore shipping. In the opinion of SRD's chief planning officer, expressed to all some years ago, this decision was taken mainly for political reasons, to demonstrate to the Asians, and to the Americans for that matter, that the Anglo-Australians were on the way back to be taken seriously. In this, the project had the wholehearted support of General Blamey.

Meantime Ivan Lyon, now a Lieutenant Colonel and awarded a DSO, had been in England testing a recently developed and highly secret miniature craft called the Motor Submersible Canoe (MSC, also known as the SB or 'Sleeping Beauty'). This vessel would enable an operative to approach his target stealthily and submerged, or only with his head above water. Rimau was intended as its first test under operational conditions. A number were brought to Western Australia for training purposes, their handling technique difficult to master, with many trainees developing claustrophobia and having to be returned to their units. It was planned to load fifteen SBs aboard a Country Craft, which was being modified in a Melbourne shipyard, for the voyage to Singapore. Although folboats were to be loaded as well, to be used for escape back to the forward base after the SBs had been scuttled following the attack on the shipping, they were not to be used in the final assult itself despite their reliability and suitability demonstrated during Jaywick the year before.

It had been made clear to Rimau before leaving Australia that the age of *Porpoise* and her size, unwieldy and vulnerable to attack in clear shallow water as she was, could make the date of her eventual return to pick them up after the attack a little uncertain, resulting in the detailing of another submarine to take her place when available. The pick-up had been provisionally arranged for the night of 8/9 November but, should this not take place, Rimau was to await for another thirty days, after which they should make their own plans to escape.

After the final departure of *Porpoise* for Australia from the DZ area on 30 September Rimau virtually disappeared from the face of the earth as far as an increasingly anxious SRD was concerned. There was no news from Intelligence sources of explosions in Singapore Harbour and no word of the party itself, despite the fact it had been equipped with two long-range radio sets.

It was not until the middle of January that a translation of an intercepted Japanese signal dated 15 October 1944 was received from the US sources revealing that Rimau had been discovered, and its members were being hunted throughout the islands. This arrived just in time for the cancellation of a rescue mission which was about to leave for the area in another British submarine.

It appears that Rimau sailed onwards towards the islands just south of Singapore in a captured Chinese junk, visiting the forward island base on the way and dropping off two men as the reinforcements for the conducting officer previously left there. Threading their way through the maze of islands they finally reached Kasu Island, about 12 miles south of Singapore, undetected, but they had the misfortune to anchor within sight of a Police coast-watching post. The interest of the Police was apparently aroused by the type of junk, unusual in these waters, and they came out in a launch to inspect her. Rimau opened fire and killed all in the launch except one man who managed to swim ashore.

Realising that the alarm was about to be given and that the whole area would be alive with Japanese air and sea patrols, it is believed that Lyon decided that the operation must be cancelled. It was very important that the top-secret MSCs should not fall into the hands of the enemy intact, so it was decided to scuttle the junk with all them inside, and escape in the folboat canoes through the islands to rendezvous with the submarine at Merapas Island.

The folboats were unpacked, assembled, and stored with food and water and the junk was sunk, presumably in deep water but the location unknown to us. One may speculate on what would have been decided if they had been provided with a custom-built and powerful Country Craft, as had been previously intended.

Japanese troops and auxiliaries, known as *hei-ho*, were quickly organised to scour the islands in landing craft. They caught up with the canoeists on about 16 October and Lyon and three companions were killed onshore on small islands fighting rearguard actions to enable the rest to escape. The Japanese caught up with the party again on 4 November at Merapas where one more member of Rimau was killed, then followed the remaining eighteen officers and men through the islands. Finally ten officers and men were captured and imprisoned at the Kempei Tai Singapore interrogation centre, awaited trial on a charge of espionage, which was conducted by a Japanese Military Court on 3 July 1945, were found guilty and beheaded four days later. Japanese intercepts in Washington archives reveal that instructions had been received from the Commander-in-Chief of the 7th Area Army as early as February, that the Rimau men were to be condemned to death.

Two books relating to Operations Jaywick and Rimau are as follows:

Mckie, Ronald (1960), *The Heroes*, Sydney: Angus & Robinson (folboat attack on Singapore Harbour 1943).

Ramsay Silver, Lynette (1991) *The Heroes of Rimau*, London (the second raid by sea on Singapore Harbour 1944).

In the interval between the surrender of Japan on 15 August 1945 and the arrival of British troops in Singapore on 5 September all records concerning the capture, interrogation, trial and execution of the Rimau prisoners had been destroyed, and even their very existence concealed. Their grave was discovered by the British authorities by accident, and the only evidence eventually obtained from the Japanese officers involved in the military court was concocted by those officers themselves, then in prison awaiting trial for war crimes. For lack of evidence against them from other sources Rimau was not included. (ALL THE ABOVE WAS RECORDED PRIOR TO 1990.)

The Ultimate Price

Despite Japanese claims that the Rimau men had been executed with full
Samurai ceremony, they were beheaded in exactly the same way as this
man, Sergeant L.G. Stiffleet of 'M' Special Unit, the intelligence branch of
AIB. Aitape, New Guinea, 24 October 1943. (AWM 101099)

The Ultimate Price

Sgt Len Stiffleeet 'M' Section Special Forces

This photograph (opposite) has become one of the most well-known of the Pacific Theatre of Warfare, as perhaps the only image depicting the execution of a Western prisoner of war.

Born in NSW Australia on 14 January 1916 he enjoyed all forms of sport. Was inducted into the Army in August 1940, and served with a searchlight unit at Richmond Airforce Base near Sydney. After three months service was released and resumed life as a civilian. In September 1941 he rejoined the Army and was posted to a signals section at Ingleburn where he completed a specialist signals course.

In September 1942, he volunteered for special duties and joined the ranks of 'Z' Special Unit, Special Operations Australia, Allied Intelligence Bureau. He proceeded to 'Z Experimental Station' at Cairns. Here he came in contact with a Dutch section of the unit, planning a mission to establish a 'Watching Station' in the mountains above Hollandia. Mission was code named 'Whiting'.

He volunteered to be the W/T operative of the party, consisting of two Netherlands NCOs and two Amborese privates from the Dutch Colonial forces. On 20 June 1943 the party embarked from Port Moresby en route to Bena Bena, central New Guinea by DC3 Dakota. They advanced on 21 January heading for Mt Hagen, travelling through the jungle over the next few months 1,100 km across the mountainous interior of New Guinea. Arrived at Lumi via the swampy valley of the River Sepik on 10 June – five months after leaving Port Moresby. A few days later they started the trek to their objective – Hollandia.

The Coast Watchers within the establishment of SOE 'Z', on 5 May 1943 became through administrative machinations recorded as being members of 'M' Special Unit.

In mid-September 1943, the Japanese garrison of Marines situated at Aitape received a report from friendly locals that Allied spies were now located in the mountains close to their Headquarters. Despite being warned by a friendly native that Operation Whiting had been compromised, the mission proceeded on towards Hollandia. About 20 September the two Netherlands personnel were ambushed just south of Hollandia. One was killed and the other escaped to warn the rest of the party. Siffleet encoded a report of the incident and transmitted it to Base HQ in Australia.

At Wantipi Siffleet's party were surrounded by 100 local supporters of the Japanese. He and his companions were captured, beaten and abused, then delivered to a Japanese outpost and exchanged for

Occupational currency and a roll or two of cloth. The commander of the area, Admiral Kamada, situated at Wewak, was informed of the capture of these prisoners. On 23 October Captain Noto, Kamada's Chief Staff Officer, reported that the prisoners were to be transported by barge to Aitape. Kamada gave instructions to the barge Captain that he inform the commander of the Marines at their destination, Aitape, 'That the prisoners be killed'.

Thus on 24 October 1943, before a crowd of jeering locals, Sgt Len Siffleet and the two Amborese privates were beheaded by three members of the Civil Service attached to the Marines. They were buried on the shore-line in a deep grave where they were executed. No trace was ever found of the grave site.

In 1943 the Army posted Sgt Siffleet missing whilst on operations. The Japanese responsible for the execution of this party stood trial and were sentenced to hang by a War Crimes Judge in 1946. A photograph of this execution was among twenty-two prints found by American troops at Hollandia, Dutch New Guinea in 1944. These were uncovered whilst deceased Japanese were being searched for intelligence information. The photograph shows Sgt Len Siffleet being bound and blindfolded on his knees seconds before he died, and is one of the most well-known of the Pacific War. It has been widely used by the Australian War Veteran's claims against the Japanese.

After the recovery of the photograph in 1944, it was originally incorrectly identified as being that of an American Airman and also as an Australian VC recipient William Newton, before confirmation naming the AMF soldier involved.

Translation of Rimau
Court Martial Documents

In January 1992 the author of this book received in the mail from Australia several documents and letters relating to Operation Rimau. The sender's name was not appended to the letter which gave the following information, 'Use this for your new book, for it has never been released in Australia to the best of my knowledge.' If this information had been known in 1991 it would certainly have changed the context of events recorded in many books on the operation.

Copy of Document

LJB/KB.

> *2 Aust. P. W. Contact & Enquiry Unit.*
> *A.I.F. SINGAPORE.*
> *8 Nov. 45*

To.
Lt. W.R. Smith. R.A.N.V.R.
Naval Intelligence.
Naval Office MELBOURNE.

1. *The attached is a translation of a Japanese Court Martial Proceeding held at Singapore on 3 July 45.*

2. *It has been considered that you will require this document for Intelligence records, and anything of a similar nature I am able to obtain during my tour of duty in this area, will be forwarded to you from time to time.*

3. *As a matter of interest, I am going on a tour of the "Rhiou" Group within the next day or two.*

> *Signed ... K. BEATIE ... Capt.*
> *(K. Beattie.)*
> SINGAPORE.

(2)

MISSING PERSONNEL OF CLANDESTINE PARTY FROM AUSTRALIA

1. *On the 11th September 1944, a party under the command of Lt. Col LYON*

which had set out from Australia on a sabotage mission to Singapore was reported missing in the Java sea. Investigations have been carried out to ascertain the fate of Lt. Col. LYON and his 22 men, and the following information is now available.

2.(a) *Some time in November, 1944 a party of about 35 British Officers and men from a certain submarine was seen by various Chinese fishermen boarding a tongkang in the water of Puloe Samboe. Plenty of firearms, ammunition, rubber boats and provisions were seen by them on board the tongkang. The men were badly disguised as Northern Indians. An attempt to land was forced at Puloe Samboe, but the Malay Policemen opened fire and many informed the Japanese. The party retreated from Puloe Samboe in rubber boats and destroyed the tongkang. They divided into two groups, one of 6 boats with 13 persons which headed for Sumatra whilst the remainder made for the Rhio Island.*

(b) *The Singapore Water Kempei Tai intercepted the party that were making for Rhio and a fierce struggle raged for 2 hours, after which, about 12 Officers and men were captured alive. The Japanese then killed 1 Lt/Cdr and 3 men on the shore of Regah Island and exposed their bodies to wild beasts. The remaining 8 survivors were taken back to the Headquarter of the Water Kempeitai in Singapore where they were tortured for 2½ months and later transferred to the Y.M.C.A. [Infamous Torture Chamber]*

(c) *The party that headed for Sumatra was also intercepted by the Water Kempeitai and about 17 British Officers and men were brought back to the Y.M.C.A. Some of these victims were known to have died from torture, but nothing is known of the rest who were still alive in July 1945.*

3. *A further report has been obtained from Singkep Island. It appears that in October or November, 1944, about 24 white soldiers landed on MAPUR Island, 6 of these were believed to have remained in the Rhio Archipelago, but the remainder moved south in December to Pompong Island where they split into 3 parties of about 6 each.*

(a) *The first party went to Temlang and thence to PENUPA SELEAR where they were captured by the Japanese Navy with the help of the locals. One was shot and buried at SELEAR, 1 died at sea and 4 were handed over to the Kempeitai at Singkep.*

(b) *The second party went to BOEIA where they were captured by the Kempeitai and Malay Police. One died while trying to escape at sea and the other 5 including 1 wounded in the shoulder were brought to Singkep.*

(c) *The third party went to SEPANGKA, but no information is available about their further movements.*

4.*(a)* *The Malay Police at Singkep Island has produced a slip of paper on which are written the names :*

Capt. CAREY
W.O. WARREN
Able Seaman MARSH
All three men are from Lt. Col. LYON'S Party.

(b) *The Singkep Police Station Admission Book shows that between the period of 18th and 20th December, a total of 9 white soldiers were admitted and subsequently removed to Singapore. The following names are shown in this record*

WALKER GORDON TAYLOR (?)
Capt. ROLAND BERNARD (?) Australians
DAVID PETER (?)
Sgt. ROBERT CHAPS (?)
Major R.M. INGLETON (Royal Marines)

Of the above only M. INGLETON was a member of Lt. Col. LYON's Party.

It may, however, be that the other men (? names) given by the prisoners were false.

SINGAPORE.   (Signed) L.F.G. PRITCHARD

13 Oct. 45.   LT. COL.

L.F.G.P. Tan.   O.C. 'E' GROUP SOUTH.

TRANSLATIONS OF PROCEEDINGS OF MILITARY COURT OF 7th AREA ARMY

Reginald Middleton INGLETON   *Major. R.M. 26 Years of age*

Born at No. 3 Richmond Rd. Wenstead London
Belonging to : No. 35 Detachment, Royal Marines

Robert Charles PAGE. Captain. Australian Imperial Forces.   *24 Yrs. of age.*

Born at Sydney New South Wales. AUSTRALIA.
Belonging to 'Z' Special Unit. AUSTRALIAN ARMY.

Walter George CAREY. Captain A.I.F.   *31 Years. of age.*

Born at Canberra City .
New South Wales. AUSTRALIA.
Belonging to the Brisbane Office of the Services Reconnaissance
Department of the AUSTRALIAN ARMY.

Albert Leslie SARGENT. Lieutenant A.I.F.   *25 years of age*

Born at No. 85 Templeton St. Wangarata, Victoria, AUSTRALIA
Belonging to the 2/14 Australian Infantry Battalion.

Alfred WARREN. W.O.I A.I.F.   *32 Years of age.*

Born at Port Billy, SOUTH AUSTRALIA
Belonging to the Services Reconnaissance Department, AUSTRALIAN ARMY

Clair Mack STEWART, Sergeant A.I.F.   *35 Years of age.*

Born at Southern Cross Town, WEST AUSTRALIA.
Belonging to Services Reconnaissance. AUSTRALIAN ARMY.

Ronald Bernard FLETCHER. Sergeant A.I.F.   *29 Years of age*

Born at Dublin, IRELAND
Belonging to 'Z' Special Unit. AUSTRALIAN ARMY.

David Peter COOLEY, Sergeant A.I.F.   *27 Years of age.*

Born at Carran Town. Victoria, AUSTRALIA
Belonging to Services Reconnaissance Department, AUSTRALIAN ARMY.

John Thomas HARDY, Corporal A.I.F.   *23 Years of age.*
Born at Naraburi Town.
New South Wales, AUSTRALIA.
Belonging to 'C' Company, Australian Ist. Parachute Battalion.

Walter Gordon FALLS. Able Seaman . AUSTRALIAN NAVY.   *25 Years of age.*
Born at Aberdeen, SCOTLAND.
Belonging to Services Reconnaissance Department, AUSTRALIAN ARMY.

....

The case of Breach of Martial Law (Stratega (or Perfidy) and Espionage) has been tried at this Court with Major Hareu Kamiya, Judicial Officer as an inspecting prosecutor, and verdicted as follows,

TEXT
The ten accused persons are sentenced to death.
1 Japanese National Flag, 1 Sketch Book, 1 Camera, and 17 Negatives (Evidence No. 1–5) which are kept in this court are forfeited.

REASONS
The accused person, INGLETON, was called to the colours in October 1940, and

joined the Royal Marines Training Camp. After graduating from the Royal Marine Academy, he was commissioned and while serving at the 385 Detachment of Royal Marine, he volunteered in June 1944, to go to Australia, to be seconded to the Services Reconnaissance Department (Hereinafter abbreviated as S.R.D. of the Australian Army) which is an institution for special operations. Upon arrival in Australia he was seconded to the 'Z' Special Unit, a subordinate institution of S.R.D.

The accused person PAGE, while he was studying at the Sydney University, joined the Sydney University Regiment in 1940. He retired from the same to joined A.I.F. in May 1942, and joined the 2/4 Australian Pioneer Battalion where he was commissioned in due course and was transferred in March 1943 to S.R.D.

The accused person CAREY, voluntarily joined the Australian Army in July 1941, and was attached to the 22nd. Australian Infantry Brigade, 8th. Division A.I.F. In accordance with the removal of the Division to Malaya, he also came over to Malaya, and was temporarily engaged in defence of the Malay Peninsular. On account of illness he was sent to Australia. Then he was given training at the Officers' Training Camp in Woodland, and was commissioned and in November 1942, voluntarily joined the S.R.D.

The accused SARGENT, joined in November 1938, the Militia of AUSTRALIAN ARMY, then was voluntarily transferred to A.I.F. Belonged to the above mentioned 2/14 Australian Infantry Battalion and was participated in fighting in North Africa and New Guinea, was commissioned in due course and in November 1943 voluntarily transferred to S.R.D.

The accused WARREN, first joined the Militia in February 1942, on his own initiative, then transferred to the Mechanical Engineers of the A.I.F. and was engaged for some time in the maintenance work of a tank regiment, and in June 1945 was transferred by order to the S.R.D.

The accused STEWART, voluntarily joined the A.I.F. and was attached to the Signal Section of the First Armoured Division, from which he was transferred again, voluntarily, to the S.R.D. in November 1943.

The accused person FLETCHER, volunteered and joined the Pioneer Battalion of A.I.F. and while he was receiving different kinds of instruction at the above Infantry training Camp, was voluntarily transferred to the 'Z' Special Unit.

The accused person, COOLEY, joined in January 1941, the 58th. Infantry Battalion by his volunteering and while he was receiving instruction at the Cannangraph Infantry Camp, voluntarily joined S.R.D.

The accused person HARDY, was called to the colours in December 1942, attached to the Transport Section, AUSTRALIAN ARMY. Then transferred to the First Parachute Battalion, from where he was transferred again by his own volunteering to the S.R.D.

The accused person FALLS, voluntarily joined the Royal Australian Navy in April 1942, and while he was at the Navy Reinforcement Section, volunteered to join the S.R.D. and was granted.

All the accused persons above mentioned, were receiving special instructions at the S.R.D. as the members for special operations, when in September 1944, there was planned a special project of infiltrating into the port of Shenan (Singapore) and by making special use of submergible boat called S.B. make surprise attacks on and destruct the Military ships within the port. This plan was named 'Rimau' project from necessity of security. All the accused persons were selected as members of the part of this project and the party consisted of 9 Army and Navy Officers, 11 N.C.O. and 3 Seamen, headed by Lieutenant-Colonel Lyon, British Army, left Fremantle on the 11th. September on-board a British Submarine 'Porpoise' and arrived at an Island called 'Merapas', one of the islands of the Rhiou Groups, where they established their base, unloaded necessary rations, Signal equipment etc., left Captain Carey in charge of these stores and the rest of the party left the island by the same submarine.

On the sea beat Pontiak, Borneo, the party captured a native junk of about 100 Tons, towed the same to Pejanton Island, and transferred from the submarine to the junk, 15 of the above mentioned submergible boats, special magnetic charge called 'Limpet', arms, munitions, rations etc., and these preparations were completed, the party sent the 9 Malayan crew of the junk to Australia by the submarine, and started on this junk for Singapore Port on about 25th. September for attack. On passing off Merapas Island, the party landed Warren and two more member on the island to join Captain Carey, and the rest continued their navigation toward Singapore sea area for the mission.

The 1st. Charge.

The clothing worn by the members of the Rimau Project were green coloured shirts and trousers and also Beret Caps of the same colour, but except the few commissioned officers, the members from their date of departure, willingly refrained from wearing badges to show their ranks also refrained from using caps and so their appearance was such that it was difficult to recognise them as regular fighting members of either British or Australian forces. Furthermore, since the day of their departure from Pejantan Island all members applied on them so-called Commando or Demouflage dying stuff and dyed into brown, the exposed part of their skin, such as, face, arms and legs. In addition to that, Lieutenant-Colonel Lyon, Captain Page, the accused persons, and 6 more members were wearing loin cloth called 'sarong', the same as used by Malayans and continued their voyage on the junk without taking off the Japanese National Flag, which had been hoisted on the stern of the junk by the Malayan crews, and whenever the junk was sighted by the Japanese patrol plane or crafts, they displayed another Japanese National Flag, (Evidence No. I), which they had prepared before hand and pretended as if the junk was an ordinary civilian vessel, crewed by native inhabitants who were peacefully engaged in daily works under Japanese Military Administration, and with these deceptive activities they succeeded in passing the guarded area, and infiltrated into the outlying area of the Port of Singapore.

At about 1700hrs. of 10th. October, they reached near 'Casoe' Island about 20 Kilometres from the Port of Singapore, when they were sighted by staff of the observation post in Casoe of Batang Police Station, and the inspecting vessel manned by local inspector Bin Shiapal and 4 other Malayans approached the junk. On seeing this vessel, Colonel Lyon and other members deducted it to be the patrolling craft of the Japanese Force and determined quick action attack of the craft, launched sudden and heavy shooting on it by automatic rifles, and killed 4 crews of the observation post. After this attack, they felt the difficulty of accomplishing the task, and decided to give up the mission, and after removing themselves on board the holding rubber dinghies, exploded the junk, and made individual flights towards Merapas Base with a view to catch at the base, the submarine which had been scheduled to come to the base in the beginning of November. How-ever their flights were disturbed and the Merapas base was raided by the parties of Japanese garrison and while being unable to contact the submarine, they continued their flights and by the time of apprehension of all accused persons in December, they encountered with the Japanese garrison on Sere, Tapai and Merapas Islands, and killed Lieutenant Muraoka and 7 other army personnels. Thus the party was engaged in hostile activities without wearing uniforms to qualify them for fighting and also using the vessel which lacked qualifications for fighting.

The 2nd. Charge.

While acting as above, they contrived to collect information to be reported to their home country, and assigned the accused Ingleton for sketching, the accused Page for photographing, and Lt-Commander Davidson for documentary recording, and these three persons reconnoitred in their disguise clothing, the conditions of guards of islands south of Singapore, state of administration of ships in these area, trend of public mind there, strength of Japanese Navy crafts operating in Rhieu Straits, condition of Beauxite being dug out in Lingga Island, etc; and made sketching records of our fleet in Rhieu Straits and Beauxite mines, also photographed the same and engaged in collection and recording of the military information, besides, other accused persons, also in their disguise costumes, exerted to collect informations for the same purpose. Furthermore, the accused Carey, while on Merapas Island, made very detailed record of the strength of our fleet operating near the base and movements of our aircrafts over the area, and recorded the same in his notebook (Evidence No. 5). In this way they were engaged secretly and without due qualifications, in collecting of military informations within our operational area.

The above facts are fully evidenced with,

1. *Statements of all the accused persons in this court.*

2. *Affidavit of Bin Shiapal made by Police Officer of the military Adminstn.*

3. *Report made by the Chief of Garrison of Shonan, about the matter.*

4. *Existence of the 5 evidences, 1 Japanese National Flag. 1 Note book. 1 Sketch Book. 1 Camera, and 17 negatives (Evidence No. 1–5).*

APPLICATION OF LAW.

The deeds of all these accused personnel fall under Paragraph 1, Sub-section 1 of Section 2 of the Martial Law of the Southern Expeditionary Forces, and so by applying Section 4 of the same Law, they are to be awarded with death sentence, and 1 Japanese National Flag, 1 Sketch Book, 1 Camera, and 17 negatives (Evidence No. 1–5) kept in the court, are to be forfeited according to Section 9 of the same Law.

Thus the case was verdicted as per the text.

The Military Court of the 7th. Area Army.
Presiding Judge:- Colonel Mayayoshi Towatari.
Judge:- Major (Judicial Officer) Mitsue Jifuku.
Judge:- Major Miyoahi Hisada.
Executed on 7th. July 1945.

THE ABOVE DOCUMENTS RELATING TO OPERATION RIMAU ARE RECORDED IN THEIR ORIGINAL CONTEXT.

Change of Fortunes for SWPA in 1944

From September 1944 strategic decisions by the Allied governments virtually eliminated both SEAC and the Australian Military Forces from the main campaign against Japan. This was to bring about a change for the better in the fortunes of SRD who, from February 1945, would be acting in direct support of the AMF in the destruction of by-passed Japanese garrisons in New Guinea, British North Borneo, Sarawak, and the liberation of British and Dutch colonial territories in the SWPA. After a precarious existence for some years as the direct servant of a suspicious AIB, employed reluctantly on tasks for which they were not really fitted, they would now be asked to undertake their proper SO roles.

In November 1944, the Controller of AIB, who had served GHQ SWPA well over previous years, was replaced by a senior Australian Officer of wide international experience and of a more flexible temperament. He was able to obtain approval for the formation of a special flight of six Liberator long-range aircraft with RAAF crews for use by the units of AIB and this, together with the greater availability of US and British submarines, solved the problem of long-range transport.

In March and April 1945, three intelligence parties were dropped by parachute from RAAF Liberators into tribal country in the interior of Sarawak. They were commanded by British officers who had served in, or spent time in Sarawak in various civilian capacities before the Japanese invasion, and were familiar with the language and the customs of the people. They were received with enthusiasm by the tribes of the interior, who were bitterly opposed to the Japanese after three years of shortages and oppression, and proceeded to penetrate down the river valleys towards the coast, training and arming the already warlike natives in preparation for full-scale attacks on the Japanese in support of the eventual invasion by Australian Forces. They were able to provide much pre-invasion tactical intelligence for I Australian Corps but, unfortunately, their potential use was not always appreciated. However, the assault on Labuan and Brunei Bay by the 9th Australian Division on 10 June 1945 was the signal for an all-out guerrilla offensive against the Japanese forces concentrated near the coast, and this unexpected threat from the rear had the effect of discouraging the Japanese from their usual reaction, which was to counter-attack invading troops before they could become established.

Kota Kinabalu as it stands today.

After the success of the initial assult, the Australian regular forces were confined to the coastal areas of the oilfields and the main towns by order of the government in Canberra and to make no move to penetrate inland. It devolved on guerrilla forces of SRD, with the invaluable help of the RAAF, to try and contain the movement of Japanese troops through the interior and restore some sort of stable and civil adminis-tration amongst the very volatile tribes. They made no attempt to penetrate the capital, Kuching, in the south of the country as there was no sizeable prisoner-of-war camp there, and it was feared that the Japanese might be provoked into massacring the prisoners there, as had happened in Sandakan in British North Borneo. After the official surren-der of Japanese forces on 15 August, SRD continued to cope alone with a column which refused to surrender and which was doggedly marching inland, pillaging the longhouses and shooting the inhabitants. The group known as the Fujino Tai (Commanded by Capt. Fujino) com-menced their retreat inland, by breaking through SRD Semut II operational lines (Major Toby Carter NZ) and headed via Tutoh and the Sungei (River) Madalam into the Limbang area. The column commenced their jungle retreat approximately 600 strong, being continually ha-rassed by two Semut I operatives (NZ & Aus) and Dayak guerrillas upriver into the interior. They finally surrendered on 28 October 1945 in the interior of Sarawak near Semut I HQ. The remnants of this Fujino Tai party who surrendered now totalled only 358. The operatives and native guerrillas in this action did not sustain any casualties.

Altogether, SRD in Sarawak was credited with having accounted for some 1,500 Japanese troops and auxiliaries killed, and 240 taken prisoner. This was accomplished by a total, at its highest, of 82 officers and men of SRD and approximately 2,000 guerrillas at a cost of about 30 natives, and nobody from SRD. The operation was classified as cost-effective.

A similar operation was mounted in the north-east of British North Borneo (Sabah) early in March 1945, though smaller than the Semut operations and code-named 'Agus'. The party was headed by British officers with previous experience in the country, and set about recruiting and training the natives as agents and guerrillas, with the object of attacking isolated Japanese outposts. During May, June and July they were reinforced by four more parties and finally covered the whole country. They were able to rescue five of the only six survivors of the 2,500 Allied servicemen who had been killed by the Japanese in camps at Sandakan on the coast, and Ranau in the interior, when on forced marches between the two places.

From Morotai itself some sixteen short-term reconnaissance and fighting patrols operated in the Celebes and Moluccas, carried in US and RAAF flying-boats, US PT boats, and one of the Country Craft of the SRD Navy, now in service. They were not without casualties from brushes with Japanese garrisons, but were mostly successful and included the rescue of the Sultan of Ternate and his family.

During the period 1942 to 1945 ISD/SRD sent eighty-one parties into Japanese-occupied territories, of which three were despatched on behalf of SEAC. Their casualties were sixty-nine officers and men dead and missing, plus seven prisoners of war who eventually returned to Australia. To these must be added members of three Liberator aircraft of 200 Flight who crashed during SRD operations.

On 15 August 1945, at its maximum, the total strength of SRD was 1,700, of which 1,250 were Australians of all three services; 550 officers and men had been fully trained as operatives, of whom 380 had actually been sent behind the Japanese lines.

Directorate of Training SOA

The very nature of Special Operations activities in the SWPA necessitated special training of all operatives sent into the field. Special training schools, usually under a cover name, were established to carry out the instruction in SO techniques, methods and equipment. Recruits were taught special methods of insertion and infiltration, how to operate in small parties, how to maintain communications using special equipment, and how to live in the jungle and work with natives. Special instruction was given in languages, intelligence, small boat and submersible craft operation, signals, medical work and other subjects which were necessary for efficient operation of field parties.

The following training schools were established:

1. 'Z' Experimental Station – Cairns
2. Fraser Commando School – Queensland
3. School of Eastern Interpreters – Melbourne
4. Careening Bay Camp (Special Boat School) – Perth
5. Camps 6 & 8 – Mt Martha (near Melbourne)
6. Advanced Training Camp – Morotai
7. Advanced Training Camp – Darwin

By arrangement with the Director of Military Training, special operational parties were also trained at the Parachute Training Unit, Richmond, NSW; the school of Military Engineering, Liverpool NSW; and the Signals Training Centre, Bonegilla.

Lieutenant Colonel A.G. Oldham AIF was appointed Director of Training and served in that capacity until June 1945, when Major J.S.B. Finlay was temporarily appointed to that position.

'Z' Experimental Station – Cairns

'Z' Experimental Station near Cairns, Queensland, was set up by SOA in July 1942, as a wireless relay station for the New Guinea Section. Lieutenant C.H. Anderson AIF was in command. When it was decided that the Guerrilla Warfare School at Foster was unsuitable for the training of ISD personnel due to rugged climate, ZES became a training school and holding area as well. Both Australian and NEI personnel were trained. When ISD was closed in April 1943, ZES was given to AIB for use by NEFIS III. Captain Ross AMF, who had succeeded Major Trapes-Lomax as Administrative Commandant, remained in command under AIB until May 1944, when he became Administrative Commandant at Lugger Maintenance School, Darwin.

Fraser Commando School

Fraser Island, situated off the coast of Queensland, was selected as the site for the main SRD training school in October 1943. In March 1944, an addition was made to the camp to accommodate Filipino students undergoing special training with SRD. A small additional camp site was established at Lake MacKenzie in the centre of the island for further training and holding SO personnel under the direction of Special Raiding Section.

Fraser Island was selected because it afforded ample facilities for jungle and amphibious training and was relatively secluded, the only other inhabitants of the island being a small forestry establishment. Facilities were developed to accommodate 100 students at a time.

Major H.A. Campbell was in command of FCS until January 1944 when Lieutenant Davidson RNVR took over. Two months later he was succeeded by Major L. McGuinn. In April 1945 Major S.R. Leach became Commandant and held that position until the school closed in September 1945.

The main objectives of the training given at FCS were:

1. To develop the students' physical fitness.
2. To fit the students for jungle survival.
3. To make the student proficient in all weapons likely to be carried by operational parties.
4. To practice the student in small party tactics.
5. To give training in small boats and navigation for the insertion of parties by sea.
6. To impart an intelligence background, giving as much instruction as possible on Japanese identification and Japanese equipment.
7. To train specialists in signals communication and to give all future operatives at least the minimum of signals knowledge necessary to maintain communications.
8. To train certain specialists in meteorology and medical work.

As operational experience was obtained, the training course was revised. Greater importance was attached to the teaching of Malay, less emphasis was laid on instruction in raiding activities, and instruction in the technique of receiving stores from the air was added.

In addition to the basic training, three other courses were given in Queensland under the direction of FRS staff. A short course in cavern-making was given to certain selected parties of students. As operations developed, cavern living was of little importance and was discontinued after five months. A special course on jungle foods, jungle living and jungle tactics was held at Cairns in March and May 1945. A special medical course for further training of medical orderlies for the field was given at FRS and in Brisbane hospitals. With the growth of medical work in operational areas, all students going through for the last courses at FRS were given a ten-day medical course.

On 14 August 1945, instructions were given that all training was to cease and in September 1945 FRS was closed. A total of 909 students, including some 250 officers, had then passed through the school. Nationalities represented in this total included Australian, New Zealand, British, Dutch, French, Canadian, Chinese, Malayans, Filipinos and Ambonese.

School of Eastern Interpreters ('B' School)

The syllabus for this school was modified from that of the 'B' School in England where training in planning and building an intelligence organisation, in clandestine work and in espionage was given to selected students. The course was at first given in a separate wing at FRS, transferred to Mt Martha, and finally at Park Orchards near Melbourne.

Under the cover name of 'School of Eastern Interpreters', students were given courses dealing with intelligence information, its importance, the type required and how to obtain it. Enemy counter-intelligence systems, interrogation methods, description of persons and surveillance were dealt with at the same time.

Other subjects included planning and organisation, recruiting agents in the field, methods of internal communication, use of secret inks, simple disguises, lock-picking and methods of entering and searching buildings. Party leaders were given separate tuition as far as possible with an additional course in cipher. All students who required it were given a course in Malay and one party of foreign-born Chinese studied their own language.

A complete library of information booklets, giving conditions in occupied territories, topographical information etc., was built up. In January 1945, photography was added to the syllabus. A total of 122 students, including Australian, British, Malay, Dutch, Indonesian, French and Canadian-Chinese passed through the school which was closed in August 1945.

Careening Bay Camp

Training at this base, located on Garden Island, about fifteen miles south-west of Fremantle, Western Australia, was concerned primarily with small submarines. The newest of these, the motor-submersible canoe (MSC) was a steel canoe, decked in, and driven by a small electric motor. Batteries were protected in a sealed compartment. Ballast and trim tanks enabled the craft to submerge. Underwater, the craft was controlled by hydroplanes and rudder, an amazing manoeuvrability being achieved. The offensive weapon of the MSC was the 'Limpet', a six-pound charge held by magnets to the side of the target. Up to nine of these charges were carried, sufficient to sink two 10,000-ton ships if correctly placed.

The training began with instructions in diving, followed by a six-week MSC course. In October 1944 the first Welman submarine arrived from England, and Welman pilots received instruction in the use of Davis submarine escape apparatus for several days before commencing the course in Welman operation. The submarine was simple to operate and pilots were able to run underwater in a few hours. Since there were no Welman operations in view, very little of this training was carried out at Western Base. Folboat proficiency was expected of all pilots and was an important part of the training course.

Mount Martha – Training Camps 6 & 8

Small parties were given pre-operational training under their party leaders, with assistance from the Technical Section at Mt Martha Research Station, near Melbourne. The planned training programme, to exercise each party in its operational role, to test out all operational equipment, and to make necessary modifications, was curtailed due to lack of instructors until early 1945 when a small staff was made available. Training Camp 6 was established in June 1944 and by early 1945 seven operational parties were receiving final training. Arrangements were made with the Department of Navy for a 40-foot workboat and crew which was attached to the school for carrying out water schemes, folboat operations and navigational training. An advanced Signals Training Wing was established in December 1944 to give instruction in the technical maintenance of sets. Regular practice in long-distance working with special equipment was arranged over a link especially set up with Mt Martha and FCS. In addition to operational rehersals, training was given in Malay, sniping, cypher instructions, enemy equipment, and sabotage of industrial installations.

In February an additional camp (Camp 8) was set up in an adjacent command. Training at Mt Martha was discontinued in April 1945, however, and Camp 8 was never really used.

Advanced Training Camp – Darwin

Pre-operational training at Darwin was organised by party leaders under the direction of the Group Commander until the formation of a separate Training Establishment in June 1945. The exercises carried out in the surrounding area and on nearby islands provided conditions as near as possible to those visualised for the actual operations. Four parties were trained for insertion and extraction by Catalina in conjunction with 20 Squadron, Darwin. Cooperation with this squadron proved most useful for SR students who practised embarking and disembarking of stores and personnel by rubber boat.

Signals training was carried out at Leanyer Station in two phases: (1) individual training in preparation of Nos. 1, 2 and emergency operators; (2) collective training as a party using signals on operational rehearsal exercises.

Parachute Training Unit – Richmond

Facilities for training of SRD personnel were provided by the Parachute Training Wing, Richmond, until May 1945 when a separate parachute training establishment was set up. The course included extensive and strenuous ground training which was shortened from one month to two weeks when operational demands for students became imperative. Seven jumps were required to qualify. Certain personnel were trained in stores dropping and followed a jump-master's course.

Beginning in June, instruction was given to SRD personnel at Leyburn. Four jumps from Liberators were required to qualify. Training in Eureka/Rebecca and S. Phone was also given.

Naval Directorate SOA

With the appointment of Commander G.C.F. Branson RN on 29 January 1944, headquarters were established in Melbourne and the organisation of the Naval Directorate of SRD began. Shortly thereafter, Lieutenant W.H. Walker RANVR was placed in charge of personnel and administration.

At the time only two vessels were under the control of SRD: the 'Krait', a former Japanese wooden vessel of approximately 74 tons, and the 'Atlanta', an Australian pattern 62-foot sea ambulance launch of 28 tons, modified with additional fuel tanks. The AMF had formed a Water Transport Unit and had taken over a portion of the US Small Ships program of constructing 66-foot trawlers of the Seine net type. With structural modifications, these vessels ('Snake Class') would resemble native craft used extensively in Singapore waters.

Lieutenant D.R.N.M. Davidson DSO RNVR (SP) was transferred from FCS where he had been Officer in Command and Chief Instructor, to Melbourne to take charge of building 'Country Craft', as these vessels were called.

The lugger 'Heather' was temporarily secured for SRD's use. Four 66-foot trawlers were approved for release to SRD and engines were obtained from the USN. Due to delays in the construction program, however, the first vessel, 'Tigersnake', was not launched until June 1944.

At a conference held on 25 May 1944 (RAN, AMF, SRD and Felo participating), it was agreed that:

1. Small craft requirements of 'Irregular Operations' (i.e. SRD and Felo) be pooled.

2. All vessels other than 40-foot workboats etc. were to be commissioned as HMA ships in command of naval officers and with naval crews as far as possible, the personnel to be drawn from those allotted to irregular operations.

3. Commander A.E. Fowler RAN, Plans Division, Navy Office, Melbourne, be detailed as 'Staff Officer Irregular Operations', and be available for advice and assistance.

4. All vessels to be brought under the control of Coastal Craft Section of Naval Ports.

5. Army facilities for servicing etc. be made available where no such Naval facilities existed.

6. NOICs be responsible for control of movements of all ships engaged in irregular operations.

7. All NOICs be notified of these arrangements and act accordingly.

8. Irregular organisations be responsible for the supply craft and original fitting out, RAN to supply any items of naval supply not available elsewhere, and the organisations themselves to be responsible for supply and special stores.

Commander Branson was replaced on 1 October 1944 by Squadron Skipper P.E. Scrivener DCM, Lieutenent Commander Thain became Senior Officer (Flotilla) and Lieutenant H.E. Josselyn DSC RNVR, joined the staff as Naval Intelligence Officer. Gradually more personnel were assigned to SRD until, on 31 January 1945, the strength of the Naval Section had increased to a total of 39 officers and 150 ratings and ORs.

Construction of vessels proceeded slowly due to labour troubles and difficulties encountered in obtaining materials and necessary parts. By the end of July 1945, 'Grass Snake', 'Sea Snake', 'Riversnake', 'Coral-snake', 'Diamondsnake', and 'Tigersnake' (66-foot trawler class) had been released to SRD. Various other vessels were assigned to SRD. Two 62-foot Fast Supply Vessels, the 'Nyane', and the 'Misima', were obtained. Other vessels assigned to SRD were the *Mamba*, an 85-foot wooden cargo vessel, the *Tarneit*, a 200-ton steel motor vessel, the *Anaconda* and the *Mothersnake* – 300-ton HQ ships – the 'Nichol Bay', a powered lighter, the lugger 'Swallow', a 38-foot fast supply vessel and six 40-foot workboats. The 'Taipan' (formerly the 'Bandoeng') was a captured Chinese junk which was used for missions.

As operations moved further away from the Australian mainland, it was decided to establish a forward base at Morotai. The Commanding Officer of the Naval Base had agreed to place base repair facilities at SRD's disposal. These included a floating dock capable of taking vessels of 100 tons and up to 90 feet. A Naval Director, Naval Liaison Officer, Flotilla Maintenance Officer and Liaison Officer for Group B were appointed to head the staff at the forward base.

Technical Directorate SOA

The technical activities of SOA commenced in August 1942 with the arrival of Major P.H. Moneypenny RE to take up the appointment of Instructor of Special Operations and adviser to ISD. Major Moneypenny divided his time between ISD HQ Melbourne and ZES in Cairns. Due to limited facilities and lack of staff, he concentrated, at this stage, mainly on training and the consideration of technical problems likely to arise in future operations.

In addition to Planning, Training, Air and Technical duties, it was necessary for the same staff to undertake a certain amount of intelligence and administrative work.

In October 1943 Flight Lieutenant Cook joined the establishment as adviser on matters relating to Air, his previous posting being Officer I/C a flight of DC2 transport aircraft used for jump training at Parachute Training Unit, Richmond, NSW.

As a fledgling unit, operating in an unknown theatre of operations, special investigations were undertaken to perfect various military equipment suitable for SWPA operations. The following will give some indication of that which was achieved during SOA's short period in the conflict against 'The Sons of Tojo'.

Developmental Boats

Folboats

The first Australian folboat was produced in November 1942 with the intention of producing a collapsible canoe to carry three men and 300 lb of stores. The first model was found to have several weaknesses, and so over the period from June 1943 to January 1944, further designs were evolved by this directorate in collaboration with Design Division, resulting finally in the production of Folboat Mk III (Aust). Early in the development of the folboat, it became evident that a suitable cover was necessary to prevent the boat being swamped by heavy seas. Development on these lines continued over an extended period, finally resulting in the cover which incorporate the various features considered desirable in the light of operational experience, particularly a quick release arrangement in the event of the boat overturning.

Outboard Motors

In order to increase the speed and range of the Folboat Mk III, a projecting motor bracket was developed upon which a small outboard motor could be mounted. This led to the development of a rubber fabric well which was fitted to the folboat immediately aft of the stern cockpit. The outboard passed through this well and was clamped to a short motor bracket secured to the stern post. These two arrangements worked perfectly. The successful development of the well fitted to the Folboat Mk III led to its adoption as a standard item of equipment, and, as such, was given the designation of Folboat No. 2 Mk I (Aust). This enabled the fitting of motors up to 3.3 hp, resulting in greater speed. A rudder was also fitted to this folboat to eliminate the necessity of steering with the outboard motor, thus providing easier turning and less tendency to capsize.

Other Canoes

The Folboat Mk III (Aust) and No. 2 Mk I were the only canoes developed in their entirety by the Directorate, but a considerable amount of work was carried out on the technique of handling, load-carrying capacity, range and performance figures for the following types of canoes imported from overseas:

> Canoe Mk I
> Rigid Canoe Mk III
> Canoe Mk VI
> Canoe Mk VIII
> American Kayak

This work took place during long exercises carried out from Catalina aircraft, submarines, SRD ships and PT boats. Information concerning these exercises has been well recorded by 'Z' investigating Depts.

Rubber Boats

Work associated with rubber boats consisted primarily of producing technical information concerning performance and methods of use in the immediate proceeding paragraph. Work was carried out on the following types of inflatable rubber boats:

> US 5-Man Boat
> US 7-Man Boat
> US 10-Man Boat
> English 'Y'-Type Dinghy
> Wheelwright Courier

In addition certain accessories were developed for use with these boats.

Silencing of Outboard Motors

Considerable attention was given to this problem and silencers were manufactured for some low-powered motors. Limited success was only achieved, and at the close of hostilities, when it was learned that this problem was being investigated by large overseas organisations, local development was stopped.

Carrying Folboat Equipment

A method was devised for carrying the FBE Mk II on the deck of a minelaying submarine. The boat was launched by opening it on deck, releasing clamps, and submerging the submarine, whereupon the boat floated off.

Airborne Equipment

The supply by air to parties in the field required the development of special equipment and techniques. Work carried out with this object in view included linked containers. To facilitate the recovery of stores a system of linking containers together was evolved, which was quite successful when used by DC2 and DC3 aircraft, but was not applicable to containers dropped from the bomb bays of Liberator aircraft.

Carriage of Canoes in Catalina Aircraft

Development work was carried out on similar lines to be the method adopted in UK for carriage, launching and recovery of Mk VI Rigid Canoes in a Catalina. Experiments were similarly undertaken with regard to folboats, but the method proposed was not fully developed.

Parachuting of Personnel

Considerable investigation was carried out to determine the most suitable type of aircraft likely for parachuting operations of the SRD type in the SWPA and it was eventually decided that the Liberator was the most suitable. However, there was no information available on parachuting from them in Australia at that time, and it was subsequently ascertained that the technique for jumping from these aircraft was being developed overseas concurrently with development here. On Major Holland's trip overseas, a method had been observed of using a slide for exiting from Hudson aircraft, so the staff then concentrated on evolving a similar technique for use with the Liberator. Arrangements for the initial tests were made by Flight Lieutenant Cook with a detachment of US Liberators at Darwin. A series of dummy drops were carried out, and a party consisting of Captain Carey, Lieutenant Lees, Sergeant MacKenzie, and Lance Corporals Filewood and Taylor successfully carried out live drops soon afterwards. Jump lights were installed and a complete exit drill was meticulously worked out. Cook trained the flying personnel for these experiments and developed a flying technique and a course of instruction. This parachuting technique evolved during these experiments at Darwin remained basically unchanged throughout SRD history, and, to our knowledge, there has not been one single casualty in either experiments, training or operations resulting from faulty exit equipment.

Weapons

Silent Austen

A method was devised for fitting Sten silencer units to the Austen SMG with highly satisfactory results, reducing the noise of firing and removing the muzzle flash.

Modified Sten

A large number of Sten bodies and Austen barrels being available, a method was devised to combine the two producing a sub-machine gun which was much lighter than any other sub-machine gun made. This was given the name of Barsten. Later a conversion was carried out using Sten bodies and Sten barrels which had been modified for fitting silencers, but for which no silencers were available. Reconversion of these barrels to normal firing produced some hundreds for operational use.

Demolition Equipment

Wing charges – charges that could be placed through the inspection ports, and on or adjacent to petrol tanks – were required for attacking grounded Japanese aircraft. The charge consisting of PE Mk 2 and Eutron turnings was developed. For attacking aircraft without suitable inspection ports the charge was also fitted with four rubber suction pads which were capable of supporting the charge, when properly applied, for a period exceeding twelve hours. This charge was successful.

Marspike

To permit the rapid attachment of charges to wooden vessels, a devise called the Marspike was developed. This devise would silently drive a pin, through a bracket on the charge, into the target when it was tapped against the side of the target. It was silent, simple to operate, and had a highly satisfactory underwater performance. Only thirty-six of these devices were produced before the cessation of hostilities, although specifications and drawings had been prepared for large-scale production.

Air Directorate SOA

In October 1943 Flight Lieutenant F. Cook RAAF was appointed to the staff of SRD to assist in planning and launching a series of operations involving aircraft and paratroops, parachute supply and dropping, and flying-boat personnel.

Knowledge of parachuting was limited and it was not known whether descents could be carried out from the B-24 (Liberator) which was the type of aircraft available in the SWPA considered capable of bringing the target within its radius of action. Experiments were conducted and it was found that exits from the B-24s could be made at speeds up to 160 miles per hour. An aircraft and crew were available at Darwin for a period of three weeks in December 1943 in order to develop equipment for aircraft modifications, paratroop exiting and flying technique.

The supply of parachutes was extremely short at this time and only twenty were allotted for the tests and operations. The first experiments with Liberators were carried out with the cooperation of the 380th Bomb Group, US. The insertion of the 'Hawk' party was disastrous, but a few weeks later the NEFIS 'Crayfish' party was successfully inserted by parachute.

Repeated requests for the information of a special unit for air support of SRD operations were made by SRD throughout 1944 with negative results. To meet the need for air support, therefore, a small Parachute Maintenance Group and Paratroop Training Unit, known as the 'Para Wing', was established at FCS under the direct control of the newly formed Air Section. Personnel and equipment were furnished by the RAAF.

Although the internal SRD control of air operations was very clear cut and a workable process, the system was constantly hindered because AIB lacked appropriate officers to conduct liaison with higher command and to express the precise requirements in the forward areas, this approval being necessary. Later, AIB appointed the SRD Air Section OC, its direct representative with the RAAF, to discuss and make all requests on behalf of the Controller of AIB for operational conduct of a project. This system worked without difficulty from February 1945 until hostilities ceased.

In January 1945 GHQ approved the formation of a special unit to meet the requirements of the operations involving air insertion and supply. This new unit, known as '200 Flight' was established with six B-24s modified to SRD requirements. SRD moved the enlarged Para Wing to Leyburn where 200 Flight was based. Air crew training, paratroop training, parachute maintenance, pre-operational training, briefing for both paratroop and air crews and operational despatch were included in the programme. Air liaison officers were posted to the various SRD operational groups to collate all necessary information pertaining to a projected plan, submitting it to the OC Air Section for planning purposes. The final appreciation was submitted to the RAAF Command who issued the operational instructions to 200 Flight. Although Air Section, SRD, had no active interest in the management of 200 Flight, it was directly responsible for the activities and policy of Para Wing; 200 Flight was operationally responsible to RAAF Command, but since RAAF Command had no operations officer with the knowledge of this type of work, OC Air Section SRD virtually held this position.

Air and Sea Maintenance of SRD
Field Parties – January to August 1945

Project	A – Submarine B – Surface Craft C – Aircraft D – Catalina	Total No. Storpedoes and Parcels Dropped or Delivered	Weight in lbs.
AGAS I	1-A		
	1-B		
	13-C		
	1-D	112	27,082
AGAS II	2-B		
	15-C		
	10-D	196	70,606
AGAS III	1-C		
	5-D	51	11,308
AGAS IV	2-B		
	4-C	49	13,397
AGAS V	1-B		
	1-C	10	4,487
SEMUT I	34-C		
	3-D	371	75,110
SEMUT II	12-C		
	8-D	97	35,852
SEMUT III	1-B		
	10-C		
	8-D	147	46,445
SEMUT IV	3-B		
	1-D	—	2,122
PLATYPUS	2-B		
	10-C		
	3-D	160	26,918
MAGPIE	1-B	—	3,376
HIPPO	2-D	—	6,566
TOTALS	1-A		
	13-B		
	91-C		
	50-D		
	155 Sorties	1,193	323,269

Note: Of these 91 aircraft sorties, 78 of them (accounting for 144 tons of supplies) were accomplished by 200 Flight. All surface craft sorties were made by SRD Fleet.

Agas III. Resupply 800ft. 11-07-45. 200 Flight.

Ops 7981. Agas IV. Resupply 29-07-45. 1025z, 800ft. 200 Flight.

New Zealand Army Members Involved with 'Z' Special Unit – SOA

Special Operations Australia
South-West Pacific

The first party of New Zealanders were selected from the lists of the 11th Reinforcements awaiting embarkation at Trentham Military Camp, for service with 2 NZEF, Middle East. Major D.J. Scott DSO & Bar had called for volunteers on two occasions, but had received a negative result. After their selection the party reported to Auckland, flew by 'Teal' Sunderland flying-boat – Aotearoa – Flight AW 310 to Sydney on 15 July 1944. The group consisted of eight members. The OC and two other members followed at a later date.

VNZ 20681 AK 257   **Major D.J. Stott**   **AUCKLAND**
                          DSO & Bar

Operation Robin I/Platypus I. Balikpapan, Borneo   **20–03–1945**

Was firstly a member of 2 NZEF and captured in Crete. Placed behind the wire in a POW camp in Greece, and escaped. Took many months to regain his unit in North Africa. Was seconded to SOE – parachuted back into Greece, managed to achieve an almost impossible mission, destroying the 'ASOPOS' Viaduct with plastic explosives. This operation denied the Germans direct access into Athens by rail of valuable equipment for their desert campaign.

Entry by submarine USS *Perch* 20–03–1945. Two of the first party of four were lost, presumed drowned, whilst going ashore in heavy sea conditions. Second party was detected by a Japanese lighter in the bay, whilst still aboard the submarine. Lighter destroyed & operatives arrived shore DZ. Mission continued.

VNZ 64785 AK 258   **Captain L.T. McMillan**   **AUCKLAND**

Operation Robin I/Platypus I. Balikpapan, Borneo   **20–03–1945**

Was with Major Stott in his rubber boat which was lost in Balikpapan Bay. Court of Enquiry at the end of war stated: 'Presumed drowned at Sea'.

VNZ 444165 AKS 182   **WOII R.G. Houghton WELLINGTON**

Operation Robin I/Platypus I. Balikpapan, Borneo   20–03–1945

Captured in the vicinity of Dotan on 30 March and taken to Sanga Sanga. He was then transferred to Balikpapan Prison on 4 April. Was stricken by beriberi, and reported to have died on or about 20 April 1945.

VNZ 22884 AK 259   **Lieutenant   DARGAVILLE**
R.M. Morton MC DCM

Operation Robin I/Platypus I. Balikpapan, 20–03–45 to 03–05–1945
Borneo

A member of 2 NZEF captured in Crete, and imprisoned in Greece. Met Major Stott there, where the two prisoners evolved a plan to escape by pole vaulting over the wire perimeter fence. This was accomplished without accident, and both returned to their unit in Africa. Seconded to SOE, they parachuted back into Greece with the British Military Mission who were operating there against the Germans.

Landed by US submarine *Perch* and was unable to become established in their operational zone. With the presumed loss of party leader, he took control of the main party to come ashore and became subjected to intense Japanese patrol action. Party finally escaped to sea in a 16ft native ocean-going perahu, was sighted and recovered by a PBY recovery aircraft on a mission to locate a downed fighter plane in the area. They were returned to Morotai after being on the run for ten weeks inside Borneo. Was awarded the MC for this operation, had also received a DCM for Greece with the British Military Mission. Settled overseas after the war.

VNZ 76162 AKS 181   **Sergeant W. Horrocks   AUCKLAND**

Operation Robin I/Platypus I. Balikpapan, 20–03–45 to 03–05–1945
Borneo

Originally with Signals in the Pacific area, and situated at Fiji. Trained in Australia with the group, then to Balikpapan, Borneo. Survived ten weeks in the jungle before joining up with Lieutenant Morton's main group, having come ashore with Major Stott in the second boat of the first insertion. Escaped by perahu to sea, and there recovered by a PBY Catalina and flown to Morotai Base HQ.

VNZ 452668 AKS 179   **S/Sgt   CHRISTCHURCH**
G.R. Greenwood

Operation Agas I   **N.E. Borneo 03–03–45 to 23–07–1945**

The object of the mission was to establish a mission on the east coast of British North Borneo. Landed by the submarine USS *Tuna* in Lubuk

Bay, they immediately set up radio communication with Darwin. Intelligence reports were received from local natives about POW camps at Sandakan. Native guerrilla units were formed and training of natives about the modern weapons that were supplied to them. A successful mission commanded by Major Chester UK. S/Sgt Greenwood was awarded an M.I.D. for his part in the operation.

VNZ 446826 AKS 180	Sergeant	CHRISTCHURCH
	V.E. Sharpe	
Operation Agas I	Sandakan area	12–01–45 to
	N.E. Borneo	24–02–1945

The first attempt to land operatives in this region failed, as the enemy were observed in large numbers. This submarine operation was aborted and the party returned to base in Darwin. Sergeant Sharpe was admitted to hospital on return, and on recovery was returned to New Zealand and did not take any further operations of 'Z'.

VNZ 275480 AKS 260   Corporal J.K. Harris   WELLINGTON

Diesel mechanic and weapons specialist. After returning from the Middle East with 2 NZEF, volunteered for work as a specialist for repairing diesel motors & weapons, on 'Z' Special craft in Australia. Overhauled 'Snake' and Fairmile craft for the forward areas at Garden Island, Careening Bay area, W. Australia. Worked on our top secret Sleeping Beauty craft also. Wounded in the hand whilst removing a 9mm round from a S & W .38 pistol.

VNZ 549709 AKS 198   Sergeant P.J. Boyle   WELLINGTON

Did major overhauls on our workboats at Garden Island and in the forward areas of Morotai and Labuan Island. Served on the 'Black Snake' from Morotai and Labuan Island, inserting operatives and supplies into enemy-held territories including Borneo. Was a diesel specialist and workboat operator.

VNZ 636815 AK 153   Sergeant R.J. Newdick   OPOTIKI

Diesel specialist and workboat operator. Trained and worked at Garden Island, Western Australia on our naval craft, including our top secret SBs. Did a tour on a 'Snake' boat in the Timor region.

VNZ 66570 AKO 447   WOII L.N. Northover   WANGANUI

Seconded to 'Z' after serving with the British Military Mission in Greece. Captured by the Germans in Crete – escaped twice from POW Camps in Greece and Crete – joined the Partisans and was awarded the MM for his demolition work in that area. Joined 'Z' in Australia 12–07–1945 and did not take part in operations in the SWPA.

The 'SECOND PARTY' were volunteers accepted from members of 3rd Division returning from the Pacific, after two years of active service in that area. Major D. Stott interviewed and selected the personel at Trentham Military Camp during November 1944. The group received special leave and embarked for Australia onboard the USS freighter *Waipouri* in December 1944. They were to be known as the second section of Operation Robin I, designated for insertion into Balikpapan, Borneo. The group consisted of eight members, infantry and signals personnel.

VNZ 66570 AK 256   **Lieutenant**   **CHRISTCHURCH**
                             F.J. Leckie

Operations Undertaken:
Stallion V: Weston, Sipitang, Brunei Bay Borneo; 08–06–45 to 11–06–1945.
Stallion VIII: Palau Saat, Brunei Bay, Borneo; 13–06–45 to 14–06–1945.
Both operations recorded intelligence information for 9th Australian Division's attack June 1945.
Semut I: Sarawak & Dutch Borneo; 25–06–45 to 28–10–1945

Entry by workboat at Lawas with two other Kiwis, after AIF landings in Borneo. Then into the interior of Sarawak and British North Borneo (Sabah). One of the last of 'Z' operatives to vacate Borneo after becoming involved with a Japanese non-complying force which disregarded the surrender requirements. This was the party of 600 known as 'Fujino Tai' who infiltrated the Semut II area (Major Toby Carter NZ ex-Shell Oil) and travelled through the Tutoh to the Limbang river. Here they continued destroying kampongs and killing and raping the natives whilst on their march into the interior, at a severe cost to themselves by another Kiwi and Aussie operatives' guerrillas.

VNZ 280669 AK 235   **Lieutenant R. Tapper**   **PUKEKOKE**

Operations Undertaken:
Platypus II-III-IV-XI, all Balikpapan, Samarinda, Dutch Borneo; 16–06–45 to 24–06–1945.
For intelligence information prior to the landing of the 7th Australian Division in June 1945. All insertions were made from Morotai by PBY Catalina, workboat and folboats.

Phase III
Was to deceive the enemy by focusing attention on the area north-east of Balikpapan. This was done by having the natives passing the desired rumours, by flying over the particular area at zero altitude as if making a reconnaissance, and by dropping a marked map of operational instructions,

together with beach markers on the area near Senipan where they would be picked up. The success of the mission was proved when large native patrols were sighted in the area.

Phase IV
Was the extraction of eighteen informants from the Balikpapan area and distribution of rumours as in Phase III.

Phase XI
Semoi, Mentawir and Sepakoe areas. To obtain information of POWs in the district.
Reliable native informers made it possible for the recovery of sixty-three Indian prisoners. On 25 July the party recovered Flight Lieutenant Alan Martin RAAF of Phase VII who had been missing since 30 June. He had received pelvis damage in his parachute drop, also losing three of his party to the Japanese including Signalman Ernie Myers from New Zealand.

VNZ 616204 AKS 176   **Signalman**   **INVERCARGILL**
                                  E.H. Myers

Operation Platypus VII Mt. Mentawir area, Balikpapan, Borneo; 30–03–1945.
A parachute insertion into Balikpapan, Semoi, Mt Mentawir area for intelligence purposes. Locality was situated 13 miles west of Balikpapan. They chuted into the area without firstly being able to check on the DZ, and the mission consequently failed. Three adverse features were: the wrong height, the wrong time, and all operatives released in one stick not two. Three of the operatives landed inside a Japanese camp area. They hurriedly discarded their boiler suits (to protect their gear from entanglement in shroud-lines whilst chuting) and fought their way out, causing many casualties. The Australian in the party, J.J. O'Dwyer, was shot at a river crossing but his body was not recovered by the Japanese. It was later found by friendly natives who placed it in a grave on the river bank. The Malay Sergeant interpreter of the party, Ma'e-roffbin Said and Signalman Ernie Myers (NZ) were tortured for three days, then executed by Samurai. Lieutenant Bob Tapper (NZ), working with the War Graves Commission immediately after the surrender of the Japanese on 15 August, recovered the bodies of the two operatives from their graves. He reports finding their heads in one grave and their torsos in another. Natives gave the Commission all the necessary information of their recent deaths, and the Japanese members involved in it paid the penalty for their atrocity. Ernie Myers was the second member of the Kiwi group to have parachuted into enemy-held territory

in the SWPA; the other survived the experience of 'Within' and returned to NZ.

The party leader of Platypus VII was the last to exit and was blown off-course from the first three operatives, landing in a 100ft tree in the nearby jungle. He sustained a broken pelvis and evaded the searching enemy patrols by remaining where he had landed. Later that evening he managed to cut his shroud lines and descend to the ground, then made his way to the river bank. Two days later, local natives recovered him and managed to reunite him with a 'Z' patrol on the coast under the command of Lieutenant Bob Tapper. Flight Lieutenant Martin was returned to Australia and took many months to recover.

VNZ 441420 AKS 177   **Signalman A.J. Campbell**   **STOKE**

Broke his leg whilst undergoing the parachute course at Richmond NSW. He did not take part in any of the operations in the SWPA with 'Z'.

VNZ 233068 AKS 172   **Corporal G.R. Edlin INVERCARGILL**

Operations undertaken:

Swift NW Halmaheras. Raoe Island. Intelligence on enemy radar; 06–05–45 to 18–05–1945.

Stallion VIII Palau Saat, Brunei Bay, Borneo with Kiwi party, Intelligence info.; 13–06–45 to 14–06–1945.

Workboat W/T operator, supplying equipment and inserting operatives into Borneo; 16–06–45 to 24–06–1945.

Semut I. After the landing of 9th Australian Division in Borneo, took over the 'Z' W/T link at Lawas transmitting to Labuan Island in Brunei Bay. Then moved into the interior with two other Kiwis. Returned to New Zealand Labour Day 1945 on the Hospital Ship *Andes* with two other Kiwi operatives, Bob Morton and Graham Greenwood.

VNZ 271450 AKS 174   **Sergeant R.R. Butt**   **AUCKLAND**

Operations undertaken:

Stallion V: Weston, Sipitang, Brunei Bay, Borneo; 08–06–45 to 11–06–1945.

Intelligence operation under Lieutenant Frank Leckie.

Stallion VIII: Palau Saat, Brunei Bay; 13/14–06–1945.

Intelligence Operation under Lieutenant F. Leckie.

Semut I Entry into Borneo via Lawas by naval workboat, after 9th Australian Division landings. Then into the interior of Sarawak and British North Borneo (Sabah) with Frank Leckie to join up with operatives of 'Z'. 25–06–45 to 10–08–1945.

VNZ 45794 AKS 175   Signalman   **HENDERSON**
N.G. Flemming
Operations undertaken:
Stallion V: Weston, Sipitang, Brunei Bay; 08/11–06–1945.
Stallion VIII: Palau Saat, Brunei Bay; Recording intelligence information
with Frank Leckie; 13/14–06–1945.
Platypus IX: Balikpapan Oil Fields, SE Borneo; Proceeded to northern
point where radio communications were set up with HQ Morotai Island.
Report for 9th Div. re enemy activity in area.; 12/18–06–1945.

VNZ 422668 AKS 173   Sergeant F.A. Wigzell   **HAMILTON**

Operation Semut I: Sarawak, British Borneo; 08–06 to 27–09–1945
Main operation inside Borneo. Parachuted into the interior of Sarawak
and landed just over the boarder into Dutch area, Bawang Valley,
Belawit. Kelabit Tribal area. Second reinforcement of eight. Total
operatives now in party: 24 (20 Aus, 3 GB, 1 NZ)
   One of the last four operatives in action against the Japanese non-
surrendering party known as the 'Fujino Tai', 'till late 1945.

VNZ 412556 AKS 178   Sergeant R.B. Shakes   **AUCKLAND**
RNZAF
Enlisted in the RNZAF as a radio mechanic with previous experience.
Following training at Wigram, he was sent to the RAF for advanced
training in RDF (Radar). Posted to an operational station in East Fife.
Was recruited in May 1942 to Special Operations Executive UK.
Volunteered for service abroad, arriving at Meerut, North of Delhi,
December 1942. Subsequently served with M.E. 9, M.E. 25 and FORCE
136 SEAC. Returned to NZ on leave then was seconded to 'Z' Special
Unit. Was flown to advance base Morotai in the Halmaheras in June,
then to Labuan Base in Brunei Bay. Operated W/T communications
with groups inside Sarawak and returned to NZ at the end of hostilities.
   After searching the records of the unit on 6 December 1991, two
further names of Kiwis appeared on the nominal rolls:

VNZ 635600 AKX 102   Major K.K.L. Brown   **WELLINGTON**

Operation Magpie II   Majoe &   **29–06 to 03–07–1945**
Tifore Islands
Planting of stores dumps on the latter island. Was not in the main
parties seconded to Australia. Became SRD's Deputy Director of Planning late in 1945.

VNZ 325731 AK 223   Lieutenant A.G. Palmer   **HAMILTON**

Seconded late in July 1945 to 'Z' Australia. Did not undertake a mission.
Became staff officer in charge of Semut stores. At the end of hostilities

was sent to Singapore to try and obtain information re lost 'Rimau' party.

The above personnel who were seconded to 'Special Operations Australia – "Z" Special Unit', up to the point in time of recording this information (1996) have never received recognition for their services, either by their Corps, NZ or Australian governments. Nothing has ever been released by the NZDF that the group ever existed. Their Commanding Officer was lost going in on his first operation, and subsequently all requests for recommendations for promotions, as agreed, were never realised. The group was the first SAS Para Commando Unit on operations for New Zealand, being in action in the SWPA area during 1944/45. Two members parachuted behind enemy lines in Borneo. One was captured in the Balikpapan oilfield area, was tortured and beheaded. The other survived the war uninjured. The unit was released from the Official Secrets Act late in the 1980s.

Operations in the SWPA in 1945

In 1944, with the Allied forces concentrating on a direct attack against the mainland of Japan, certain areas occupied by the enemy were by-passed, thus leaving large controlled land masses still containing considerable Enemy Forces, consisting of sea, air and army units. It was considered that in Borneo a serious threat would transpire from the Brunei area, Labuan Island, a known naval and airforce base. On the mainland, consisting of Brunei, Sarawak, Dutch and British North Borneo, substantial forces of Japanese were still in occupation under the command of General Masao Baba. The Allied General Staff and Allied Intelligence Bureau, who were the controllers of SRD and 'Z', required an efficient Intelligence network of operatives in this specified area, to provide the 9th Australian Division with accurate information relating to the strength and location of the enemy forces, prior to the invasion by their troops in June 1945. These occupied areas of colonial islands, being off the direct line of attack against Japan, had now become the sole responsibility of the Allies of the US, as General MacArthur did not wish to commit his American forces in this direction.

The fortunes of SRD received a major change in early 1945 as they would now be acting in direct support of the AMF with intelligence and guerrilla action against the by-passed enemy garrisons, and would undertake their proper SO roles. Thus the SOA operations were placed on the priority list for entry into Borneo. With the Allies in control of Morotai Island in the Halmahera Group, Borneo was now in the area which could be penetrated by long-range aircraft, and the B-24 Liberators of 200 Flight RAAF were the correct type of aircraft for these missions. They could remain in the air for considerable periods of time, were economical on fuel and with great carrying capacity of supplies and bombs were easily adapted to requirements for the dropping of guerrilla-trained parachutists into occupied territories. Flying times recorded to Borneo and return to base were logged at between eleven and fifteen hours depending on existing conditions prevailing before and whilst airborne. Submarine entry into the areas was considered a bad risk as the coastal Malays and natives were unreliable, and the element of surprise would be at risk with the necessary transportation of equipment and supplies into the interior. The Japanese controlled the coastal regions, but not the interior tribal lands of the 150-million-year-old virgin forests and the indiginous peoples, 'The Headhunters'. News of enemy forces landing on the coastal regions would soon come to the attention of the Japanese and large parties would seek out our operatives prior to their establishment in the interior.

Borneo is a hot, sultry island of lush vegetation, tropical birdlife and a great variety of animals. It is situated in the Malayan Archipelago, bounded to the east by the Sulu Sea, the Celebes Sea and the Straits of Makassar; to the south by the Java Sea; and to the west and north by the South China Sea. It is a mountainous land in the north and central regions, with Mt Kinabalu in the NW, rising to over 13,000 feet and a known marker for our 200 Flight RAAF, flying B-24 Liberators on their missions of supply and reinforcement of operatives into selected locations under SRD control.

It is a land of indigenous tribes with about 350 different dialects, but one language taught by the *hadjis*, teachers of Islam, who had roamed the *ulu* or interior of Borneo for hundreds of years, was *bahasa Malayu* (Malay language). Being able to communicate with the headhunters of Borneo was one of the main factors for the survival of all operatives within the interior. Animals such as elephants, several species of monkey, hornbills, orangutans, wild oxen, tigers, honey bears, porcupines, flying squirrels, foxes, big bull ants, various species of deer and pig abound. The reptile group included the crocodile, lizards and enormous python. In some of the rivers the deadly and lethal piranha fish abound. The interior is one of the most disease-infected areas of the tropics, with BT and MT malaria, scrub typhus and blackwater fever abounding. The slightest scratch could become infected and even life threatening if unattended. Without medical attention over the three years of occupation, the general health of the indiginous peoples of the interior was affected.

Recognition must be accorded the 'White Rajas of Sarawak', the 'Brooke Regime', for the successful 'Semut' operational groups to survive the first entry into the interior of Borneo and Sarawak, after the Japanese occupational forces controlled the area. The Brooke government had instituted various regulations and laws prohibiting any interference by outsiders with the indigenous peoples of the 150-million-year-old virgin rain forests, thus protecting their customs, rituals, and tribal laws of 'Within'. The European (*Orang Puteh*) was respected and accepted in their domains when moving through the many tribal areas. The groups of 'Z' who parachuted into the interior (*ulu*) were immediately accepted as members of their communities and families, and were shared amongst the various longhouses in the kampongs. In all areas, unbeknown to the operatives, the *Penghulu* or *Kepala* (Headman) of the tribe, allocated two of his members as personal bodyguards to each '*Orang Puteh* from the Skies', with instructions to protect their charge at all costs. When in action against the Japoon they were but an arm's length away.

If the Malays, coastal natives and the Chinese throughout Borneo had not been maltreated and abused by the Japanese, Allied operatives would have experienced considerable difficulty in obtaining their assistance and required intelligence information for the Australian Divisional attack, set for June 1945.

Missions During 1945

The five 'Agas' missions constituted one of the more successful major operations carried out by SRD. The original Agas party, under the command of Major Chester (UK) of Python fame, left Darwin on 24 February and landed at Lubuk Bay, Borneo, on 3 March. (The first attempt to land operatives in this area by submarine in early January failed, as the enemy were sighted in the DZ in large numbers. The mission was aborted and the party returned to Australia.) The objects of the mission were to establish a base on the east coast of British North Borneo with radio communication to Australia; to set up a native intelligence network, particular importance being attached to detail information on the POW camp at Sandakan and the high-priority target indicated by GHQ at Kudat; to establish friendly relations with the natives; and ultimately to organise such armed resistance in that area as might be authorised by GHQ. The intelligence objectives subsequently were increased by military developments to include, in addition to the original area, the north-west coastal area of the Sarawak border and the Japanese concentrations at Ranau and its approaches. The party selected a jungle base for its radio station and stores, and made reconnaissances of Sesip, Sugut, Mamahat, Arbar and Paitan rivers by folboat. The party leader contacted natives through a former Customs House boatman. A hospital was set up with a Chinese Doctor in charge at Lokapas. By 17 May, 150 natives were being trained as agents and for police duty. The party killed several score of the enemy, rescued Allied prisoners, and, during the course of the mission, more then 600 Japanese were destroyed as a result of air strikes directed by Agas spotters. Major Chester was evacuated on 21 May and Captian Sutcliffe (UK) took command of the party.

Agas III, led by Flight Lieutenant G.C. Ripley RAAF, was inserted on 23 June for the purpose of supplying general intelligence and making a reconnaissance for the rescue of POWs at Rinau. The party was unable to rescue the small group remaining at Rinau because of their very weak condition. Arrangements were made for a large white arrow to be placed on the hillside in a jungle clearing to indicate the camp, for possible rescue by paratroops.

Major R. Blow (AIF) led Agus IV which was to obtain intelligence in the Tawau area, located in the extreme south-east of British North Borneo. Headquarters were set up at Semporna on 14 July and the

BETTER BUSINESS, July 1, 1945

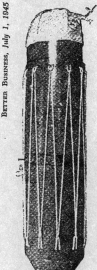

★ *An Australian industrial triumph in getting rations, ammunition and medical supplies to isolated jungle fighters is revealed in*

THE STORY of the STORPEDO

W. S. Lowe

IT SEEMS a long time now since the yellow tides of Japan were sweeping irresistibly through the Western Pacific to the very shores of Australia and New Zealand. With hardly a pause, Malaya, Singapore, Borneo, Java and the rest were overrun and Australians learned with a shock that Japanese forces were in New Guinea, that they had crossed the Owen Stanley Range, that Darwin had been bombed and that an invasion of the continent was imminent.

But the tide, was stemmed and turned and now that it has been rolled back, another story may be told of how food, ammunition and medical supplies were delivered to the fighting, sweating jungle units.

Imagine what happens to a sack of potatoes dropped from 500 ft., by a swooping plane travelling at a speed of 150 miles per hour. No need to mash them after that! How then would tinned supplies or bottled drugs survive the ordeal? In practice there is at least a 50 per cent destruction of durable stores plummeted to advanced units in this way; among the more fragile supplies, the survival rate is much lower.

The obvious answer is the parachute but, with the use of the of the

'chute, the loss is equally as great for other reasons. The falling chute is subject to wind drift. Accuracy in dropping supplies is thus impossible. In the European airborne invasion at Arnhem, British troops were able to recover only 5 per cent of supplies dropped to them by chute because of the inaccuracy factor—and there were no jungles or scrub to hide the precious supplies from view. They were, in fact, too well in view, under withering fire from German units but too far away for the needy British troops to secure.

To this difficulty of accurate supply dropping many minds had given thought. The basic problem was to absorb the shock of supplies hitting the ground. The 'chute reduced this shock effectively but at the cost of accuracy and of scarce and expensive supplies. One solution offered was to fit the load with a substantial spring which would depress beneath the package on impact with the ground. The recoil of the spring proved as damaging to the supplies as the original impact, so that didn't work.

Then a group of Australians got together on the problem. There was R. P. Morris, young general manager of Mor-

BETTER BUSINESS, July 1, 1945

civil engineer; Colonel Lennox, the aeronautical expert of the group; Captain Frewin, well-known test pilot; and E. R. Campbell, chief engineer for Morris and Walker. They finally evolved a successful scheme and with magnificent enthusiasm sold the idea to a sceptical Air Department. The firm of Morris and Walker, printers, poster makers, box-makers and general experts in paper and cardboard, spent over £2000 in preliminary experiments and manufacture.

Today, all over the Pacific in the Allied Air Forces, the result of their endeavours, the Storpedo, is a familiar sight to men and units in isolated positions. Everything from cartridges to electric light globes, from tinned beef to fresh eggs, can be successfully dropped in the Storpedo. Thousands of units have been supplied and there has been 95 per cent success in the accurate and safe delivery of supplies.

There are two essential items in the Storpedo's equipment—a small 'chute and a specially designed percussion nose which absorbs the impact. Of the two, the nose is the really revolutionary invention. Some understanding of the shock to be absorbed on impact with the ground can be gauged from an example.

A load of 200 lb., dropped from a plane 500 feet above the target, has to absorb a shock equivalent to the dropping upon it of two tons from a height of one foot! The same kind of shock would be felt by the passenger of a car which struck a brick wall head on while travelling at 25 miles per hour.

The Storpedo nose is constructed of layers of cardboard (chip-board, more accurately) formed into a cone about 16 inches in diameter and 12 inches from apex to base. When this nose, surrounded by a load of supplies, strikes the ground, the nose crumples under the pressure and the shock or energy is absorbed in compressing the air within the nose, which bursts when the internal pressure reaches 30lb. per square inch. The shock is thus not transmitted at all to the supplies above, which come to rest as delicately as if handled on ground level by some careful aircrafts-man.

The Storpedo 'chute increases accuracy because it is only half the diameter of a standard 24ft. 'chute and is equipped with a vent in the canopy which acts as a pilot in its downward fall and ensures that the Storpedo will strike the earth directly on the point of the per-

A Storpedo before assembling and loading. The cylindrical body can be extended by use of the additional sections. Discs in the foreground are used to separate portions of the load. A loaded Storpedo ready for the plane, showing single lacing system, is pictured on the opposite page.

BETTER BUSINESS, July 1, 1945

cussion cone. The accuracy obtainable by this, 'chute is 10 times as great as that previously used and supplies can be dropped with absolute accuracy within an area 25 yards by 100 yards from a height of 500 feet.

★ *Prelude to Success*

THIS is the finished story – a success that has speeded up the Pacific operations, brought fresh food and supplies to troops out of touch by land communications, and supplied medical necessities to forward units. But success did not come at once; not by any means.

The inventors' largest task was to work out an experimental design for the percussion nose – when the cardboard was too thick or too strong it was merely crushed by the impact; when too weak or too thin it burst too soon and, in either case, supplies were dam-

aged. Many an experimental Storpedo was tried out by dropping it down a light well in the Morris and Walker factory. Size and design of 'chute and Storpedo body, best weight for loads, tensile strengths of ropes, 'chute materials and cardboards, height and speed of launching from planes and methods of releasing the parachute after launching – these were some of the minor difficulties considered and overcome.

Nor was it easy to convince the sceptical experts that the Storpedo was the answer to their prayers; perhaps it was Morris' salesmanship or Lennox' mathematics, or maybe it was just a desire to get rid of them both which at last brought permission for official tests. With an eye to a spectacular demonstration Lennox went all out for a salvo drop – half a dozen Storpedos shot out

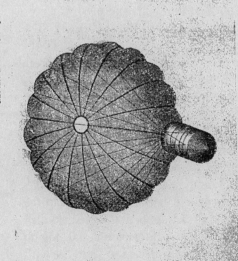

BETTER BUSINESS, July 1, 1945

22 inch Storpedo dropped from 500ft. Picture taken from ground nine seconds after release.

BETTER BUSINESS, July 1, 1945

of the bomb-bay togeth-er. A heart-to-heart, brother-if-you-love-me-at-all talk to the pilot brought this off and the brass hats were duly impressed as the whole salvo with undamaged supplies landed within a narrow circle.

Another spectacular idea didn't come off so well. This was an experimental drop into the sea to test the usefulness of the Storpedo used like a bomb without a parachute, in dropping supplies to shot-down airmen or to lifeboats. The load, unknown except to the inventors, consisted of bottles of ginger beer and glasses, and the idea was for the waiting launch to whip up to the Storpedo and then the duly impressed officials were to be treated to a drink. The Storpedo landed with a great spout of spray. The launch raced across and Morris prepared for his climax; but something had misfired – the glasses were intact but the bottles had kept on going all the way to Davey Jones!

★ *Peacetime Uses*

HOWEVER, one failure is a small matter when you can successfully demonstrate the dropping of fresh eggs, without making an omelette. The Storpedo won its place and the Morris and Walker factory roared into the production of unrevealed thousands. New models and

adaptations followed in quick succession and soon the air-borne supply problem ceased to exist.

Now the inventors are working on a scheme to use the Storpedo for peacetime needs. Isolated settlers will need supplies and small towns will appreciate at least an inward air mail postal service in the post-war air age. The Storpedo is being adapted to use for dropping from any height. It will bring its load in an unbroken fall to within 500ft. of the ground and then the 'chute will come into operation to check the descent. Units will be returned to the factory for nose replacements and re-packing of the 'chute. Perhaps they will even perfect a model for dropping off passengers – you never know!

The idea would certainly seem to have possibilities in New Zealand – dropping supplies and mail, I mean; not passengers. At the least it might be feasible as an intermediate step whereby small but airminded communities, lacking landing facilities or the funds to provide them, could still share in the air age.

Meantime the Storpedo is another of those remarkable achievements which have been on the secret list; achievements which, taken together, have literally won the war.

☆ ☆

party completed several successful patrols before ceasing operations when the war ended.

Agas V, under Captain R.K. McLaren, operated in the Lahad Datu area (Darbell Bay region). An intelligence system was established and a hospital dressing station were set up.

The 'Semut' were the principal parties operating in the Brunei Bay territory and in Dutch Borneo. These operations were planned to obtain pre-invasion intelligence. As originally planned, the project comprised two parties: a reconnaissance party and a main body to follow up after two weeks. The whole operation was to have been controlled by Major G.S. Carter (GB/NZ) from a headquarters in the Baram river area, but difficulties in intercommunication and the need for decentralising the administration of such a large area, which at that time included not only Sarawak but also portions of Dutch and British North Borneo, contributed to the subdivision of Semut into separate commands. Major Tom Harrisson of the original reconnaissance party was firmly of the opinion from the start of the operation that he could control his area by himself, and not be restricted by another person in the area.

Since the Dutch Christian natives were much more numerous than the Sarawak pagans and intensively more violently anti-Japanese, it was decided to move the headquarters eastward to the Sarawak border behind Kabak. All personnel in the party had been giving medical assistance to every village visited, a major factor in winning and holding native goodwill. By the end of July over 1,000 members of tribes from the interior were under arms, equipped either with captured Japanese weapons or with rifles which the party had been able to supply. The arrival of 300 rifles had a further effect on raising the moral of the natives. The main problem was to restrain these new guerrillas from taking the offensive in an indiscriminate way. Excellent discipline was observed due to the careful plans made for the distribution of arms and control. Each of the valleys comprising the main lines of approach into the area was under the control of a white operative, who had with him fifteen to twenty-five 'regulars', natives who were treated as fully-fledged soldiers. Weapons were assigned to individuals on a 'loan' basis, with the specified number of rounds of ammunition. Weekly inspections were made to see that rifles were properly cared for, and that the ammunition had been used only for purposes intended. Guerrillas killed a number of Japanese who penetrated into the interior but did not go in search of the enemy. They also took prisoners including several notorious collaborators. A site was selected in the Bawang Valley and cleared, levelled, the rice fields drained, and a new runway of split bamboo constructed. The first plane (an Auster from Tarakan Island) landed nine days after the project commenced.

Semut I agents penetrated to Brunei, Trusan, Lawas, Sipitang, Tenom, Keningau and Beaufort. An efficient fifth column operated over a wide coastal area. In addition to sending a daily report of enemy movements, information regarding air targets was provided enabling the RAAF to attack these with conspicuous success. The Japanese local food supply was cut off and numerous natives were induced to abandon the Japanese working instead for Semut I. According to prior arrangements, Semut took the offensive on 9 June, the same day the AIF landed on the coast, taking the Japanese completely by surprise when they were attacked from inland and from the coast.

Results of Operation Semut I were excellent. In addition to the collection of intelligence prior to the AIF landing, over 1,000 Japanese were killed and enemy opposition to the landings weakened. Civil order and temporary administration was restored throughout northern Dutch Borneo, the inner areas of northern Sarawak and south-western British North Borneo. At the time of the Japanese surrender, Semut I controlled an area of approximately 16,000 square miles with nearly a quarter of a million population. Large numbers of Japanese documents and maps were forwarded to ATIS, Labuan Island. Major I. Lloyd of this unit flew into Borneo by Auster landing on the bamboo strip, then proceeding northwards to Long Miau, lower Sabah area. Here he inspected and documented material freshly supplied to him by the operatives in that area. From these he translated the information of the Japanese intention to fortify and defend the Sapong Estate in the northern region of Sabah.

Much new geographical information was collected on large tracts of previously unmapped and unexplored country. Some 300 intelligence reports were responsible for the successful bombing of important targets in the area until August 1945. One Japanese force known as the 'Fujino Tai', under the Command of Lieutenant Fujino, consisting of approximately 600 including women, children, medical staff and nurses, broke through the Semut II lines of Major Toby Carter (GB/NZ) in the Baram river area south-east of Brunei. This group headed through the Belait and Tutoh areas in a direct line towards the Sungai Limbang to the north. They continued to defy the surrender order, believing that the information contained in the leaflets was incorrect, and a ploy by the Allies to make them surrender. The documents, according to Fujino, did not have the Emperor's chop (seal) attached, hence their non-acceptance when dropped from the air.

They continued into the interior, killing, raping, destroying anything of value including extra food supplies and kampongs. The two Semut I operatives (one NZ, one Australian) and their Iban and Dayak guerrillas, after walking away from the group on four occasions, finally responded, causing the 600 Japanese many casualties and pushing them up into the interior, to the headwaters of the Limbang river. From this location the group travelled into the interior and finally surrendered on 28 October near the HQ of Semut I and the bamboo airstrip in the Bawang Valley, Belawit. It was a costly trek into the interior for the Fujino Tai, losing approximately 200 of its members to guerrilla action and sickness.

Semut II was to operate in the Baram river basin, an area almost covered by thick jungle swamps in the coastal region. Travel throughout the area was almost entirely by river with the result that control of the river system was essential if Semut II was to be penetrated from central Borneo and the coast. Eight members of the party, commanded by Major Toby Carter (GB/NZ), landed by parachute on 16 April. Reinforcements were landed later, increasing the party to twenty-three by 30 August. Headquarters were established at Long Akah (Baram river area), the old government fort. The natives were very cooperative as captured records and intelligence information poured in through their efforts. When the Japanese pushed through to the Tinjar river, the natives panicked and it was then learned that the Ibans were effective only while they were winning. Weapons served as a moral booster only, the natives' success at killing Japanese was not due to bullets but trickery. They would decapitate the enemy whilst he was asleep or drunk. Against organised resistance they were useless. With the assistance of the AIF, Semut II was able to restore law and order in this region pending the arrival of the Military Affairs Unit.

The nucleus of Semut III was originally inserted with Semut II. Captain L.W. Scochon (UK) and two others left this section to establish a new party which was to operate in the Rejang river basin of Sarawak. The native Dayaks of this area had their own methods of killing Japanese, using deadly blowpipes (*sumpitans*). The party's policy was to form an armed body made up of rangers, police personnel and native volunteers. The force had a standard army organisation and no arms were issued to anyone outside the group. Heavy casualties were inflicted on the enemy during the period of operation, 16 April to 23 June.

Semut IV was made up of personnel assigned to 'Crocodile' and was to operate temporarily until Operation Crocodile was ready to commence. The primary mission was to obtain intelligence on the coastal area of Sarawak between Baram Point and Tanjong Sirik. The party under Major Jinkins included two ex-government employees of Sarawak. Inserted in August 1945, they had hardly begun to operate when the war ended.

Another Borneo operation of considerable dimensions was coded 'Platypus'. Like Agas and Semut, Platypus was highly rewarding. The quality of continuous information returned by various subdivisions of the party had an important bearing on the decisions of the Allied Commander in the Balikpapan area. Platypus was to be carried out in a series of phases.

Phase I (Robin) was to build up an intelligence network over Balikpapan and Samarinda areas to gain all types of military intelligence, including information of the POW camp north of Balikpapan. This operation was under the command of Major D. Stott (NZ).

Phases II, III, and IV were carried out by a party led by Lieutenant Bob Tapper (NZ). Phase II was most successful in removing natives from sea-going perahus in the Balikpapan area for interrogation, and later selected well-informed natives from Balikpapan itself for interrogation at Morotai Headquarters. Phase III was to deceive the enemy by focusing attention on the area north-east of Balikpapan. This was done by having the native operatives pass the required rumours, by flying over the particular area at zero altitude as if making a reconnaissance, and by dropping a marked map and operation instructions, together with beach markers on the beach near Senipan where they would be picked up. The success of this mission was proved when large native patrols were sighted in the area during the later missions, and by a broadcast from Tokyo that a landing had been made in the area. The object of Phase IV was the extraction of informants from Balikpapan and the spreading of rumours mentioned in Phase III. Eighteen informants were extracted and the enemy deception plan was completed.

Phase V was to provide inter-communication between field parties, divisions and brigades for the purpose of passing last-minute information; to control movements and tasks of the field parties according to the tactical situation; to provide an extra intercommunication link for Divisional Headquarters as required; and to organise a safe withdrawal of field parties to their own lines. The party was to furnish a special detachment of eight operatives to accompany Divisional Headquarters in order to carry out any special task required. This special detachment under Captain M.L. Drew (AIF) was attached to HQ 7th Australian Division to supply close liaison between field parties and the invading forces. Platypus V acted as an advance party for Group C which arrived in Balikpapan on 12 July and took over the control of SRD Forces.

Phase VI was led by Captain McLaren. The party was parachuted into the Riko Bridge area near Balikpapan on 30 June. Owing to the height and wind draft, the party overshot the DZ and landed 50 yards from a Japanese guardhouse. They escaped detection, but supplies dropped near this garrison over a mile from the selected area, were subsequently lost. One member of the party was captured; the others evacuated on 6 July without having been able to accomplish their mission.

Flight Lieutenant A.R. Martin (RAAF) was in charge of Phase VII, which was to carry out a reconnaissance of the Mt Mentawir area about 20 miles north of Balikpapan. The party of four was inserted half an hour after Phase VI, from the same B-24 Liberator delivering Phase VI. They parachuted into the area without having been able to check the dropping zone and the mission was consequently unsuccessful through its failure to follow correct methods and procedures within enemy-held territory. Three of the party were lost – one was shot at a river crossing and killed, while a New Zealand signalman and a Malay Sergeant were captured, tortured and beheaded. The leader of the party was blown off course and landed 10 miles from the DZ location. He landed in a 100-foot tree, was badly injured, but managed to escape with the help of friendly natives. The whole mission consisting of Phase VI and VII was doomed to failure from the beginning.

Four parties operated under Phase VIII, led by Captain V.D. Prentice (AIF). As a direct result of the activities of this party, air strikes were made on several important targets. At Kotabangeon, the HQ occupied by Admiral Saburo Nomiya was completely destroyed and much of the town demolished. Local food supplies were cut off from the enemy. Valuable post-war contacts with native chiefs were made on behalf of the Dutch Government, and intelligence regarding Japanese escape routes was obtained.

Platypus IX, with Captain McLaren in charge, left Balikpapan on 12 July, proceeding up Balikpapan Bay to a northern point where radio communications were set up with SRD Headquarters to report on enemy activity in the region.

Phase X of Platypus landed in the Riko river area on 16 July. Due to enemy activity in this region, the party was unable to complete its mission and was withdrawn on 20 July. The party of four was under the command of Lieutenant Chambers.

Platypus XI commanded by Lieutenant R. Tapper (NZ) was inserted on 22 July to obtain intelligence in Semoi, Mentawir and Sepake areas, and to obtain information about POWs being held by the Japanese. Information from natives made possible the rescue of sixty-three Indian POWs in the area. On 25 July Flight Lieutenant Alan Martin, the leader of Phase VII who had been missing since 30 June was found. Whilst natives were bringing him downriver to the coast by perahu, they encountered Lieutenant Tapper's patrol who arranged for him to be uplifted and returned to Base Hospital at Morotai.

In the final Phase, Platypus XII entered the Pegiah area to ascertain whether or not any POWs were in that locality. They found no trace, but were able to gather information concerning defensive positions of the enemy.

Two large cooperative projects were planned during this period in conjunction with other AIB sections. 'Salmon' was the joint plan of SRD, SIA and NEFIS III, and envisioned a complete chain of communications from Darwin to Java with the intervening islands serving as links. It was intended that these secret island bases could service a fleet of small surface vessels, thus eliminating, or at least reducing, the existing complete dependence upon submarine transportation for operational purposes. All stores and supplies were assembled and personnel were ready to move in and establish three bases according to plan, when the imminence of the Japanese surrender caused GHQ to order these movements to halt. Eventually the entire project was cancelled.

SIA Operations, 1945

In addition to the participation in the Salmon project, SIA was charged with a number of operations in the NEI under the heading of the 'Town' Plan. Five parties were established: 'Caen', 'London', 'Bath', 'Dover' and 'Crewe'. London was inserted on Cocos Island on 5 June, with Lieutenant Chater (AIF) as leader. Operating till after the war ended, this party served as a repeater station for other parties, obtaining general information on the enemy as well. Dover, commanded by Lieutenant Gillett was inserted into the Semenka Bay region, Sumatra, on 3 July. Crewe was to work in Java at Tanjong Pela Bunan with Lieutenant Nicholson (RANVR) in charge.

All three of these parties were composed of Indonesian personnel and obtained general information on enemy activities in their assigned areas. Bath was composed of specially trained Arab operatives and commanded by Lieutenant Drake (RANVR). This party operated in the Sunda Strait area, West Java. Caen was also composed of Mohammedans and operated successfully in Surabaya from 9 August until the end of the war. All of these parties were already in place and maintaining an initial flow of information by the time the war ended. It is believed that these contacts would have been quite useful had field operations continued. Party 'P6F', consisting of two Indonesians, was sent into Kendari in the Celebes on 26 January but failed to report and was presumed lost.

The dismal success rate in the Dutch New Guinea/Timor area provides a lesson in special operations. The Dutch insisted that a Dutchman command all operations in their former colonial areas; the Portuguese also attached personnel to operations in their section of Timor. Special operations require the participation and support of the local populations, and the Dutch were hated colonial masters. Almost every mission that contained Dutch operatives failed. The Semut operations were scattered over the Borneo-Halmaheras-Celebes area and in the lower NEI. Withdrawal of these persons was delayed mainly because of extreme transport shortages and also because the 9th Australian Division operating in Labuan, and the Semut group, were instructed to continue their operations on the North Borneo Coast. Both Agas and Semut assisted in obtaining information regarding POWs and the collection of surrendered weapons. The Tawi Tawi base of SRD under Captain J.L. Chipper was closed early in September and the party was assembled on Morotai by 14 September.

Summary of Field Operations

CODE NAME	LEADER	OPERATIONAL AREA	DATE OF MISSION
Adder	Grimson	Portuguese Timor	21 Sept 45
Agas I	Chester	Sandakan Area	3 Mar–28 Aug 45
Agas II	McKeown	Kudat area, BNB	3 May–21 May 45
Agas III	Ripley	Ranau, BNB	23 Jun–11 Oct 45
Agas IV	Blow	Tawau, BNB	14 Jul–13 Oct 45
Agas V	McLaren	Lahad Datu, BNB	27 Jul–10 Sep 45
Bintang	Buxton	Semarang, Java	19–20 Jun 45
Brim	Crombie	Dilor River, Timor	5 Aug 45
Carpenter I	Martin	Johore State	22 Sept 44–25 Feb 45
Carpenter II	Hart	Johore State	7 Feb–31 Dec 45
Cobra	Cashman	Guruda, Timor	29 Jan 45
Crane	Gluth	Batoe Daka-Togia	14–15 May 45
Crayfish	Overweel	Wissel Lakes-NG	26 Feb–26 Jul 45
Crocodile	Jenkins	Natuna-Anambis-Tembelan	6–13 Aug 45
Flathead	Nicholls	Asia Is., Ayu-Vogulkop	Sept–Oct 44
Giraffe I	Trappes-Lomax	Taboelandang Is.	17 Mar–18 May 45
Giraffe IIa	Trappes-Lomax	Majoe Is.	26 Mar 45
Giraffe IIb	Gluth	Majoe-Tifore Is.	27–29 Apr 45
Hippo	Cheng (Canada)	Kuching, Borneo	10–15 Aug 45
Jaywick	Lyon	Singapore Harbour	8–12 Sept 43
Lagarto	Ellwood	Portuguese Timor	1 Jul–29 Sept 43
Largharout	Johnson	Dilot/Luca River, Timor	15–17 Jul 45
Lizard I	Broadhurst	Sth Coast, Timor	17 Jul–17 Aug 42
Lizard II	Broadhurst	Beaco	2–12 Sept 42
Lizard III	Thomas	Sandimingo	17 Nov 42–11 Feb 43
Magpie I	Lambert	Sangihe Is.	11–12 Jun 45
Magpie II	Brown (NZ)	Majoe-Tifore Is.	29 Jun–3 Jul 45
Menzies	Prentice	Serong-Samate-Batana	Jun–Sept 44
Mugger-Sounder	Paddick	Portuguese Timor-Babaris	Feb–Jul 44
Opossum	Brunings	Hiri, Ternate Is. Halamrs	8–11 Apr 44
Optician	Kennerd	Sth China/Java Seas	7 Mar–15 Apr 45
Perch	Lees	Dutch New Guinea	13 Aug–23 Sept 45
Platypus/Robin I	Stott (NZ)	Balikpapan	30 Mar–10 May 45
Platypus II-IV	Tapper (NZ)	Balikpapan, Dutch Borneo	16–24 Jun 45

Platypus VI	McLaren	Riko river area, Balik/pn	30 Jun–7 Jul 45
Platypus VII	Martin	Mt Mentawir, Balik/pn	30 Jun–25 Jul 45
Platypus VIII-1	Prentice	Samairinda, Borneo	1 Jul–12 Aug 45
Platypus VIII-2	Thompson		
Platypus VIII-3	Chalmers		
Platypus VIII-4	Martin		
Platypus IX	McLaren	Balikpapan	12–18 Jul 45
Platypus X	Chalmers	Riko river, Balikpapan	16–20 Jul 45
Platypus XI	Tapper (NZ)	Balikpapan Bay	22 Jul–6 Aug 45
Platypus XII	Biggs	Begiah	28 Jul 45
Politician	Jenkins	Sth China & Java Seas	Dec 44–Jun 45
Python	Chester	E. Borneo, Tanbisan	6 Oct 43–8 Jun 44
Raven	Stringfellow	Rando, Celebes	14–20 Jun 45
Reaper (Copper)	Cardew	Muschu Wewak	11–20 Jun 45
Reaper (Gold)	Nicholls	Cape Moem, E. of Wewak	8–9 Apr 45
Rimau	Lyon	Singapore Harbour	11 Sept 44–7 Jul 45
Rimau (Extract)	Chapman	Merapas-Singapore	22 Nov 44
Semut I	Harrisson	Sarawak, Borneo	25 Mar–28 Oct 45
Semut II	Carter	Barum river, Brunei	16 Apr–20 Jun 45
Semut III	Sochon	Rajan river, Borneo	16 Apr–23 Jun 45
Semut IV	Jenkins	Makab, Bintulu, Borneo	27 Aug–11 Oct 45
Squirrel (Phase I)	Prentice	North Borneo	3 Apr 45
	Prentice	Moeara, Sebawang	24 Apr 45
		Djoeta Oil Fields	3 May 45
Squirrel (Phase II)	Hands	Brunei Bay, Borneo	1–20 May 45
Stallion II	Hands	Mempokulto, Tg. Sakat	15–19 May 45
Stallion III	Prentice	Usukau Bay	20 May 45
		Jesselton, Borneo	2 Jun 45
Stallion IV (Agas III)	Chester	Beaufort-Papar-Kimanis Bay	8–17 Jun 45
Gelding (Stallion V)	Leckie (NZ)	Weston, Sipitang, Brunei Bay	8–17 Jun 45
Mare (Stallion VI)	Drew	Mempakul, Brunei Bay	8–11 Jun 45
Stallion VII	Mollard	Labuan	2 Jun 45
Colt (Stallion VIII)	Oldham	Sipitang, Brunei Bay	16–18 Jun 45
Filly (Stallion VIII)	Leckie (NZ)	Palu Saat, Brunei Bay	13–14 June 45
Foal (Stallion VIII)	Hardwick	Brunei, Kimanis area	23–27 Jun 45
Starfish	Black	Lombok Island	14 Mar–3 May 45
Stork	Gluth	Tifore, Majoe Is.	25–28 May 45
Sunable	Williams	Ocussi, Dutch Timor	27 Jun 45
Sunbaker	Wilkins	Timor	17 May 45
Suncharlie	Marshall	Doefoei Islet, SW Timor	23–30 Apr 45
Suncob	Wynne	Guruda, Timor	2 Jul 45
Sundog (Phase I)	Austin	Sth. Coast, Frontiera Prov.	21 Jul 45
Sunlag	Stevenson	Vemori, Timor	29 Jun–5 Aug 45
Swift	Betington	NW Halmaheras	16–18 May 45

Operation Agas I –
British North Borneo (Sabah)

This recording of the above mission is from the manuscripts of S/Sgt Graham Greenwood, who was a member of the 2 NZEF seconded to SOA in August 1944. His group of eight Kiwi Army personnel travelled to Australia by Sunderland Flying Boat 'Aotearoa'.

The first mission into North Borneo area by submarine was aborted. On approaching the DZ during daylight at periscope depth, the area was observed to contain heavy concentrations of enemy forces. At this stage it was not possible to make new operational arrangements, as no reconnaissance photographs had been taken except this particular area. The only alternative available to the party was to return to Darwin base. However there was a major snag – this particular submarine could not make the return to Australia, as it had a rendezvous to keep elsewhere. The Commander contacted by radio another Allied submarine in this locality, and arranged for the party to be uplifted and transported back to their base. The transference of stores and equipment proved to be a nightmare. The crossing between submarines by rubber boats in pitch darkness and heavily loaded was accomplished through choppy sea conditions at the time.

Unloading was extremely difficult, having to scramble up the heaving sides of both vessels to stow everything away. The whole traumatic experience took over two hours, and the operatives were all thoroughly exhausted, demoralised and experienced seasickness.

The Second Attempt of the Mission

Back in Darwin again, the equipment all checked and in readiness, another submarine had been laid on for 24 February – in five days time. Waiting in Darwin's mid-summer conditions was an exhausting and trying experience for this Kiwi. To those from more southern climes, summers in Darwin are almost unbearable. Our green-clad party of four officers and three other ranks just sat at our demarcation camp area and awaited for the arrival of our transport to the submarine. On arrival we heaved on-board our personal gear, and were taken a short distance down to the port.

VNZ 452668 S/Sgt G.R. Greenwood

The first sight of the huge submarine nestled against the wharf brought home the stark reality of what lay ahead. The truck drove onto the wharf, giving us a closer look at this business-like American submarine tied up alongside, with Stars and Stripes hanging motionless from its stubby mast in the still afternoon air. I had never seen a submarine before except on the movies, and its size – what could be seen of it – was staggering. Most of its three hundred foot length (91 metres for the metric mind) from stem to stern lay low in the water, with only its duck-board decking above sea level. All that rose above the deck was a four-inch gun in front of its ammunition locker, the conning tower, periscope and radar antenna, now both fully retracted, and a stumpy mast supporting aerials and the wire stretching fore and aft. The whole craft was painted a dull, dark grey. I felt a flush of excitement at the prospect of the seven of us joining the crew of about seventy on what would be a seven-day journey into the unknown.

The seventy-odd green kerosene tins containing our supplies, each with a rope handle tied around it, the deflated rubber dinghy and the two unassembled folboats were already stowed away in the ammunition locker behind its watertight doors, now firmly clamped shut. The arsenal of rifles and guns and our personal equipment were all passed down through the conning tower and stowed away below.

After the farewells to the few whose business it was to know about our mission, we walked down the gang-plank onto the submarine's deck, climbed up a short ladder into the bridge, and down through a hatch into the conning tower, then down another steel ladder to the control room to be greeted by the Commander and his officers. No sooner were these formalities completed that the order was given to get under way. The four diesel engines jumped into life one after the other, the shore lines cast off, and the submarine, with nine tenths of its bulk hidden below the water, slowly edged its way into the channel. We were allowed on deck to witness our departure, which seemed a gala occasion. Everyone in sight was waving good-bye, and every ship that boasted a hooter expressed its farewell long and loud. Even the RAAF mechanics working on the Catalina flying-boats scattered at anchor around the harbour joined in the spirit of the moment. There was certainly no secret about our departure, but few if any would have known we were on board or the nature of our journey.

Rapidly gaining speed, the US Submarine *Tuna* headed for the boom gate at the entrance of Darwin Harbour, passing a frigate at anchor on our starboard side. As we approached, her crew all stood-to along the rails, and those of us on deck returned the compliment by doing likewise. Then they too sent us on our way with a long series of 'toots'. Ahead of us the boom-ship lazily prescribed a quarter circle to allow us to pass through into the open sea, and when we were clear, it immediately retraced its path to replace the heavy anti-submarine steel net across the channel entrance.

The low hills around Darwin gradually sank below the horizon behind us, and it was good-bye to Australia. When would we see it again? So we were at last on our way. This was 'Day One' – 24 February 1945.

It was very pleasant on deck, with the water swishing past a few inches below our feet at about 20 knots, and the cool breeze fanning us. Very welcome after Darwin's 95 degrees in-the-shade only an hour or two earlier. As the sun headed for the sea on our port beam we decided to go below and settle into whatever quarters had been allotted to us. Of our party of seven only three of us were not commissioned, and we learnt that there were only two bunks between the three of us, and we could fix things up any way we liked. Well, we didn't particularly like this situation, so one of our members who had travelled on the previous trip, and knew his way around, went up to the forward torpedo room and found himself a bunk amongst the racks of stored torpedoes. Thus we all had sleeping quarters we could call our own, which was just as well as there was little else to do most of the time, but doze or read in bed.

The *Tuna* was one of five Tambor class long-range submarines that had been built and commissioned between 1939–41, and all named after deep-sea fish. It was extremely well appointed, with chromium and stainless steel fittings everywhere, a gadget-fitted kitchen, a walk-in freezer stocked with all kinds of goodies, and infinitely more spacious than its British counterparts. Its displacement was around 1,500 tons, with a crew of 60 to 70. Its sting consisted of six torpedo tubes forward, four more aft, the four-inch gun on deck, plus two Oerlikon anti-aircraft guns.

The interior was divided into seven compartments, all separated by watertight bulkheads. Starting from the bow and working aft, there was first the forward torpedo room. Shining levers and gauges were massed around the six closed breeches (looking like great pressure cookers on their sides), and on either side of the narrow central passage were steel racks carrying the 'Tin Fish'. On top of this the duty crew lay on mattresses. Next came the officers' quarters consisting of a wardroom big enough to seat eight comfortably around a table for their meals; for their entertainment a sideboard containing a library, a radiogram and the usual liquid refreshments. About four small cabins on each side of the passageway were the officers sleeping quarters. Through the second bulkhead was the control room, situated directly below the conning tower and the bridge, where the officer of the watch on duty directed operations – on the bridge when on the surface or at the periscope when submerged if there was anything to observe. This control room was a mass of gauges, levers, dials and two huge hydro-plane wheels, and the walls and ceilings were completely obscured by rafts of pipes, tubes, cables and ducts. Electrical switchboards, automatic position finders, electronic navigational aids, radio compass, anti-radar detector, depth-pressure and temperature gauges, all the paraphernalia associated with the tricky business of under-sea navigation and warfare, were grouped around a handful of seamen whose skill and training allowed them to interpret and use this mass of technical gadgetry.

When the craft was submerged at 'periscope depth', that is at a level where the periscope in the 'up' position is just above the surface, the keel was 60ft down. In nautical terms, therefore, it could only dive in a minimum of 10 fathoms. On approaching our DZ locations up north, we would have to be exceedingly careful of the shallow coastal areas.

Passing on towards the after end, the next bulkhead led to the kitchen and the men's mess, heralded at most times of the day by the smell of cooking. The compact all-electric kitchen occupied about 8ft by 4ft, and it was from here the hot meals for the 70-odd crew three times a day were produced. Four tables allowed 24 of the crew to eat at any one time, and as soon as one finished another took the vacated position. When meals were finished the same tables were used for recreational purposes – playing cards or writing letters or whatever. Keeping one's mind active and not becoming bored was the most essential thing for all members. From the mess, pushing away the heavy curtain, one came into dimly lit sleeping quarters. Three tiers of steel bed-frames were hinged on the 'wall', their outer edges supported by chains, each being fitted out with mattress, sheets, pillows and the odd blanket. As the temperature was seldom below 70 deg, F, the need for a blanket was not a requirement or necessity under these conditions. At the end of this area was the shower room or cubby-hole, where a man needed a book of instructions to work out the sequence of valves and taps, and the same went for the 'heads' (loo) alongside, where doing things in the wrong order had disastrous results. The next bulkhead led into the engine room with its four shining diesel engines and electric generators. The diesels, obviously only usable when on the surface, could be used either to drive the craft along or to recharge the batteries; when submerged the generators could be used as motors to propel the sub at three or four knots, drawing power from the batteries. These huge batteries ran the full length of the submarine beneath the floor decking.

The seventh or last compartment was the aft torpedo room, similar to the forward one, but with only four tubes.

The crew accepted us into their midst, and showed real friendship and hospitality for which their service was renowned. They admired our courage in going on such a 'crazy mission', and treated us like some sort of heroes. Most of them had been right through the war in this submarine, and we felt that they were the heroes not us. One seaman

Air New Zeland's first terminal, the flying-boat base at Mechanics Bay, as it appeared in 1939. The airline's first aircraft – ZK-AMA Aotearoa – is moored on the right of the picture in front of the terminal, hangar and engineering buildings. The 19-seat flying-boat (an S.30 Empire Class) had a top speed of 138 mph, and took nine hours to fly the Tasman, a trip which today takes only two and a half hours by Air New Zealand DC-8. The other aircraft in the picture is a Pan American flying-boat.

'Spirit of Progress'
Air-conditioned, stream-lined, all-steel train. In service between Melbourne and Albury, Southern Cross Series P4504.

called 'Tiny' had been with the *Tuna* since she had been commissioned, and in the process had grown to a mighty 23 stone! He would eat two full-sized dinners to our one, and being so heavy he had a special spot amidship where he had to stay whenever the sub dived or surfaced! His girth was so great that, sleeping on a lower berth, the bunk above him could not be used and was permanently folded up.

After nightfall the general rule was to travel on the surface at full speed, with two of the engines being used for propulson and two recharging the batteries. During the evening of the first night we were allowed on deck for a breather, and for an hour or so watched the tropical lightning and realised that, after all the frustrations and delays, this was really 'it'. At about 8 p.m., we were ordered below as there was to be a trial dive, the usual procedure when leaving port was to ensure all systems were properly operative. Suddenly a loud klaxon horn blared through the sub, and everything seemed to happen at once. The officer on watch on the bridge dived into the conning tower, pulling the hatch closed behind him, taking up his position at the periscope as it rose smoothly and silently out of its well. At an order given over the speaker system, the diesel engines became silent, to be replaced by the quiet hum of the electric motors now driving the craft at only a few knots, plus working the ventilator system. More control orders followed, 'Close ports and recirculate'. Being now closed, the air within was recirculated by the electric fans. At the same instant, the ship tilted forward, as the tanks flooded and the sea swished over the decks above.

'Level at 60' came booming over the intercom, and the sub leveled off with its keel 60ft below the surface and the periscope being now fully extended was just above the surface. Operators at their assigned duty positions trimmed the vanes using the hydroplane wheels, with all their attention directed on the depth gauges on the control panel. 'Correct', reported all stations relating to individual functions of the dive.

After thirty minutes the great 1,500 ton 'fish' surfaced after the tanks were blown; diesels roared back to life; ports were opened; fresh night air wafted through the ducts diluting then expelling the moist air that members had breathed for the period of the trial dive. That was the final action this day the 24th February. After listening to the radio news bulletin we were ready to try out our new accommodation 'Navy Submarine' style. Sleep was no problem, the steady humming of the engines and ventilation system lulling us off in an exceedingy short period of time.

February 25th. All day we continued to speed along the surface, heading towards the Eastern tip of the Japanese-held Timor, and during the night passed within twenty miles of its coast. We were permitted

Map showing the route from Darwin to British North Borneo, 24 February to 3 March 1945, on the US Submarine *Tuna*

to go deckside again, but only two at a time in case of emergency action. As it transpired this was to be our last walk 'topside' until DZ disembarkment which eventuated seven days later.

February 26th. At 6 a.m. we were awakened by the diving klaxon, and from this day on, standard operational orders were observed. During daylight hours we were to remain submerged to avoid detection by radar, patrol ships and aircraft, as we were now in the land and sea controlled by our enemy forces. This was to be our first experience of being submerged for a period of twelve hours. By the evening the air 'within' was getting decidedly thick, and to our delight the cook decided to treat us with grilled steak for dinner on this occasion. Oh for the 'Navy' rations! Acrid smoke soon pervaded every corner of the craft, making ones eyes water and smart. The cook wasn't the most popular person on board

THRESHER. (Gun now mounted forward of c.t.)   1941, U.S. Navy, Official.

4 *Electric Boat Co.:* **Gar, Tambor, Tautog, Thresher.**
1 *Mare Island Navy Yard:* **Tuna.**

Displacement: 1,475 tons. Dimensions: 299 × 27 × 13¾ feet. Guns: 1 – 4 inch, 2 – 20 mm. Oerlikon. Tubes: 10—21 inch
(6 bow, 4 stern) Machinery: G.M. Diesels in first 3, Fairbanks-Morse in others, with all-electric drive. B.H.P.:
6,400 = 21 kts. 22 kts. reached on trials). Complement: 65. Differ from *Sargo* type in silhouette, hull form, and
internal lay-out. Double-hull construction, with external control room as in German submarines. Bilge keels are fitted.

Name & No.	Laid down	Launched	Completed	Name & No.	Laid down	Launched	Completed
Gar (206)	27/12/39	7/11/40	14/4/41	Thresher (200)	27/4/39	27/3/40	27/8/40
Tambor (198)	16/1/39	20/12/39	3/6/40	Tuna (203)	19/7/39	2/10/40	41
Tautog (199)	1/3/39	27/1/40	3/7/40				

War losses: *Grampus, Grayback, Grayling, Grenadier, Gudgeon* (207, 211), *Triton* (201), *Trout* (202).

Above: Courtesy of *Jane's Fighting Ships*, 1944–45

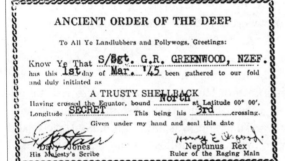

ANCIENT ORDER OF THE DEEP

To All Ye Landlubbers and Pollywogs, Greetings:

Know Ye That S/Sgt. G.R. GREENWOOD, NZEF.
has this 1st day of Mar. '45 been gathered to our fold
and duly initiated as

A TRUSTY SHELLBACK

Having crossed the Equator, bound North at Latitude 00° 00',
Longitude SECRET. This being his 3rd crossing.

Given under my hand and seal this date

Davy Jones
His Majesty's Scribe

Neptunus Rex
Ruler of the Raging Main

Left: King Neptune's
Certificate for crossing
the line.

Right: The badge of the US
Navy Submarine Service, worn
on the white summer uniforms.

at this time, and when surfacing was finally ordered at about 7 p.m.
the fresh air intake was a profound relief to us. The course was now
due west along the Flores sea, and reasonably far from land.

February 27th. We were still travelling west, submerging again
during the day, and on the surface during the real travelling at night.
It was at this stage of the trip that the seven of us gathered around

our maps and aerial reconnaissance photographs spread out on the table of the officers' wardroom, graciously vacated in our favour by the ship's officers. Gort expressed his serious doubts about the security arrangements back in Melbourne, and felt that there was insufficient grounds for changing our sealed orders, which by this time he had opened. To do this without consulting the 'powers that be' was indeed sticking his neck out, but, as he pointed out it was better to have the knowledge than not to be prepared for that which may eventuate in occupied territory. 'Check and double-check' in open and close warfare is undoubtedly a means of survival. As one of the objects of our operation in this initial phase was to investigate the situation at Sandakan-BNB, where about 2,500 Australian and 600 British were interned in a POW camp, and landing reasonably close to this town was essential. After poring over the reconnaissance photographs (which this time covered the coast for approximately 100 miles) it was decided to go to an area north of Labuk Bay, some 35 miles north of Sandakan near Trusan. The intelligence photographs clearly identified three rivers, the two outer ones with villages (kampongs) on their banks – and probably Japanese controlled – but the middle one with no signs of life near it. Our proposed aim was to go up this as our point of entry into BNB, but HQ for security reasons were not to be informed of the change, till after we had safely landed.

The commander of the submarine was consulted, and he produced his charts which provided the information that a long shallow shelf ran out from the shore in this location. He was not prepared to risk taking his charge into waters less than 10 fathoms in case of having to make evasive and emergency dives. Analysing this situation, meant, we would have to be off-loaded approximately 10 miles out at sea. This caused some consternation as we could only make or propel our clumsy flat-bottomed dingy at about one mph. Our rubber dinghy carrying more than a ton of supplies plus seven bodies, and towing two loaded folboats into the bargain, would not reach cover of the shore before daybreak The alternative was to set off as early in the evening as possible, hoping we were not sighted or detected. It was a calculated risk and one that would have to be taken. The die was now cast, therefore this was the location we sought.

February 28th. The night the new course was abruptly corrected northwards into the Makassar Straits, with the enemy now situated on both sides – Dutch Borneo on the port side, and the Island of Celebes on the starboard.

March 1st. The trickiest part of this operation at this stage lay ahead, as we headed for the narrow section of the straits when both shores were visible through the periscope. As darkness fell, and the time for surfacing drew near, the radar detection antenna (which went up and down behind the periscope) showed the presence of enemy radar, probably on the coast on one side of the straits. The frequency was quickly determined and proved to be Japanese, so it was necessary to continue submerged until out of range. At about 4 knots (4½ m.p.h.) this took about three hours, and as the evening wore on the effects of breathing the same air for almost fifteen hours began to be felt. Those who were not performing necessary duties were ordered to lie down, smoking was forbidden, and as a final step metal trays were set out with sodium peroxide spread on them. When water was added the mixture fizzed away, producing oxygen and absorbing the surplus carbon dioxide out of the air. This action greatly relieved the breathing process, but the temperature was still uncomfortably high.

When the radar operator finally reported that there was no longer any radar signals detectable, and preparations were being made to surface, the sonar operator reported engine noises. These were plotted for a few minutes – long enough to learn that a ship was heading straight for the sub. The Captain ordered 'Crash dive to 30 fathoms' (180ft) and at that depth it levelled off, the engines were cut, and complete silence was ordered. Every ear strained. The faint churning noise of a marine engine grew louder and louder until it was directly above. Had our periscope or radar antenna been picked up by their radar? Were they going to drop depth charges? Nobody breathed. Gradually the noise receded and in three or four minutes all was quiet again. Returning to ten fathoms the Captain peered into the darkness of the night through the periscope. Seeing nothing and the radar being clear, the order to 'Surface' boomed loud and clear through the intercom system. Observation and the radar being clear, the order to surface was given. Fresh air came wafting into the sub. Full speed ahead on the surface took us through the straits without further incident, then far from land out into the Celebes Sea.

March 2nd. Sailing due north, heading for the straits between Tawi Tawi and the eastern-most portion of Borneo; this was the last dangerous piece of navigation. Nothing untoward occurred, however, and at daybreak the next morning the sub submerged again into the depths of the Sulu Sea.

March 3rd. The last chance to check our gear, which made us feel like a walking QM store! Each of us had to carry a back-pack, which contained our personal gear, our dress consisting of jungle battle-dress, boots and anklets, for me a black beret with NZ badge on it, web gear, armament consisting of 'Sten' gun (fitted with a clumsy, heavy silencer), a silenced pistol, rubber cosh, plus a .32 or .45 pistol in a holster or back pocket. Strapped to the right leg, the commando's friend, the

7½-inch stiletto. The pouches of our web-gear contained ammunition, two grenades, emergency rations, signalling mirror, mosquito repellent, atabrin tablets, pocket knife and spare torch batteries. From our belts hung a sheathed parang (large native knife), water bottle, waterproof torch, compass, first-aid kit and kosh (a short length of rubber hose fitted with lead shot). On our wrists we had expensive, luminous-dial issue wrist watches. The officers in the party had Luger pistols, Leica cameras, binoculars, US semi-automatic rifles, and two walky-talky radios for possible use later on. Quite an arsenal and weighty too!

After darkness fell about 7 p.m., it was 'Surface–Surface' and up we came. The Captain had been cajoled into taking us to within five miles of our shoreline DZ, despite the depth only being about seven fathoms and too shallow to dive if anything happened. (He didn't want to have any incidents on this trip, as it was their last operation before being homeward bound to San Francisco for refitting and leave during that period of time.)

The seven of us scrambled up the conning tower out onto the deck, which was wet and slippery; the rails had been removed, so there was nothing to support or hang on-to, but fortunately the sea was calm and no wind. It took several minutes for our eyes to become accustomed to the conditions that existed, relieved by the brilliant stars in the totally clear tropical sky; the only thing in sight was a faint line on the horizon which was presumably our DZ area. It looked an awful long way away. We each had our specific job to do, and speed was the

Maruf and Kanun, with a full 'load'.

essence. The huge black rubber dinghy was extracted from the deck ammunition locker, and one's job was to inflate it with a foot-pump. Meantime the two folboats were put together, much quicker and easier than we had imagined. The sub commander was standing over us, trying all he knew to hurry us up. He was quite jittery – far more nervous than we were! The three boats were then gently slid down the sloping sides of the deck into the water, and then the task of loading commenced. This dinghy was far larger than the one we practised with; a full twelve feet long by about seven wide. The middle would be filled up with our gear and sausage-like sides would be our seats. The seventy-odd kerosene tins were stacked three deep and four across; these contained all of our food, ammunition, radio gear, medical supplies and were all numbered for reference. On top of these went all our guns and packs, some of the surplus going into the two folboats which would be towed behind. The job was finally completed without incident, and we were ready to go. Where to? The unknown?

Final farewells were exchanged, and a two-gallon jar of water was passed over to us as a passing gesture, also cartons of cigarettes for the smokers and chewing gum for the non-smokers. It was now 8.20 p.m. when all was completed as we left the safety of the sub. Three sat along each gunwale and Jackie positioned himself facing the stern so he could do his sculling act with the oar. Paddling with canoe paddles, the dinghy was extremely difficult to handle. For a start it spun in circles, got mixed up with the folboats, in fact did everything but go straight ahead. It took several minutes to co-ordinate the paddlers and coax the flat-bottomed barge on any resemblance of a steady course.

Looking back from about fifty yards at the sub, it looked like a black destroyer just sitting there. Suddenly its diesels came to life, shattering the stillness of the night with colossal noise, and disappeared into the darkness. We now felt and realised we were alone in enemy-held waters, and of the opinion the noise would have been heard from the shore, thus warning of our presence. The sub-captain's concern was obviously the safety of his craft and crew rather than us; crazy adventurers, bobbing around in his wake. And so the great haul to shore and what ever began, six paddles stirring up pools of phosphorescence in the warm sea, and the oar sculling away at the rear. We were just settling into the routine when the wooden bracket, tied at the back for the sculling oar to ride in broke one of its straps. As it was below the waterline nothing could be done to tie it on again, and Jackie decided to scull without it. A few minutes later it slid away sidewards and out of his hand, disappearing into the night. This was a good start! Seven pairs of eyes strained to see the oar as we milled around in circles for a full five minutes. If we left it to be found by the Japanese later, they would realise that something was afoot, probably setting up a patrol over the whole area.

Finally, giving the situation at hand as being hopeless and time consuming, a valuable commodity at this point of the operation, a decision was made to abandon the search and press on. Back on the correct course and a few strokes of the paddles, the truant oar hit the side of the dinghy. It was welcomed home by all hands. It was now used as a rudder only, which added considerably to the stability of the course, assisting the six paddlers to push the two-ton load along at 1.5 knots.

For half an hour or so we kept going, then paused for a rest and quenched our thirst from the water bottle supplied from the sub. Whilst talking the feeling came over us that it was becoming lighter; or was it we were becoming accustomed to the dark? Looking behind us we saw the answer, a large almost full moon was coming above the horizon, creating a silvery track down which we would be travelling towards the shore! This condition would make us stand out like 'a pimple on a pumpkin' to any observer from shorewards. Moon rising in the east, our course due west! As we set off again, Jackie and I in the rear seat called for a silent prayer session, as this situation could be our undoing. An uneasy silence settled over the crew with the realisation of just how we were exposed at this moment with the possibility of being sighted by a Japanese patrol boat in this area. After approximately ten minutes, seemed a life time, the brilliance of the moon began to fade. Glancing in that direction, showed that a cloud had formed on the east horizon and had temporarily obscured the offender. It was mercifully dark again, but how long would it last?

After a further hour's heaving on the paddles, a rest and drink period was called for. The moon was now 15 degrees above the horizon and, as it climbed, the easterly cloud bank followed it up. We were still in comparative darkness. Details of the coastline now began to show up. Several miles away to starboard was the dark shape of a headland, which showed that we were in a large bay, and on portside another small headland, past which was nothing but empty sea (Labuk Bay). By midnight, having paddled for 3½ hours, we were getting decidedly stiff through not being able to change our positions or even stretch our legs, and our arms ached from the unusual and prolonged exercise. The drinking water finally disappeared, and the empty bottle filled with sea water was consigned to the deep! The faint noise of the surf became audible, plus odd clumps of trees began to detach themselves from the dark skyline. If our navigation had been accurate (?) we should be in the vicinity of the mouth of the central river of the three photographs we had so closely examined in the sub. We didn't want to travel up the other two, as villages or kampongs existed on the banks, probably occupied and controlled by Japanese.

As the sound of the surf increased, we stopped to observe our position! Still about 400 yards from the shore, the white sand of the DZ could clearly be discerned. A break in the light strip of foreshore indicated a river mouth, which we paddled cautiously and silently towards. Guns and grenades were laid out for instant use should we be spotted or attacked. This was our most tense moment of entry into enemy held territory. No-one spoke – ears were strained – hearts beat loudly as to be almost audible! Expecting having to ride the surf, we were totally surprised when its noise suddenly ceased, and in perfect silence – except for the noise of crickets in the trees – we passed over the bar into the tree-enshrouded estuary of the tidal river. Still with our oars muffled, and the group scarcely breathing, the clumsy craft and its two canoes in tow were eased around the corner, then pulled into the mangroves and hidden from being sighted from the seaward direction.

As if this was the end of the show, the whole area became floodlit when the moon came out from its bank of cloud and drenched the area in its brilliant light. Almost immediately the clouds that had followed the moon to its zenith completely disappeared, to be replaced by the stars again. Not only was this a staggering answer to our prayer, but it seemed to be an omen for the future. We had arrived unseen and in one piece. This was Japanese-occupied Borneo (BNB). The nearest help was 1,500 miles away.

It was now 1 a.m. Stillness prevailed in this remote British North Borneo area known as Sabah. No-one spoke – not even a whisper – the air and water seemed to be asleep knowing that the 8 tense paddlers were intent on listening and resting tired muscles, after five hours of continuous exertion. Quietness was broken by the life in the jungle nearby, with the crickets and night-birds creating their own continuous concert of noise. It was through this that all ears were straining to identify human beings being present at this location.

The moon was now positioned high overhead – the brightness magnificent. One could certainly read a book under these conditions. The landscape was clearly visible and in peace time would have been thoroughly appreciated. Just opposite where we had stopped was a large conifer-type tree covered with thousands of little twinkling fireflies; they would all 'switch-off' with any sudden noise from within the jungle below. Quite fascinating when one observed this view for the first time.

After about half an hour's rest, and being reasonably sure after this period of time that our arrival had not been detected, Gort ordered a further move up river as we would be visible to anyone approaching the estuary from the sea. The heavy clumsy dinghy was coached into motion once again with muffled strokes by the paddlers. Progress was slowed up by the two folboats in tow which insisted on tangling with the protruding roots of the mangroves. In desperation their contents were transferred to the big rubber dinghy, then two of the party climbed into them, propelling them up stream. Five members now remained to push the larger craft up the rapidly narrowing stream.

After struggling for about two hundred yards, it became clear that further progress in these darkened conditions was impossible, but as we were now well hidden from view it was decided to stay where we were till morning. Making ourselves as comfortable as possible whilst now situated in the mangroves, we dropped off to sleep which wasn't difficult after our lengthy and difficult experience just completed.

It was broad daylight when we awoke, and looking out of our surroundings we were greeted by a rather disturbing sight – nothing but mud – mud – mud! In the intervening four hours that we had slept, the tide had receded leaving us high and dry on a tidal flat. The full significance of the situation gradually began to dawn on us, that this was not a river at all – but a tidal estuary.

As such we were not likely to locate any fresh water to quench our thirst with. The two-gallon bottle given to us by the submarine commander was only a tantalising memory; as the bottle had been filled with sea water and consigned to the deep long before we reached the shore. Now all that was left to be consumed was what remained in our personal water-bottles attached to our web belts – about a pint apiece.

Gort and Jack went for a quick scout around, looking for signs of water and a suitable camping site. They returned after about half an hour looking rather glum, having found neither. The area was covered in low, sparse coastal jungle which offered little or no cover from above. We knew, from aerial reconnaissance photographs of the area taken a few days prior to our departure, that fresh water rivers were on each side of us, but kampongs (villages) were located there. Japanese would certainly be in occupation of these and would be considered hostile until we had made contact with the local natives. We would soon know if they were sympathetic towards us, or report our arrival in the area to the Japs!

A temporary sight was chosen amongst a patch of scrub somewhat thicker than the rest, and high enough to be above the high tide line, and to this point we unloaded all the contents of the dinghy and folboats – tin stores, packs, arms, and various essential necessities of war. Finally the folboats were dismantled and the dinghy deflated. Hopefully this craft would not be required again. After consuming a small cold meal and a careful pull at our now precious water supplies, the plan of the day was worked out. Two of us were to stay with the gear and spend the rest of the day making fresh water from sea-water, using the emergency chemical apparatus that had been brought with us for that purpose. The rest of the party would go off in different directions to locate fresh water, returning to the temporary base when successful – or at four in the afternoon, whichever came first.

Just ten days earlier we had been in snowy, wintry conditions in Melbourne, and here we were six degrees from the equator in the steamy jungle with the temperature permanently between 35 and 40 deg. celsius in the shade. Using the conversion equipment for sea to fresh water whilst wearing our lightweight jungle green clothing, the heat of the tropical day and the effort, took the stuffing out of us. The process consisted of pouring about a pint of salt water into a metal canister and adding a measured amount of the chemical; the lid was then screwed on, and for twenty minutes the can had to be shaken up and down like a cocktail-shaker! The resulting mixture was then passed through a gauze filter to remove the precipitated solids (which now included the salt in the form of an insoluble compound), and the pint of not very tasty fresh water poured into one of the kerosene tins. Then the process was started all over again. Taking it in turns we kept this up on and off for almost all of the day, producing about two gallons of liquid thirst quencher for the members of the group. Not much to show for a day's work to the returning patrols who reported that there were no signs of fresh water in this location.

It was a serious group that sat down to their first cooked meal that evening. By the time that the dehydrated meat, vegetables and dried fruit had been soaked and cooked, our cups of coffee made, there was little water to share around for our water bottles. We obviously could not exist and survive for long on that quantity of treated water. Besides which, there wasn't enough chemical to last for more than a few days.

Before darkness enveloped our location, we slung our hammocks between two trees – our first night's sleep ashore. These were American made, with a double layer at the bottom, a very fine mosquito net right around and which closed up from the inside with a zip fastener, and a rubberised tent-top roof which was stretched out with guy-ropes and tied to the branches of nearby trees. One 50–50 wool/cotton blanket was the sum total of our bedding, just to keep the chill from us as the temperature sank down to around 70 deg! This drop in temperature was sufficient to produce a dew, so heavy that it could be felt falling on one's face soon after sunset, and anything left out in the open became too damp to wear.

About 2000 hrs, not daring to have a fire burning during darkness or using our torches more than was absolutely necessary, we decided to turn in, and Gort's final word to all was that, if any of the group knew how to pray, now was the time to get busy and offer such, for if we didn't find water soon the situation would become serious. But he explained, as it was not a monsoon season there was little hope of rain. But someone with more faith than the rest suggested tying the hammock roofs up instead of down, to catch any rain if such did eventuate. This we all did, climbed in – zipped up – then settled down in the humid cooling night air.

For a lengthy period I lay awake, too thirsty to sleep, thinking of all the places where I had partaken of fresh cool drinks! Oh, the iced orange cordials in Queen Street Auckland – the Melbourne huge pineapple/orange thirst quenchers from the pavement stalls, and the half-pint glasses of chilled milk at ...! Nothing in the world seemed more important at that moment in time than a long cool drink ...! Oh, God, let it rain!

It must have been about 2200 hrs. with sleep just turning the thoughts into dreams, when a strange noise on the roof of my hammock woke me up. At first it sounded like some large insects playing hopscotch on the roof, and then the truth dawned – it was raining! Unzipping the hammock I hurriedly clambered out – and sure enough there were big heavy drops of lovely cool rain falling, getting more and more numerous every minute. I awakened all the rest of the party, who were startled at being so silently being brought back into the world of the living, thinking we were being attacked by the Japs. They, too, quickly realised that this was a momentous moment in our operation. Our prayer had been answered from above! All members hurriedly emerged from their hammocks to join in the rejoicing. Within minutes there was a regular downpour, and the upturned roofs began to fill and sag under the weight of the 'nectar from the skies'. We filled every available four-gallon tin, water bottle, and anything else that could possibly hold this much unsuspected and appreciated gift from above. Then in the excitement I stripped naked and had a shower-bath. Gort severely reprimanded me for doing such, for this was evidently the quickest way in the tropics to catch a chill, and he did not want a casualty on his hands at this point in time. Still it felt great to be clean and fresh after the previous sweaty night and days.

The rain abruptly stopped and soon the stars were as bright as ever again; that was it for the night. A quick rub down with my only towel, a thirst quencher from that which had fallen from above, then back to the hammock for a rest and sleep. That was three times in twenty-four hours that we had experienced a miraculous intervention of the handiwork from above. First it was the missing oar retrieved, the cloud over the moon, and now out-of-season rain. The latter was not experienced again in this area whilst we were there.

For another two and a half days the search continued without success, and by then our new supply of water was sadly dwindling. Then success – if you could call it that! Fresh water pools were found about a mile away – dark red brackish water lying in the thick of the undergrowth. Drawn off quickly and boiled it was quite drinkable, despite the reddish colour absorbed from the roots of the palm trees and flax-like bushes surrounding the pools. But under the circumstances it was a lifesaver and most welcome.

An area near the water-holes was found that would make a suitable bivouac, with tall trees all round, something we needed to allow an aerial to be rigged for communication to and from Darwin. So started the immediate and mammoth carting contract of struggling through the trackless undergrowth with seventy-odd kerosene tins, each weighing 20 or 30 pounds, our packs, hammocks, arms, and of course the dinghy and two folboats. As it was quite impossible to carry the dinghy in one piece (it weighed about 150 pounds) we chopped it up into chunks with our parangs (native knives)! There was no turning back now – we had burnt our bridges, or more accurately 'chopped our method of withdrawal', behind us! The folboats were dismantled and taken along, as they would be needed very soon for clandestine night trips up or down the coast to contact the natives. There was no question of leaving the boats behind, as natives or Japs might have stumbled over them and triggered off a manhunt from which there would have been little hope of escaping. After completing the return trips about ten times we were all totally exhausted, but at least there was no tangible evidence of our arrival; all of our belongings were now domiciled in one main area, plus we had water to drink, cook and wash in. After preparing and consuming a good meal, we again slung our hammocks and retired behind the protective mosquito netting. Sleep was an essential requisite, in preparation of what might be around the corner. Tomorrow would be soon enough to sort things out in this new location.

Not knowing how long this bivouac was to be in existence as our headquarters, we set about making it comfortable with the available resources at hand. Beneath the hammocks small racks were made from bamboo on which to store packs, boots and weapons. Apart from keeping them dry, this reduced the chances of insects great and small from invading our clothing. A table and bench seats were quickly assembled by using small Nikau palm trees, cutting them to length and splitting them in half. The flat areas were put uppermost and fixed to a log framework, using vines to secure same. Covered with a black rubber sheet which was recently part of the dinghy, it became a table of sorts for our eight operatives.

Our cooking stove consisted of four or five steel rods (which were general issue for such) stretched across a convenient hole in the ground; there was no shortage of firewood, as one of the daily tasks was collecting this for the day's needs of cooking and billy boiling for hot drinks.

After assembling various structures, our bivouac area contained all the necessary jungle comforts that were needed. Communication with the outside world was the next important step. The T-shaped aerial assembled in Melbourne had now to be slung between the highest possible trees, correct distance apart and directional facing. Two tall Saraya trees seemed to fit the requirements, but the problem was, just

"KAMPONG TAPOKAN" 19ᵈ June 1945.

INFORMATION FROM "AH. TET."

FORMERLY EMPLOYED AS CLERK PITAS ESTATE.
FOR 6 YEARS. IMPRESSED LABOUR BY JAPS
1942 Japanese occupied Pitas estate
Oct 17ᵗʰ under command of YAMAKUCHI who
is 2 i/c of ("THE NISSAN NORIN COMPANY")
("Enemy Property Estate" " ")
This man was also manager of
Langkon + Bliaping Estate.
Head Manager being OSHIRO (came Kudat 1944)
(NOW LANGKON)
1943 Japanese named INEMOTO was
manager Pitas Estate.

1944 (oct) Japanese named FUJAHARA was
manager Pitas Estate. now in
Jesselton. Left Pitas 29ᵗʰ April '45.
Left his 2 i/c a lad of approx 16
years of age named SASA HARA
in charge. now imprisoned
this camp
The CPO. of this N.N. Coy. named ONOMA
payed a visit to Pitas from Kudat
28ᵗʰ or 29ᵗʰ May 42. Whereabouts at
present not known.

Mr. Payne F.L. former British manager
Pitas Estate was arrested by Japs
25ᵗʰ May 1942. Ah Tet was very
recently informed Mr Payne is
interned at "Kuching." still

Intelligence report submitted by HQ at Pitas.

how to climb them. The trunks at ground level were approximately three feet in circumference, and the first branches fifty feet aloft. This was a common situation in signals training, and a pair of spikes were always included in the jungle radio gear. These were strapped to each leg with a large spike protruding down the inside of each ankle. A length of strong rope was tied in a loop around the tree and the waist of the climber and the stage was set to clamber up these trees. Jack

2

Following are the names & Ranks of 6 Japanese soldiers (army) killed at Litho 14th June 1945.

NAME	RANK (RED/YEL BRAID)	APPROX AGE	REMARKS
TASIMA	CPL (NEWLY PROMOTED)	31 years	I/c party
ISONO	PTE 1ST CLASS [RED]	29 "	
ONO	(not known)	29 "	new addition to party
HONCHO	SUPERIOR PTE [RED]	25 "	3 I/c party
NARIZUMI	LEADING PTE [RED YEL BRAID]	34 "	2 I/c "
MATSUMOTO	PTE 1ST CLASS [RED]	32 "	

These men were sent to Litha, as an outpost to gather information re planes & shipping in MARADU BAY. They occasionally made a trek to TELAGA. Their arms were 1 KEKE (M.G.) & 6 rifles. These arms were found in their quarters unloaded — No M.G. mags loaded. These arms now in our possession & being used by our men. They were also fully equiped with Gas equipment.

They payed with Jap 1 dollar notes for all employment & food. A copy of their receipt was forwarded fortnightly to Tanjong Batu. It is believed they were sent from Tanjong Batu, but not confirmed.

volunteered to attack the situation at hand (with his merchant navy experience) and positioned the rope loop. After about twenty minutes of climbing with the rope and use of the spikes, he was almost exhausted with the effort when he reached the first branch and attached the aerial to it. Looking downward from a distance of 50 feet, his thought was of the downward passage and safe arrival on the jungle floor. The whole process was again repeated to complete the erection at the other end. Off to the side of the two trees selected, the ground was cleared for the radio transceiver shack. Another palm tree table was created, again

2

A seventh killed same date — one of 2 who arrived Litho from Langkan 1700 hrs H.14th June 45 — was a Marine. Navy blue cap:— N.BLUE. WHITE WITH BLACK ANCHOR. Rank & name not known. The second was a NYISAN man. Rank & name also not known.

NOTE. None of these 8 men were wearing unit identification plates or patches.

Enclosed is a copy of "an order of the day" sent from Langkan to this outpost. Capt May's interpretation says it reveals something about an enemy plane dropping something in this vicinity on 11th May 45. On the back of this is an account of payments to natives for food

with a rubber sheet cover. The transceiver and morse key were positioned, plus the hand operated generator on the ground nearby. An awning of green parachute silk was then erected over the area to keep off the night dew and sun – and possibly prying eyes from reconnaissance aircraft. Branches of bamboo were now placed and used to camouflage the structure.

It was only five days since our arrival in enemy territory – our bivouac was complete and contact with HQ was now the main mission. To be or not to be was the question! Our schedules with base station situated at Darwin some 1,500 miles away were pre-arranged for contact on the hour plus a listening watch would be maintained twenty-four hours a day. We took it in turns to wind the hand generator, which produced 12 volts, providing power for the transceiver. (Batteries and recharging equipment were too heavy to transport into occupied territory. When finally established these could be chuted in). After adjusting the transceiver to our operational frequency, Darwin could be heard coming in at strength 5 – perfect on our first effort. We now transmitted our call sign, time and time again, but received no confirmation of receipt of such. This situation continued for nearly two days, and in between calls Fred frantically checked and rechecked the transmission side for faults that would cause non-functioning. (The hand generator was similar to a child's rocking horse; one sat upon it and turned the handles situated where the neck was positioned.) Working the generator became a tiring effort whilst being totally bathed in perspiration. With continued contact trying to be made with HQ, on the seventh day of our landing in this occupied area we were finally acknowledged and given the correct code. Sweet success! They did not expect contact to be made so soon, and had not been listening for our call – which explained our vain efforts over the previous two days.

With the all-important communications link now established, the rest of the operatives set off in the two folboats to make contact with the native population seeking information as to their attitude towards us, and about enemy troops in the immediate area. Urgent intelligence reports were needed to ascertain the location and condition of 1,800 Australian and 700 British prisoners of war held in a POW camp at Sandakan! These soldiers had been captured at Singapore when the Allied Forces had surrendered to the Japanese in that area.

First native contact with the operatives of the scouting party was a local chief (Hadji) who was overwhelmed and delighted to see them. Importantly, he was willing to co-operate, thus luck was still on our side. It transpired that the Japanese were deeply hated by the local tribesmen and Chinese for they had confiscated all their valuable belongings, animals and food supplies, in exchange for worthless occupational money. Women and girls were raped, and anyone who showed the slightest resistance to their orders was murdered. The natives referred to the enemy soldiers as 'binitang', the Malay word for 'animals', which gave some indication of their feelings towards them. On the slightest provocation, lowly ranked soldiers would bayonet and kill the tribespeople, and not be answerable to their officers for such practice.

Gort and three operatives would be out on intelligence seeking trips for two or three days at a time using the folboats, then return to this locational bivouac. The total information recorded was then laboriously coded using the double cypher method in use, and transmitted during the next schedule period. Grinding at the hand generator for an hour or more in this tropical heat, was not one to be looked forward to. There was little for us to do whilst the operatives were away, and time used to hang heavily on our hands in those early weeks. Out of sight and security within the area was the order of the day. One dared not wander far from the camp environment or approach the beach shoreline,

Above, and opposite page: The Dusan Rungas Tribe, Kudat, Sabah, B.N.B.

which was a mile away. When the sea was rough the surf could be clearly heard on a calm day. During the night, chopping noises could be heard from the direction of the kampongs along the river banks close at hand. We kept our silence from within the jungle base.

On several occasions I wandered through the nearby jungle (fairly open and not too dense as we were later to experience) and the wild life was quite fascinating to observe. There were hoards of small monkeys romping about the lower branches above my head as I walked beneath. Once I stood and watched as several gathered on one branch, intent on observing and pointing at the strange creature below. It was just like a zoo, only I was the exhibit! A little later a tremendous crashing and screaming noise commenced, about a hundred yards away. It made me curious enough to climb 30 or 40 feet up a tree to locate and find out just what was eventuating. Observed a unique sight! A huge gorilla, probably weighing half a ton and about seven feet tall, was high up a fir tree swinging it madly from side to side and working up his excitement at the same time. When its swaying reached a maximum he would let go at the top of the swing and fly through the air to the next large tree which would then bend almost double under the impact of his great weight. During the aerial part of his act the gorilla would let out a nightmarish shriek of delight. I soon had to vacate my position in this tree I had climbed, as an itching sensation on my hands was being caused by hundreds of tiny red spiders which were using their ability to bite, objecting to my intrusion of their domain.

Puru Puru, 'first base' in the coastal scrub country north of Labuk Bay near Sandakan, in British North Borneo, 6°N, 117° 35′ E.

Left: Fred at the transmitter and receiver on the table made from palm tree trunks, and the author on the hand generator. The awning of green parachute silk was brought along to keep off the tropical sun and the prying eyes of reconnaissance aircraft (Feb 1945).

Below: The American-type hammocks, with mosquito nets and waterproof 'roofs'. Dress for the day (every day!) was a cotton sarong and green leather "sneakers". In the picture 'Skeet' (corporal) Hywood (left), and Fred (Lieutenant) Olsen, both of the Australian Army Signals.

On another of these walkabouts, hearing a loud rustling in the undergrowth, I turned around to find myself face to face, quite literally, with a large orang-utan, standing on his hind legs and almost my height. (Orang-utan is a corruption of two Malay words meaning 'Jungle man'.)

We just stood and stared at each other! He was so human I was too fascinated to be scared, although they are not normally vicious. Having no firearm with me, I decided the only course was to stare him out. For some reason I talked quietly to him as I looked intently into his beady, soulless eyes. It was undoubtedly the first time that this had happened to either of us! A fascinating experience, but it ended when he turned on his heel and quietly walked off into the jungle and disappeared from sight.

Animal life of all descriptions shared the jungle with us — snow-white leopards, woodpeckers, pigeons, monkeys to mention a few — but some were not quite so harmless. Two that we had to be continually on the alert for were centipedes whose interlocking front mandibles packed a highly poisonous bite, plus the dreaded scorpion whose sting killed its prey with a rapidly acting poison. They had a delightful habit of climbing into unoccupied boots during the night, and we soon learnt to take evasive action by shaking our footwear each morning before putting them on, plus zipping up our hammocks immediately we vacated them, day or night. They were not fancied bed-fellows. What with scorpions, centipedes, snakes, ants, the malaria-carrying anopheles mosquito, the tropical jungle is no place for the concrete environmental types like ourselves!

The only visible sign of the Japanese military at this stage was a solitary aeroplane that flew near our bivouac area one afternoon. The sound of its engine was clearly heard whilst it was still a long way off, and by the time it was overhead I had climbed a nearby tree to try and obtain a good look at it. The density of the foliage prevented a complete sighting, but I was able to identify the red discs under its wings and body. By this time the Nips no doubt suspected our presence, and were investigating up and down the coastline for any sign of us. This aircraft patrol did not happen again, so obviously our encampment was not detected.

A week or two after this incident, a reliable Chinese lad who had been contacted by Gort in his travels, arrived breathless early one morning whilst we were having a snack for breakfast. (He was the only Bornean knowing our location.) In rapid 'Bahasa' Malay, he reported that about thirty Japanese soldiers were assembling at a kampong about twenty miles away called Paitan. Their intention and instruction was to seek and locate us. Perhaps a new unknown radio transmitting in the area had given them an indication of our presence. We immediately encoded a signal to HQ on the next sked, asking for an airstrike on Paitan. Within a matter of some four hours the sound of aircraft engines could be clearly heard approaching from the north. Through the overhead branches of the jungle we saw a flight of three twin-bodied Lightning F36 fighters pass overhead. Bomb racks below the wings were full plus rockets protruding. We had no idea from whence they came, perhaps an American carrier? It certainly made us feel a lot less isolated in the Sabah area of Borneo, to know we had a back-up assistance only a few hours away.

Within a few minutes of their passing over, we felt rather than heard a series of muffled explosions coming from the direction in which the aircraft had flown. Later we were to learn that most of the enemy soldiers at Paitan had been either killed or wounded in the bombing, and as a result a decision had evidently been reached to leave us alone in future. Our radio link had now proved itself as our insurance against attacks from the Japanese. However, a combination of events, including this incident, made a move to another site necessary.

Despite our isolation, our small radio communications receiver (MC. I) with its changeable waveband units which plug into it, allowed us to receive most short-wave stations, including the very powerful US Armed Forces station broadcasting news bulletins for the Allied troops in the South-East Asian battle zone. BBC programmes were also beamed and received by us.

These kept us in contact with the outside world, and the progress of the war in our theatre of operations. We became aware of the situation in the M.E. in the last week of April with the capitulation of Germany – VE Day. We may yet get home in one piece!

Plans were now afoot for us to relocate further up the coast, and 3 May. was decided for the day – or night – movement. This would make it exactly sixty days since our arrival onshore from the submarine. As our rubber dinghy had been consigned to the trash pit, and the folboats were insufficient to do the task, two native fishing boats had been commandeered for the movement complete with volunteer crews. At sundown these craft were to enter the estuary where we had arrived, and load all our gear located there.

As 'D' day drew nearer, more and more equipment and stores were made ready and repacked. The tree climbing ordeal was repeated to recover the aerial for future use. The seven of the party were on hand to trudge through the trackless undergrowth to transfer all of our possessions etc., to the embarkation point situated in the estuary. Darkness descended, but there was not a sign of the commandeered native fishing boats. Then faintly drifting through the still night air, one heard the high-pitched chatter of excited natives, then the glimmer of oil lamps flickering through the mangroves and hanging vines, which indicated their approach line to us.

The natives quickly attacked the handing of all the gear, and rapidly stowed it on the larger of the two boats. Five of the party boarded this vessel whilst another of the party and I went in the smaller boat with the radio gear plus our personal belongings. Once again it was a still, quiet night with no moon, reminding us of our DZ arrival just two months previous. We edged our way down the estuary, and once clear of the trees the sails were hoisted to help us on our journey. Sails were simple affairs, tied along one edge to a pole about ten feet long and raised up the mast to a point about two-thirds along its length so that it hung at an angle. The lower end was tied with ropes to the gunwales.

Gently paddling, we passed over the bar and into the open sea. Gort had placed me in charge of this boat, but with this young Arab boy Ali, who owned it, being more conversant with the sailing and local location, there was little that we could do in the way of giving advice or instructions. Finally we were on our way to 'Base Number Two'. We turned north outside the estuary and edged along the shoreline just beyond the breakers. What breeze there was soon died away, leaving the sails hanging limply down, thus propulsion from then on was by punting, with poles being pushed on to the sandy bottom by the native crew.

Thinking that there might be a useful breeze further out from the shore, I asked Ali to steer out into deeper water. (This was my first contact with a Malay-speaking native, and I succeeded in being understood). We had moved out some two hundred yards away from the other boat when we heard a shout from their direction. Suddenly we saw the reason. A native fishing boat, fitted with an outboard motor, was bearing down on us on our port side. Ali quickly turned the tiller to swing our vessel inside of their track, and it passed within thirty yards. The only visible human form on board sighted by us, was a native holding the tiller, and showing no sign of recognition of our party as it passed. Japanese soldiers must have been inside the cabin, as no native would be at sea with an outboard under his control, or even own such?

Being now alerted to the danger at hand, we now had armed ourselves with Sten SMG's in readiness for that which may eventuate. A grenade pin was withdrawn, but the boat continued on its course and disappeared into the night. Phew! We quickly pushed back to the rest of the party, to be met with a barrage from Gort. 'What the bloody hell do you think you are doing?' plus a few well deserved uncomplimentary comments. We certainly kept closer together after that. Slowly, very

Above and following page: Base 2, Lokapas.

Top: The radio hut built by the local Dusuns. Not one nail was used in its construction. Note the "kitchen" on the left. The trees are all mahogany.

Bottom: The view from the shack looking north across Paitain Bay towards Jambongan Island. The house at the lower left of the picture belonged to the Chinese 'tauki' or merchant, whose young son taught us to speak Malay better than any other instructor we had.

Bottom: 'Tuan Doctor' inspects a Dusun child with a tropical yaw on its head.

Top: This native hut housed three generations of Dusuns, a total of twenty persons, two dogs, and half-a-dozen fowls under the floor.

slowly it seemed, we wended our way up the coast for the next three hours in total silence, the jungle shoreline visible in the starlight.

About midnight it was decided to drop anchor amongst a group of other native boats in a shoal where they were catching flounder, as we would be less conspicuous and hopefully get some sleep. Our little perahu had a tent-like roof made of 'atap', a type of palm leaf laced up in a thatch arrangement. We made ourselves as comfortable as possible in the cramped space, dozing off and on until daylight eventuated about six o'clock. On awaking we felt stiff, sore, and generally felt unkempt, like one does after a night on a train. Ali lit a little earthenware fire, which is the 'galley' on these native boats, and prepared to cook his breakfast of rice, flavoured with fish that had been hanging from the mast for weeks, drying rock-hard in the tropical sunlight! We brewed ourselves a cup of coffee and ate a couple of biscuits from our ration packs. No weight watchers problem for us! The morning was calm, and a very thick fog hung over the water limiting our visibility to approximately fifty yards. This soon vanished as the sun rose above the horizon, revealing the shoreline about a mile away with golden sandy beaches lined with palm trees. If we weren't fifteen hundred miles behind the enemy 'front line', what a wonderful location to spend some time here. Real travel poster stuff!

Putting such irrelevant thoughts from our minds, we set the sail in the now gentle morning breeze and headed for Jambongan, a large island now visible about three miles up the coast – our first port of call. (It was here that Gort had made his first contact after our arrival with the Hadji (local chief) who had invited us to stay with him.) We pulled into the landing of the little kampong and received a welcome with all oriental politeness and ceremony. Led to the Hadji's *sulap* we were invited to sit on the floor, and provided with cups of sweet china tea without milk. Surprisingly it tasted great, and most refreshing in the growing heat of the day. We were invited to stay the night here, so whilst Gort and the Hadji had another conference, we wondered off to enjoy the scenery and taste the tropical fruits that were in abundance everywhere. We had our first introduction to pawpaws, and the gigantic water melons which grew to about a foot and a half.

The evening meal was quite a formal affair. The Hadji and his bevy of beautiful wives (three) sat with us on the grass mats, in the cross-legged pose common to Muslims, inviting us to partake and join in the self-service feast. The centre piece was a huge dish of chicken pieces, that had been cooked whole inside green coconuts. This was surrounded by dozens of little plates containing tasty tit-bits, mostly fried in coconut oil – sweet potatoes, tapioca cakes, shell-fish, crabs, fish roe, pickled pineapple and other sumptuous delicacies which really were out of this world. We finished off this unexpected feast with a fruit salad containing pineapple, pawpaw, melon – washed down with the native brew Arak (brewed from rice polishings). A gourmet's delight. One to remember and relate if possible to our families back home.

A large wooden building erected over the landing had been prepared as our sleeping quarters. As we settled down for the night, the only thing between us and the floor boards was a grass mat about an eighth of an inch thick! It was the thinnest mattress I had ever slept on, but it was surprisingly comfortable and sleep was not a problem.

An interesting piece of information emerged during our stay on Jambongan; this related to our incident two days earlier. It transpired that the motor-boat we had so narrowly missed on the way up the coast was carrying two Japanese officers, and had mounted on the bow a Lewis gun. Known as the 'Barang' boat, it did a regular run up the coast from Sandakan to obtain supplies of fruit and vegetables from nearby kampongs, and was on its way back when we sighted same. The natives informed us that the officers were probably so drunk on 'Arak' by the time they passed, they would not have sighted us. The pilot of the boat did not give any sign in case he gave us away. It had indeed been a near thing. As Gort remarked, 'Someone is looking after you, lad.' I heartily agreed.

Further information was given that a week before, two young Japanese soldiers had arrived at the island in the late afternoon demanding to be fed and given a bed for the night, as they were too late to get back to their base at Sandakan before dark. The pair were given a good meal, after which they demanded to sleep in the Hadji's house on his gigantic mattress (on which he and his three wives slept). This was granted, but before they turned in for the night they became completely inebriated on the native brew 'Arak'. Whilst they were sleeping, two of the young warriors of the village climbed up into the rafters of the house directly above the sleeping soldiers, and taking careful aim dropped a heavy ploughshare on them from above. Both were neatly decapitated. In case of reprisals or a search by their unit, their bodies were buried in the deep of the nearby jungle, and their boat hauled out and burned. Their uniforms and personal possessions were hidden, and upon request by us, they were produced for inspection. I was permitted to keep a few of their personal letters, a serviceman's newspaper plus rank badge and star off a steel helmet. The bloodstained mattress and floorboards were still there, however, as moot evidence of the dark deed. The following day we bade farewell to the Hadji and his family at Jambongan, continuing our travel up the coast again.

By mid-afternoon we pulled into a wharf on Pulau Musa (Pulau – Malay for island). There was a large store shed situated there containing tons of conch shells and a wooden house overlooking the bay which was open and deserted. This had to be the home and trading post of a wealthy, hard-dealing Chinese merchant called Puk Min Chu, whose business was buying conch shells from the native divers, and selling them abroad for the manufacture of buttons and ornaments. He had been notorious for paying low prices, and the natives had evidently 'put his weights up' to the Japanese who had come to his island, arrested him and his family and transferred them to somewhere on the mainland. The house was erected entirely of wood – floors, walls, ceilings, doors, roof and all. It had obviously been a lovely place, but everything moveable had been taken by the Japanese or the locals. All that remained were a lot of papers and rubbish lying all over the house. The scene was rather pathetic, and it did not take much imagination to see just what had transpired. There were broken children's toys and torn books, smashed crockery and expensive ornaments just lying scattered in every room of the house. We stayed for about an hour then climbed back into our small boat, setting our course for the next and final stop at Lokapas, a kampong of Dusun and Bajau natives situated on the coast. This position was considered suitable for our purposes and future activities in this area.

The waterline at Lokapas was a tangled mass of mangrove roots, except for a small wharf, which had been used by the timber boats to transport away the milled mahogany planks. Our small boat was tied up between the even smaller Dusun craft, and as the light was failing we unloaded or gear and clambered up the steep pathway to a large clearing about a hundred feet above sea level. There was very little shelter, as nearly all the trees were just dead trunks and the under-growth had been cleared by fire or by previous occupants.

This location was to be the site for our radio station, and the Dusuns had offered to erect a *sulap* for us to live in and accommodate our radio equipment. Before darkness enveloped us, our hammocks were quickly slung between the stark trunks of huge, dead mahogany trees.

For the next few days we slept and prepared our food in the open. This was no great hardship, as the temperature remained pleasantly constant day and night. A neighbouring Chinese 'tauki' (shop-keeper) sent his small boy up the hill with many delicious plates of Chinese foods.

This tauki was a high-class Mandarin who had married a beautiful Dayak princess, and their eight-year old son was most handsome and intelligent. Their hospitality knew no bounds, and at any time during the day or night the lad would materialise with tapioca cakes, cooked in banana leaves and still piping hot. With a little sugar added these were delicious and a welcome addition to our meagre intake of carbohydrates which for the last two months had consisted of water crackers and rice. Scones made from rice flour produced by the kampong, and banana fritters were but some of the many dishes made available to us.

Three days after our landing, a group of native carpenters arrived on the scene, accompanied by a horde of locals whose task it was to enter the jungle and bring back the necessary materials. This was the first experience to witness a native *sulap* being built, and was a real education in the art and craftsmanship of the natives. Not a single nail or bolt was used, no tools of any kind were needed for the construction, except parangs – long, straight-bladed, heavy knives. They commenced construction at nine in the morning, and we moved into it at four in the afternoon.

To begin with eight posts were sunk into the ground, protruding up about three metres and arranged in a square. Heavy poles were then lashed to these about a metre above the ground level to form the floor joists. On top of these were laid some of the planks left behind from the pre-war milling operations, being mahogany about four metres in length and 250×50mm. The roof framework of lighter poles was soon lashed up and a thatch-type roof was ready to be tied on. The leaves of a palm tree (called atap) were folded over long thin sticks and attached with thin vines. Many dozen of these were made, and then one by one lashed to the roofing structure, starting from the bottom and finishing at the top, just like thatching. The completed result was a water-tight roof, but open enough to allow ventilation. The front steps for access were made by lashing three bits of wood to three poles, whose lower ends were buried in the ground, and the tops lashed to the floor framework. The last things placed on were the grass-mat side walls, which the women folk brought to the scene of operations in time for them to be tied on for the completion of the *sulap* before nightfall. We extended and added an annex for cooking and washing, a few days later.

The commanding view of the whole area was indeed a change after looking at nothing but jungle for the past two months. From our new position perched on top of the hill, the view extended right down the coast past Jambongan Island, and away inland to the highlands which were dominated by the twin peaks of Mt Kinabalu (13,451 feet) some 60 miles away. On many clear nights the sky over these mountains was lit up almost continually by great flashes of lightning as tropical storms raged on the western slopes.

It was a novel experience to have natives moving around us, and they were quite obviously delighted to have our company rather than the 'binatang' in the area. This rapport was greatly increased as a result of a chance incident. One of the areas of my responsibility that fell to my lot was the care of the medical first aid equipment, the whole supply of which was in a kerosene tin and intended for our own use. During the construction of our *sulap* I had noticed one of the older members of the tribe with a tatty bandage on his right leg a few inches above the knee, and on enquiring he informed me that it had been bad for two years. (Medical help in this area was discontinued with the Japanese occupation about mid-42.) He was requested to report back one day and I would see just what I could do for him. He eventually did so. I very gingerly cut away the bandage, then cleaned up the wound area with cotton-wool and disinfectant. It was a firm belief amongst Muslims that cowdung makes a good compress for open wounds, and this was what I was removing! Eventually after a good half hour of bathing and scraping the wound lay exposed – a hole in the flesh about three quarters of an inch in diameter right down to the bone and clearly visible. The skin around the area had hardened, and I was of the opinion it looked hopeless for it to recover and heal over! I smeared the sides with vaseline and then literally filled the hole with sulphanilamide powder, which at this point in time was considered a completely new 'wonder drug'. After finalising the bandaging of the wound, the old warrior was instructed not to undo it, and report back in four days for a renewal of the dressing.

On removal of the dressing on his second visit, I was utterly amazed at the progress. The skin had softened, and the healing process was quite clearly under way. The treatment was repeated and he was told the next inspection was to be in another seven days time. On his return, the improvement was quite unbelievable. The hole had completely healed over, and only the healthy scab remained. A dry dressing was attached and held with sticking plaster. In a further week all that remained was only a scar to show where the once deep hole existed.

News of the 'miracle cure' spread like wild fire, and first three or four, then twenty or thirty, were lined up every morning to see the 'Tuan Doctor'. Now I was no doctor! But by using common sense I managed to satisfy most of the problems. Anyone reporting with 'Sakit parut' (stomach ache) got an immediate dose of Epsom salts; headaches, toothache or fevers received aspirins; skin wounds or infections got the sulpha treatment. Those with hacking coughs had a dose of good old 'Linctus G', the Army stand-by. 'Number Nines' never failed to produce results for constipation, plus sulphadiazine which was the remedy for dysentery.

This was my repertoire! No-one complained about the treatment and very few came back again – killed or cured! Very soon our supplies of medication dwindled and were running dangerously low, even for ourselves. Fortunately we all kept fit and healthy during this period.

In preparation for the arrival of reinforcements from 'Z' by parachute, and also to enable our supplies to be replenished, a dropping zone (DZ) had to be cleared in the valley adjacent to our camp, about half a mile westwards. Clearing commenced of an area three hundred yards long by a hundred yards wide from the primary jungle, including huge trees. This became a daunting task, considering the floor of this area had to be smooth enough for receiving the reinforcement parachutists who would arrive by our '200 Flight' Liberator Aircraft from Morotai, Halmahera Island group, forward base.

Some 80 or 90 natives and Chinese hacked away with their parangs and burnt rubbish for four days, and were still dragging away branches when the first B-24 Liberator flew overhead. Firstly the 'Storpedos' came down attached to small chutes, these contained our necessary supplies and those of the reinforcements to our group – Nick, Maruf and Kanun. The natives watched in awe, as the new arrivals came floating down under their white or green chutes on successive runs by the Liberators. Nick twisted his foot whilst landing on the uneven surface, but otherwise the first drop went off without a hitch. Controlling a 32ft circular chute from a 1,000ft exit is most hazardous compared with the modern-day chutes. A few of the storpedos missed the DZ and finished up in the nearby trees, but these were soon retrieved by the wildly excited natives. They considered this a most enjoyable experience, having not known about just what could come from the skies!

After the welcomes and reunions had run their course, Nick shared a very disturbing piece of information with us. Major Don Stott (from SOE) and his party of Kiwis and Australians, who had started their mission of 'Robin I' a week or two prior to our departure, had travelled by submarine to the South Borneo Oil Fields at Balikpapan. Stott and another Kiwi officer MacMillan, were considered drowned whilst landing in rough and stormy weather in their rubber dinghy. The rest of the party suffered casualties before being rescued by a PBY float plane and returned to Morotai Base.

Gort was more sure than ever that poor security in Melbourne had been to blame, and that the Japanese had prior knowledge of their arrival. He was of the opinion that our uneventful arrival had been ensured by his last-minute change of plans whilst still on the submarine (for which he was castigated by signal from HQ).

Our work on the radio became more and more intense as the organisation started to operate properly. Supplies for the native guerrillas had to be ordered – green uniforms, boots, arms, ammunition etc., and information was coming in steadily through the network of agents (mainly Chinese) who were now on the payroll. All this intelligence material had to be quickly relayed back to HQ. Other Agas groups had entered and established themselves further down the coastline, and their ciphered traffic was being transmitted to base through us, as we were now the control station.

It was during this period that news about the 2,500 Australian and British POWs at Sandakan came through the network, that they were being guarded by a handful of Japanese soldiers – about 20. Gort had strongly recommended to Base HQ Australia, that a Naval Task Force group should land there and rescue as many as possible, before the Nips took aggressive action against them.

The problem of medical treatment for the natives became so acute that a doctor was requested to be sent in. Two weeks later one was dropped by parachute from a Liberator of 200 Flight RAAF. Dr May was an American Chinese who had given up his practice in a Los Angeles suburb, after hearing the plight of the natives in the occupied parts of Borneo. Well in his forties, short of stature (about 5ft nothing) he was a ball of energy and determination. After operating from a tent for a period of about a week, he organised the local carpenters to build a hospital for his many patients in the jungle, using the logs and cut timber left behind by the former mill owners. It must have been the only hospital completely built of mahogany in the world. Two Chinese girls who had been school teachers before the occupation were con-scripted as nurse aides. Their first involvement was the making of sheets from our parachutes, green and white – silk sheets on mahogany beds, what a hospital!

Aerial drops were now coming in twice a week, which frequently included mail from home which had been addressed to a 'Special Box Number in Melbourne'. Our families had no idea where we were, and at this stage we had no method of getting mail out of the country. 'Official letters' were being sent to our 'Next of Kin' each month, stating that we were in good health and on a 'Special Operation'. Many of the other New Zealanders in the organisation did not have the same treatment repeated for them. There was a breakdown in the system somewhere!

The natives in this BNB region known as Sabah had no contact with the outside world. Radios were something out of this world. On occasions we would pick up on a small MCR I receiver, bulletins in the Malay language from the powerful Armed Forces radio station, firstly from Darwin and later from the forward base at Morotai in the Halmaheras. We tuned up the volume to the fullest, and allowed the natives to listen to the wonders of the 'Orang Puteh'! There was always a large gathering when they observed the sun in the right quarter of the sky (native time piece), and listened to the news. This tribe lived mainly on their small boats, handled and ate their stinking and dried fish, and never seemed to wash either their clothes or bodies. You could smell them coming from yards away.

For the first time since our arrival at this new base, a couple of the locals came running up the hill hurriedly informing us that three boats were approaching us from up the coast. Using the powerful binoculars we could clearly identify three motor torpedo craft travelling at about thirty knots, heading directly for our base. Flags were not flown identifying the craft, and members of the crew could be seen 'standing too' on the fo'c'sle swivelling gun action station, presumable a .50 calibre MG. Were they Niponese or Allied vessels? The Union Jack was now flying above our *sulap*, but this might or might not be of any helpful identification to the approaching unknown force! Added to this emergency, our operatives were now away on a mission down the coast.

Quickly putting on my tropical uniform, collecting my Sten plus a couple of grenades, I ran downhill with the two natives to the shoreline. We pushed a perahu out into the deeper water, and commenced paddling towards the oncoming boats. Even at this distance of about a mile away, I could not identify with the binoculars the nationality of the vessels. The natives held aloft a small Union Jack, hoping beyond hope that they were Americans not Japs! No machine-gun fire was received, and the crew did not appear on deck until they came closer. It was indeed a tense moment, and butterflies in the stomach were the order of the day. Then a loud-hailer with a distinct American accent boomed out. 'Who the hell are yuh?' Cupping my hands I replied 'Allied Intelligence'. As they drew alongside I gauged from their expressions that this encounter was beyond belief! I was hauled aboard and introductions followed. All had no idea that Allied Intelligence was located inside Japanese territory of Sabah! The boats had been on a mission from Moratai scouting around looking for targets to shoot up. I informed them that there were no targets between Sandakan and Kudat, but at Kudat central they were there for the asking. From their refrigerator I was given canned beer, cigarettes and chewing gum. After climbing back into our perahu, the three PT boats roared off at high speed in the direction of Kudat. The conclusion to this event after considering such later that night was, if I had not met the Americans at sea, our hut on the hill would have been a lovely target!

All good things must come to an end, and shortly after this episode and not having encountered the enemy, instruction were received that another move of this base was imminent. Our destination this time was the take-over of a large rubber estate plantation homestead around the headland. Some of the party were to be transported by Ali's craft, whilst the remainder were to walk overland through the dense Borneo jungle. The natives were keen to guide us to the estate on this occasion. So once again the packing commenced including the Doc's hospital equipment. We set off early in the morning on the 40-mile hike through the interior jungle. It was almost the longest day – 20 June – not that it made much difference six degrees from the equator. We had now been in the country 108 days, and not one enemy soldier had been encountered!

The journey to Pitas commenced. At the end of the fourth day we were not sorry to leave the jungle behind and make contact with a large village named Senaja on the banks of the wide Bengkoka River. Here we were to spend the night, and next morning advised to inspect a very secret camp recently carved out of the jungle, called Tapokan (meaning 'hidden'). This was the guerrilla training camp established by our own operatives where volunteers from the natives in the area were living and being trained to handle modern weapons of war – Brens, SMGs, carbines, grenades etc. Establishing careful security, and only entered by a tortuous access route well guarded and booby-trapped, it was well concealed from the vision of the enemy. Jap boats travelled up and down the river only a mile away. Their regular timetable made it possible for silence to be maintained at these times. The density of this jungle absorbed most noises, and such precautions were probably not necessary.

News next day provided by native bush telegraphy, informed us that a party from this training area commanded by our operatives had made a raid on the Pitas Estate homestead. Japanese there had been completely taken by surprise and annihilated, leaving the way clear for us to now move up river and take possession of this location for our HQ, as instructed. The nearest enemy garrison was now at Kudat, just across Marudu Bay some twenty miles away. This was to be our next encounter, but on a much larger scale. Early in the morning we were taken to the river with all our equipment and boarded an outboard motor-boat that had been stolen from the Japanese. This recent acquisition was much appreciated for the movement upstream of approximately five miles.

War news in the Pacific was becoming increasingly better, and for the first time we began seriously thinking of its finality. However there was one small mission to be completed, that of the proposed raid on the garrison of Kudat town. It finally got under way. The force included five Europeans and the same number of Malays and Chinese who were selected for their reliability. Three small perahus were used for the operation down river from Tapokan and the 12-mile hike across Marudu Bay. The enemy garrison offered only token resistance, after which they were taken prisoner and transported to Tapokan and interned in a specially constructed 'bamboo cage'. The captured radio station was dismantled, and also taken back with the prisoners. We were informed

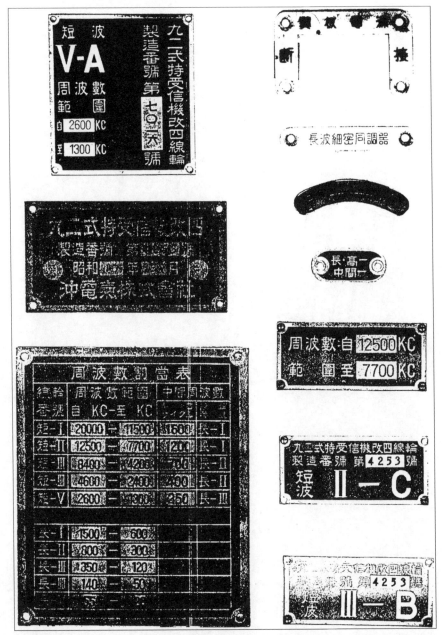

Plates removed from a Japanese radio transmitter captured in the raid on Kudat.

that they had been without supplies for a considerable period, due mainly to the sea blockade by the US Navy. Their one plane which we had encountered shortly after we had arrived in BNB was grounded through lack of fuel and spare parts. Their motor-boats were also of no value. For food they had to rely on the local population, and accordingly their

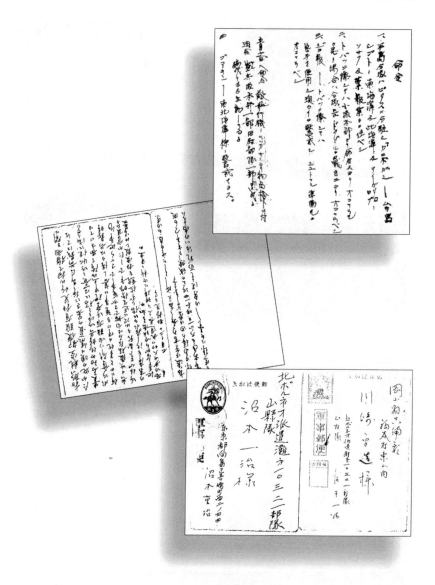

Japanese letters that never reached home.

behaviour became more civilised. Interrogation proved that their morale was very low, and that they all had agreed to surrender to the first Allied party that arrived in their area. Most businesses in the township of Kudat had been inoperative for years, and the premises in most cases were deserted and extensively deteriorated.

With this potential threat removed, a great deal of the tension and resulting precautions were eased. Diesel workboats began to make regular calls, even coming right up to Pitas with our supplies and

Right: One of two
40-foot bamboo
aerial masts
obtained for us
from the jungle.

Below: The author
at work in the Pitas
radio shack.

Left: Sarap, an Australian-trained Malay agent.

Below: Japanese prisoners.

Scenes at the training camp of Tapokan, the area carved out of the jungle, hopefully unknown to the Japanese. The natives undergoing military training.

Air travel authority for my solo return from hospital in Darwin to Mt Martha camp at Melbourne.

transporting agents and troops. In the third week of August we heard on our small MCR I's, that atomic bombs were dropped on Nagasaki and Hiroshima. The total capitulation eventuated with the signing of the 'Surrender Treaty'. At the end of August with everything that had eventuated (War over – clearing up) I became totally exhausted and developed an asthmatic cough and malaria. Dr May treated such with adrenaline injections, and showing no signs of improvement was recommended to Base HQ that I be flown out to Morotai.

From the AIF Hospital within a few days of my arrival, I was on an aircraft enroute to Melbourne and 'Z' HQ. Arrangements were made for me to travel on the Hospital Ship *Andes* which arrived in NZ and berthed at Lyttleton on 7 October 1945. My discharge after medical treatment was dated February 46.

In 1999, Graham Greenwood is one of the two extant Kiwi operatives who were seconded to the Australian Special Force of SOA in 1944. He now resides close to his family in Perth, WA. The other member is living on the North Shore, Auckland.

Operation Robin I (Platypus I) – Balikpapan Oil Fields, SE Borneo

20 March 1945 – 3 May 1945

In 1944, with the Allies striking a deadly blow against the Japanese in the South West Pacific theatre of operations, a group of New Zealanders encamped at Trentham Military Camp were selected from the 11th ME Reinforcements for special operations in this area. They were to undergo extensive training in Commando and Intelligence missions into enemy-occupied areas, and were seconded to the AIF for entry into 'Z' Special Unit, a cover name for 'Special Operations Australia'. The party was under the command of Major Don Stott DSO & Bar, who had served with distinction with the British Military Mission in Greece. The party flew by Sunderland Flying Boat 'Aotearoa' from Auckland to Sydney on 15 July 1944, and immediately commenced training at special bases situated at Fraser Island in Queensland; Parachute School, Richmond, RAAF Station NSW; advanced Commando Camp, Darwin; finally to Garden Island (Careening Bay), situated 15 miles SW of Fremantle, Western Australia. Garden Island was SOA's operational and training base for small boat instruction, and introduction to submarine methods of the assembly and handling of inflatable rubber boats and folboats (similar to modern-day kayaks) from deckside and at sea. The newly designed Folboat No. 2 Mk I (Aust) was introduced to the group. It incorporated a newly developed rubber fabric well, fitted immediately aft of the stern cockpit. An outboard motor up to 3.3 hp was passed through this well, then clamped to a short motor bracket secured to the stern post, resulting in greater speed than with the sole use of standard paddles. A rudder was also fitted, thus eliminating the necessity of steerage by outboard motor control handle. It was now stable during turning and with less tendency to capsize. Members were selected for this operation, and the remainder allocated to others including 'Agas'.

The US Submarine *Perch* under the command of Commander Blish Hills USN, was given the mission of delivering the party of 11 operatives, plus stores consisting of a total weight of 6,492 lb (signals equipment 1,271 lb) to their DZ situated just off the coast of SE Borneo Oil Fields at Balikpapan. The coded name of the operation was 'Robin I'.

The party consisted of 5 NZEF, 3 AIF, 3 NEI personnel:

Major D.J. Stott DSO & Bar (NZEF) OC

Capt. M.T. McMillan	(NZEF) 2 I/C	Lt. R.M. Morton DCM	(NZEF)
Lt. W.C. Dwyer	(AIF)	WO. L. Farquharson	(AIF)
WO R.G. Houghton	(NZEF)	Sgt. B. Dooland	(AIF)
Sgt. W. Horrocks	(NZEF)	Sgt. R.L. Dey	(NEI)
Pte. Kondoy Satu	(NEI)	Pte. Kondoy Dua	(NEI)

On 12 March 1945, with all stores loaded below deck, the folboats plus rubber boats lashed to the outside of the submarine hull – dismantled and transported in this manner whilst submerged – Commander Blish Hills set his course for Borneo: Balikpapan via Surabaya, Lombok Strait, Flores Sea, Java Sea and the Strait of Makassar, leading to his DZ and unloading of operatives in the Balikpapan area.

During the uneventful and somewhat cramped voyage, the boats were unlashed from the hull whilst the submarine was surfaced, examined and exercises instituted for their assembly within the time factor allowed for the operation. Water was found to have entered the valves of the rubber boats, thus requiring rectification prior to inflation. The outboard motors which were stored below deck were taken out and given a workout.

The voyage continued northwards unmolested and *Perch* was approaching the DZ drop area on the morning of 20 March. It now submerged in the early hours prior to daylight to escape detection by the enemy. A conference was called for all members, including the submarine Commander, and the final operational orders were read and fully understood by all.

The operational plan for the insertion of the party into Japanese-occupied Balikpapan area was:

1. Night of 20/21 March, reconnaissance party comprising of Stott/McMillan Rubber Boat # 1. Dooland/Horrocks folboat # 2. The party was to reconnoitre the insertion area; keep a low profile during the hours of daylight; then return to the submarine night 21/22, but if possible make radio contact with the party still at sea. Failing this, try again night 21/22. Folboat and rubber dinghy to keep in contact whilst at sea by means of HF walkie-talkie.

2. Night 21/22 March. *Perch* was to return to the DZ and await return of the reconnaissance party. Remain at the rendezvous until 0100 hrs. If no contact made by radio or folboat, to retire seawards for safety and concealment in the deep area.

3. Night 22/23 March. Failure of the reconnaissance party by 2200 hrs to return to the DZ, Lt. Morton was to take control of the main party and be inserted at a new location 9 ml South of Cape Tambangonot, a few miles from the original location.

    The reconnaissance party on the night of 20 March assembled their boats on the deck of the submarine which now stood off the coast 35 miles north of Balikpapan, a very shallow area for a submarine to venture into. At precisely 2200 hrs, after loading, the two boats were assisted in launching from deckside, into a choppy running sea. The night was overcast with wind increasing, indicating that a severe storm was brewing in the bay. Horrocks and Dooland pushed off with their paddles and started their outboard motor. Stott and McMillan's motor failed to fire, and after three attempts, Stott shouted the order 'Commence paddling shoreward'. The outboard motor on #2 failed to answer the throttle, just idled. The operatives were now fully operational – clothed in jungle greens, camouflage-type floppy hats, canvas lace-up Commando boots, pack carrying extra ammunition, food and medical supplies, torch, trade money, web gear containing ammunition and magazines. Attached just above the jungle boot an 8" stiletto killing knife – the trade mark of the Commando and Special Forces. Weapons which the operatives had a choice of included the .30 cal US carbine semi-automatic, Sten or Owen SMG, machine pistol, S&W .38 or US Colt .45 pistol. Lengthwise the heavier weapons were short in length, excellent for close-quarter jungle warfare, and devastating against bolt-action weapons.

Under the conditions that existed at time of push-off, Bill Horrocks was of the opinion that the operation should be aborted that night. He clearly remembered the incident many years later. On receiving the order to push off and commence paddling from Major Stott, he and his Aussie operative partner in the folboat complied. On looking over his shoulder he was just in time to see the friendly craft disappearing beneath the windswept and choppy waters of the bay. Being 1,200 yards from the foreshore, the battle now commenced against the ever-increasing waves and wind conditions being whipped up the now well-advanced storm within the bay. About midway from the insertion point to the shore DZ, lights were observed from the shore area. Don Stott gave his last ever known order by walkie-talkie: 'Enemy in sight – go for your lives'. Horrocks and Dooland immediately changed course away from the indicated area, heading for the safety of down the bay. Stott and McMillan were never sighted again. A military Board of Enquiry gave a verdict at the end of hostilities, 'Lost at sea, presumed drowned'. There have been many explanations advanced as to the loss of the two Kiwis!

Lieutenant Bob Tapper, a member of the second party of Kiwis attached to 'Z' Special Unit, whilst working with the War Graves Commission at Balikpapan after the surrender of the Japanese, forces in the area, interviewed many of the local population and enemy personnel, to no avail, regarding the fate of our two operatives. With the amazing 'bush telegraphy' that existed within Borneo, the natives would be the first to have heard of the recovery, capture or death of two Allied soldiers in their locality.

Horrocks and Dooland were unable to make contact with their OC in boat No. 1 by radio, and having travelled a considerable distance down the bay from their original course to the land DZ, now turned directly shorewards. At 0130 they heard on the HF radio a muffled Japanese voice, then loud and clear at 0145 two English voices checking frequency and reception. It could have been the other members of the party, but when trying to contact them, they received no response to requests for acknowledgement of their transmission. At the debriefing of the party that escaped back to Morotai, it was recorded that

> At 0200 hrs, we grounded in the shallow waters of the Bay, with the long haul of the folboat fully laden to the shore about 200 yds, away. We approached slowly and silently, in a stooped position, giving a small target to be observed. After a quick reconnaissance of the beach, returned and carried the folboat ashore into the concealment of the thick tropical jungle. Disassembling the folboat into four parts, we buried everything, hoping that the area would not be detected by the enemy. We kept concealed and under cover for the whole day, searching for our other operative partners but found no evidence of their being in the general area of the DZ. Enemy activity along this shoreline was nil, giving the impression that our entry was undiscovered. We awaited till the appointed time during darkness to contact the submarine at 2200 hrs. No response. We tried again the following night without success. Enemy patrols were not observed along the beach, nor any rifle fire was heard from either direction.

For the next four weeks these two operatives were continually on the run, but were befriended by several local natives who provided them with what food was available, as this was a scarce commodity which could not be purchased with money. The Japanese had confiscated the majority for their own consumption in the area, as the Allies controlled the sea links which provided the necessary transportation of food supplies to their occupational forces.

Perch returned to the DZ in the bay on the night 21/22, waited until the required stipulated hour for the return of the reconnaissance party at 0100, then returned to sea. *Perch* again approached the DZ during darkness for the third time undetected on the night of the 22nd. This was a clear and moonlit visit, with visibility of approximately 150 yards. Moving slowly and with decks just above the waterline on a glassy tropical sea, Morton and the remainder of the party now under his control assembled their folboats and rubber supply dinghy with stores in readiness to disembark at the DZ. It had been agreed that without any contact being made with the original first reconnaissance party, the second group would automatically proceed as per instructions circulated for the mission. Commander Hills now stationed on the observation platform, noticed a strange outline of a 'buoy' situated near the DZ. Lieutenant Dwyer, the Intelligence Officer of the party, was called to the platform to sight the object in question at about 150 yards range, and directly forward. He immediately reported the object in question was a semi-submerged type of enemy 'oil lighter'. Commander Hills reacted immediately, ordering the 4" gun crew on deck to 'Destroy contact'. The first two shells were near misses, but the third, using open sights, was a direct hit. The contact burst into flames, and with the ensuing barrage encountered, immediately sunk below the glassy waters of the bay. A critical period in time now existed, for with the oil fire spreading across the surface of the sea, the submarine and the main party on deck would be silhouetted against the flames, brilliantly lighting the bay and being observed from the shoreline.

The encounter with the oiler was witnessed by Horrocks and Dooland from the safety of the jungle, and the action was related to the party when they finally rejoined them four weeks later. Morton informed Commander Hills that they were ready to go and not to abort the operation. Disembarkation was accomplished without further distractions, and *Perch* departed the DZ for operational duties in the SWPA for attacks against enemy shipping.

The four rubber boats and folboats of the main party, now fully laden with operatives and supplies, departed the DZ area at 2230 hrs, and immediately experienced outboard motor failure similar to the reconnaissance party. They failed miserably, but for some unknown reason recovered and performed reasonably well close to the shoreline. They landed at their designated land DZ at 0100 hrs after hauling their loaded boats through the shallow waters for the last 150 yards. A survival perimeter was instituted and a quick reconnaissance of the area was carried out. This produced a negative encounter with the Japanese coastal occupying force. It took till 0630 hrs for all the operatives to transport the mass of equipment and stores into concealment of the nearby jungle, and to escape detection at this early stage of the mission disposed of all boats and motors in the interior.

Being now daylight, Morton and Dwyer carried out a reconnaissance of the immediate location, and much to their dismay, made a rather disturbing discovery. Their new hiding place and stores lay close and adjacent to a well-worn and freshly used native track. Recent movement on this could be clearly seen by the naked eye. Immediate steps were employed to remedy this unnerving predicament of fortune, when a native child wandered into the area. After sighting the operatives he immediately informed his parents at a nearby kampong that strangers were now in their immediate vacinity, close by, and were not Japanese.

The inquisitiveness of the youngster was indeed a fortunate encounter for the operatives, for members of the tribe nearby were soon to arrive, and proved to be friendly. Food and cigarettes were offered and accepted by them. Their services, after conversing with the elders of the tribe, were obtained for the movement of all stores into the 'ulu' (interior).

This was implemented for security and concealment from the enemy. This base camp was now located about three miles inland from the coastline, near a *sulap* belonging to a man named Hassan where, after a meal provided by him, the operatives slept in the jungle.

Bill Dwyer recalls that Hassan spoke Dutch fluently and took an instant dislike to Sergeant Dey (NEI) who treated him like a slave from the start. Hassan and I were to warm to each other. Before the Japanese occupation he had been a pilot in the Dutch Samarinda-Balikpapan service and willingly helped me learn the local dialect. On his advice we hired the carriers and transported the equipment into the interior. He did not like the Japanese but hated the Dutch even more. His people respected him to the extent that they hung on every word he had to say. Being better educated than they were, they totally relied on him for advice.

Early on the 24th Hassan awoke the operatives, guiding them to a new bivouac area a short distance further inland. Communications with base at Darwin proved a major problem, and did not eventuate. The batteries which had been transported dry-charged, failed to function when acid was introduced into the cells. From the main supply dump near the shoreline, Hassan and another native recovered and carried to the new forward camp the steam generator. When fully fired up and operational, this unit failed to recharge the batteries. The optional hand generator was not included in the signals equipment. If this had been included, it would have cut down the total weight transported on this mission, and would have not been detected by using firing methods for the steam generator.

Patrols were now sent out in all directions to obtain local information and establish contact with the missing members of the operation. Kampongs along the area were anti-Japanese, promising to warn the group of impending enemy entry into and through their territory. This help now created a network of lookouts and an early warning system. No *orang puteh* (whites) were known to be located in their vicinity. News travels quickly in the jungle, as a form of bush telegraphy really exists in these 'virgin forest' areas of the indiginous peoples of Borneo.

On 26 March a native runner brought the unwelcome news that the Japanese had arrived in the area to investigate the sinking of the oil lighter. The groups main store hideout had been located by the enemy, and a heavy guard had been placed around the area. An enemy patrol was moving through the dense jungle and heading straight in the direction of the operatives' bivouac. An immediate decision was made to move the stores held in the camp to a new location, and this was completed at a fast pace. From Indonesian sources post-war, it was learned that on arrival of the main party a local native collaborator named Abdul Rahman, who was an informer working for the Japanese

Major Don Stott DSO & Bar, SOE–SOA Party Leader of Kiwis and Robin
I.

Kempei Tai, had witnessed the landing. He had made his way secretly
to Balikpapan, and led the enemy investigation patrol to the main stores
dump. They had little trouble finding it, because some of the local
natives had pilfered much of the food supplies, and discarded the empty
remains and rubbish into the jungle.

Morton and Dwyer set off on a reconnaissance to locate a new area
for security and an operational base for the group. Farquharson and
Dey went to pick up Kondoy Dua (the lookout). Houghton and Kondoy
Satu set out to remove the remainder of the stores and make a final
clearing of the old bivouac site. Houghton did not return from this
sortie and a post-war investigation by Lieutenant Bob Tapper (NZ)

Taken before party left by submarine for Balikpapan, Borneo.

Back row, L-R: Condoy Satu NEI – Condoy Dua NEI – Sgt Dey NEI –
WO2 Farquharson AIF – Sgt Houghton NZEF – Sgt Horrocks NZEF.

Front Row, L-R: Lt Dwyer AIF – Lt Morton NZEF – Major Stott NZEF –
Capt McMillan NZEF.

Missing: Sgt Dooland AIF

reveals that he had escaped from a Japanese patrol only later to be
captured near Dotan, and eventually taken to Sanga Sanga on 30 March,
then to Balikpapan. During Morton's reconnaissance, the party heard
shots in the immediate vacinity, and Dey returned stating that he had
been unable to locate Kondoy Dua. Contact had been made with the
Japanese search patrol on a nearby hill-crest. Farquharson failed to
return, and was presumed to have been captured or killed. Dey was
unable to estimate the strength of the approaching enemy forces. After
a short period of hide and seek, Morton's party also came under
observation, resulting in a short sharp engagement without sustaining
any casualties. With the automatic and semi-automatic fire coming from
the operatives, the Japanese were of the opinion that they were en-
countering a large force of invaders.

The operatives now retired further into the security of the dense
jungle and towards nightfall changed direction directly towards the
location of the stores dump. The Japanese were not encountered during
this move, enabling the recovery of as much stores that could be

VNZ 452668 S/Sgt G.R. Greenwood. VNZ 444165 WO2 G.R. Houghton.

transported into the interior base. Valuable field rations in tins were to become of major importance in the weeks ahead, to provide sufficient nourishment for the three operatives now together in the party. Radio transmission gear was now valueless and were discarded, thus lightening their loads for rapid exit into the interior.

Being now 27 March, the Robin I party after a week in occupied territory consisted of three persons: Morton, Dwyer and Dey. With the original party still missing, plus Houghton and Farquharson presumably wounded and captured, also lost were the Netherlands

East Indies twins Kondoy Satu and Dua. (In Malay Satu is 1 and Dua 2.)

On 28 March, it was decided to carry out reconnaissances, the main objective of which was the recovery of the lost personnel of the group, and to this decision the recovery of Kondoy Satu was attributable. He was in a poor state of health, suffering from shock and exposure to the tropical climatic conditions and insect bites. A friendly native, whom the reconnaissance party had encountered, supplied the information that Farquharson had been captured and wounded in the upper arm. Morton, Dwyer and Dey continued the recce on the following day. These were short-range efforts, as the jungle tropical humidity and lack of food were the main loss of energy and fitness. Kondoy Satu was eventually located, being helped by some of our friendly loyal natives. He was suffering from exhaustion, exposure and mosquito infection. He related that he had been captured, but his native friends had managed to enter the enemy camp releasing him of his bonds, and escaped at an opportune moment when not under observation by his captors. Kondoy Satu, who had recurrent malaria and was experiencing another attack at the time, reported the fate of Houghton and party: 'He was wounded during the engagement and taken prisoner.'

On 29 March Morton and Dwyer with Sergeant Dey continued to search for other members of the group, but long-range patrols were impossible owing to the shortage of provisions. The party now withdrew further into the interior for concealment, concentrating on a low profile, thus avoiding any further contact with enemy patrols. This continued until 17 April. With reports arriving at the new base by runner from the loyal and trustworthy natives, it was known that 250 Japanese were searching the area. It soon became apparent that this was correct, for an extremely rowdy force of about 100 soldiers plus native collaborators were approaching from the north. Bill Dwyer recorded,

> They made such a bloody row that anyone for miles around would have been warned of their presence. They seemed unwilling to venture into the dense jungle from the main tracks in small parties. I inspected one of their rest areas after they had departed from such, and what a sight to behold. A bloody pigsty. It gave our morale a magnificent boost, conveying to all of us that the enemy were not prepared to venture too far from the defined known tracks. At the stores dump that they had taken control of, indications were that a major force had arrived in the area supported by substantial automatic firepower. I believe the native guides had misled the Japanese as to our location, for they certainly did not venture too close to our position.

The only contact with the outside world by the operatives was a small American MCR I radio (Minature Communications Receiver) on which they could obtain 'international news' from the Forces SWPA broadcasts. These were only used on rare occasions so as to conserve the batteries. Rainstorms were frequent and the party suffered discomfort from mosquito, leech and tick attack.

The network of native intelligence now provided information that both Horrocks and Dooland of the reconnaissance party were alive and well. They had been adopted by loyal tribespeople some distance away. Rejoining the main party was impossible due to the major Japanese force situated in the jungle between the two groups. They would await the opportunity to return unobserved, using their interior trackers for the task. Hunger amongst the operatives was rapidly taking its toll. All this time since their arrival in this area, their contact native had supplied them with various small quantities of food supplies, rice, yams, coconuts, fruit, supplimented occasionally with shellfish, bird's eggs, scrawny chickens, and on one occasion a green turtle. Soup of the 'Gods' for all. This supply of food, like many other things, came to an abrupt end when the enemy placed a standing patrol around the various supply areas. The group had grown accustomed to the daily dose of yam, starchy but filling with plenty of fibre. They started to live off the land to survive, searching the jungle for anything that was edible. Red berries which the *babi* (pigs) had eaten from the lower branches of trees came under scrutiny. These were tested on the skin under the arms and were finally eaten, causing a little loose movement of the bowel. All were losing weight quickly, and with the lack of nourishment the heavy

Folboat with raised metal umbrella for radar location. USS Submarine *Perch* is partly in photo.

undertaking of reconnaissance patrols and observation duties were now reflecting on health and fitness of all members.

For some unknown reason the Japanese now withdrew all forces except the local observers in the immediate area. Perhaps they were of the opinion that the operatives had retired further into the interior, and were not prepared to venture into this unknown 'domain' of the indiginous peoples of the 'ulu', the 'Headhunters'! This was a welcome report from the native intelligence system, and we managed to obtain two cups of rice a week plus some yams. The emergency tins of field rations were long finished and now sadly missed. Some of the party had lost weight substantially since arrival in Borneo – 42 lb plus.

Patrols were an everyday occurrence, and whilst in progress Allied aircraft passed directly overhead, but contact with them did not eventuate owing to the denseness and confines of the jungle. One chilling experience in the environment now occurred, and was recorded as follows:

> During one patrol we had the fear of hell put into us. A similar noise to that of the 'Spirit of Progress' hurtling down the permanent way (Australian Victoria Railway Train) was fast approaching through the jungle. We took cover and set up a defensive position as best we could under the circumstances. The noise became louder and louder. We were in the direct path of the advancing unknown! Suddenly, overhead in the jungle canopy passed a group of 300 plus monkeys, heading for a new feeding and mating area. Hearts were now racing and pulses high. Recovery of the group took

Hammock slung in jungle at Balikpapan. Robin I first camp.

a little while after this unaccustomed encounter with the wonders of the 'Jungle'.

On 20 April Horrocks and Dooland returned to the main party, having received substantial help from the local natives in their area also. Both were in reasonable physical condition and had obtained much valuable information about that immediate area. After all the operatives had related and discussed their perilous and present situation, it was agreed to locate and steal a native sea-going perahu. If luck held, they

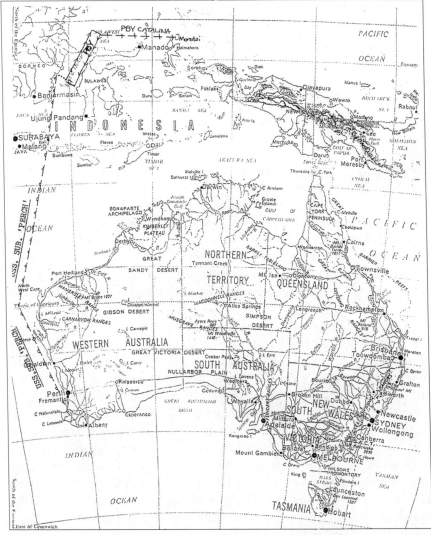

Operation Robin I (Platypus I) voyage via the Lombok Strait on the American Submarine USS *Perch* – 20 March 1945. The rescue of the surviving members by a PBY Catalina aircraft and return.

could manage to return to an Allied base in the Halmaheras. A patrol managed to contact their close friend Hassan, who informed them that after the attack on the main party by the Japanese, he was accused of providing help for the Allied force soldiers, was taken to Balikpapan and interrogated by the Kempei Tai. He was given a severe beating, but he did not disclose his association with the group. Hassan finally escaped from his captors and vanished into the ulu, then returned to his home kampong. He bought the news that McMillan and Farquharson were in custody in Balikpapan although this information was later proved to be incorrect.

Oespo, a native helper from the tribe, plus a few of the remaining members of the group travelled down the coast for several miles and located a sea-going perahu. It was amazing that the Japanese had not holed or destroyed the craft. After several days of continual haggling, a final price of 1,400 guilders was arrived at. It was 16ft in length with a beam of 6ft. Old but reasonably sound for the anticipated trip, it gave hope to all concerned that it would take them to freedom and the safety of an Allied advanced base.

The trek down the coastline commenced on 29 April, and at many kampongs the group managed to purchase various items of food for their escape by perahu. A farewell feast at a kampong near the embarkation point provided the operatives with a most welcome change of diet, though the resulting effects were long to be remembered by all. Rich food being ravenously introduced to the stomach, after so long a period, produces a rebellion from within.

Many operatives from all missions experienced this discomfiture after returning to base areas from 'Within', after living off the land and eating rice continually.

On the first day of May 1945, the perahu, now fully laden with food and water, was in readiness for the journey. The 1,400 guilders were presented to the native owner, making him a wealthy member of the tribe, and respected in the local area, provided that this information did not reach the ears of the Japanese Kempei Tai! Many of these seafaring tribespeople had volunteered to return to the Allied lines, and six were selected on the basis of intelligence and local knowledge. The point of departure was approximately 30 miles north-east of Balikpapan. At dusk the journey to freedom commenced in earnest, with the maximum effort being exerted on rowing and paddling during the hours of darkness. The furthest from land by daylight would help non-detection from the shoreline by the Japanese. Various thoughts lingered in the operatives' minds, the major one being 'Will this journey succeed? Or are we bound for a watery grave?'

The first day dawned bright and clear with a smooth unruffled surface.

At 1100 hrs two B-24 Liberators were seen approaching the coast from the direction of Morotai. The party were unable to attract attention from this flight – being just a small object in this vast area of open sea, detection from a great height would be difficult unless specifically being searched for. The perahu continued on a NE course for the remainder of the day. Lieutenant Dwyer, the Intelligence Officer in the party, produced his Mis- Ex escape kit which included a small signalling mirror, which proved to be their salvation on the next encounter with an aircraft. In the middle of the afternoon of day two, a low plane was spotted about 20 miles away. Friendly or not, they were determined to contact it – the enemy may be searching for them, having been informed of their escape from Borneo. Dwyer lined up the signalling mirror and with all the rest of the operatives offering a silent prayer, the flashing signal from the mirror was acknowledged by the aircraft, which immediately turned in the direction of the perahu.

The aircraft was now identified as a PBY Catalina flying-boat. It arrived moments later and circled the perahu, then alighted a little distance away from them. A tumultuous welcome was given to the crew of the aircraft. All members of the party plus the six natives rowed towards the PBY and boarded immediately. The pilot of the rescue aircraft was Captain Humphries of the US Navy 13th Air Sea Rescue Squadron located at the forward base of Morotai in the Halmaheras. Machine-gun fire from the blip .50 cal holed and sunk the 16-ft escape perahu. This aircraft was on a search pattern mission for a downed fighter pilot off the Balikpapan coastline which had proved to be a negative search, and the second part of the mission was the recovery of a downed B-24 Liberator crew from a beach DZ on the west side of the Celebes. The latter was duly accomplished and with approximately twenty-six persons on board including the crew, was put to its fullest potential for flight. After a prolonged full-powered take-off on the smooth off-shore waters, it finally became airborne after covering approximately 4 miles, and set course for Morotai. Their arrival back at Morotai base after nightfall coincided with an air attack in progress, although the PBY was undamaged whilst landing.

The second party of New Zealanders now situated on Morotai were in the process of assembling operational equipment for a search and rescue mission into Balikpapan for the missing Robin I party. On learning immediately of the arrival back at 'Z' Base HQ of the survivors, SRD cancelled the operation and the NZers were allocated to various other missions now being undertaken inside Borneo.

Lieutenant Bob Tapper of the second party, who represented the War Graves Commission in the Balikpapan theatre of operations at the conclusion of hostilities against Japan, investigated the disappearance of Major Don Stott and Captain Leslie McMillan. He interrogated numerous personnel of the Japanese Occupational Force in Balikpapan and Coastal Defences, but failed to obtain any information about their landing on the shores of the DZ area, or recovery of any bodies in that vicinity. With the natives not knowing of any Allied prisoners being held or found drowned, and no further reports of a person resembling Stott who had been seen in the interior, a court of enquiry at the end of the war gave the verdict that Stott and McMillan were 'Lost at sea, presumed drowned'. Of WOs Farquharson and Houghton, evidence produced recorded that they both died whilst prisoners of war.

THE FOLLOWING ARE COPIES OF DOCUMENTS

MEMORANDUM for: **7th. November 1945.**

20681

2ND N. Z. E. F. CASUALTIES – PERSONNEL ATTACHED TO AUSTRALIAN FORCES.

Movement return No. 01 covering the period 1st to 31st May 1945, submitted by the New Zealand Liaison Officer, Melbourne, contained the following paragraph under the heading 'Casualties':

'The following Battle Casualties whilst on Special Operations are reported on 2NZEF personnel attached to 'Z' Unit in Australia (S.R.D. memo F/15/1199 of 30/5/45):-

20681 Major Stott, D.J.   *Reported 'Missing' w.e.f. 21st March, 1945.*

64785 Capt. McMillan, L.T.   *Reported 'Missing believed prisoner of war w.e.f. 21st March 1945.*

444165 Sgt. Houghton R.G.   *Reported 'Missing' w.e.f. 26th. March, 1945.*

Base Records has received no subsequent information in regard to these personnel nor has it any knowledge of the area or areas in which the casualties occurred.

I understand that discussions are now in progress in connection with the search for graves of the New Zealand personnel who died, or may have died, in various areas in the Pacific War Theatre and it is suggested that further information as to where the above-named became missing be obtained from the Australian Authorities in order that Graves Units or other organisations may be furnished with all available details.

Another New Zealander attached to 'Z' Unit who is also missing is VNZ 2616204 Signalman Ernest Henry Myers. He was reported 'Missing believed Prisoner of War' by cable 5095/2ECAS3014 dated 8th September 1945 from Allied Land Headquarters, Melbourne. In his case, however, a recent memorandum from the Liaison Officer to the Adjutant-General indicates that the casualty occurred in the Mount Mentawir area, Balikpapan, and that he may have been killed and buried by the Japanese at

Semoi. Copy of the Liaison Officer's memorandum was forwarded to Base Records by the Adjutant-General on the 26th October – your file D. 339/1/4A.

The foregoing is referred to you following a recent discussion between an officer of my staff and Captain Highet of your branch.

Director
Memorandum Despatched
8 Nov. 1945.

STATEMENT BY LIEUT/COLONEL H.O. RIGG – BRITISH ARMY

RE LOSS D.J. STOTT AND CAPTAIN L.T. McMILLAN.

In addition to the statement handed to the Adjutant/General this morning, I may state that on the same night as this party was due to go ashore in the Balikpapan area on the night of 20th–21st March, 1945, a Japanese oil tanker was sunk off that coast by the submarine carrying the party.

There was a blaze for several hours before the submarine was finally sunk and it is known that this blaze made the Japanese Troops in the area on the alert, not for Major Stott's party in particular but for enemy action in general.

As a result of this activity, Major Stott's party, if it ever did get ashore, would be continuously hunted; and this is confirmed by Capt. Morton's report already on file.

As a result of this incident with the tanker, it has been considered by the Australian Army that Major Stott and party did not actually get ashore. It is understood, therefore, that the Australian Army are posting the A.M.F. personnel as 'Missing Believed Killed' – considered to be drowned at sea.

The opinion of responsible Staff Officers of S.R.D. is that more belief should be attached to the report of the trustworthy native quoted by Capt. Morton than the theory

Coastal Kampong from where the party purchased the sea-going perahu.

that Major Stott and his party never landed. Against this it must be admitted that the most careful enquiries by P.W. Recovery Teams and S.R.D. personnel trained in intelligence work has failed to establish any further evidence of Major Stott and Captain McMillan's continued existence.

(signed) H.O. Rigg Lt. Col.

[Error Para. 2 – Submarine should read Tanker]   22nd. Nov. 1945.

EXTRACTS FROM INTERROGATION OF LT. COMDR. YOSHIMURA

BY CAPT. JACOBSEN, HQ. 7 AUST. DIV.

24 Mar. 45.

Information received stated that the allies had made a landing in the vicinity of SAMBODJA, therefore, YOSHI says, he despatched WO's KOBAYASHI, NAKA-MURA and interpreter TAKAHASHI to see what the situation was – at this time there was a Coy of Army at SAMBODJA. Information concerning the landing of the rubber boat received from the natives by 101 Fuel Dept Adm Offr at SAMBODJA – the information said that there were three rubber boats with a certain amount of arms and equipment. The landing was made about 7 miles north of SAMBODJA RIVER – this information was related to him, and to the senior staff offr, YOSHI

Lt Bill Dwyer (AIF) and Lt Bob Morton (NZEF) (Robin I) arriving back at base.

says when he reported to the Senior Staff Officer, the senior staff officer gave orders for the Army to capture the enemy.

On Mar 25, he in person left with two other soldiers for SAMBODJA – he contacted Major YAMADA, CO of the Bn, and talked with him about the matter. He then proceeded on his way across SAMBODJA river – he was accompanied by the Adj of YAMADA Bn – the Adjt's name not known by YOSHI. When across the river he met his WO KOBAYASHI, who had taken food supplies from the invaders and this supply was loaded on trucks. 1 PL. of the Army had already been despatched to seek out the invaders. There was nothing else he could do so he returned to the HQ on the same day. According to later information received the Army PL that went out to seek the invaders, saw two of them in tall grass however, before they could do anything they were discovered and shot at – at this time, NAKAMURA who had gone with the Army unit was wounded very seriously. They tried to catch the two invaders, but one escaped through the jungle – the other went into the grasslands between the river and the swamps – there was no further way to escape, so he turned and fired at them – he was finally shot and captured. The person who was captured this time was shot through the shoulder – according to YOSHI his name was FERGUSSON (1) (Aust. Army).

On 26 Mar YOSHI went to Sambodja again and met Major YAMADA and talked about this matter. He then went on to look over the vicinity where the engagement had taken place – he had to make a report to the HQ at Balikpapan. In regard to the prisoner – he was wounded, so Major YAMADA and he decided to send the prisoner to BALIKPAPAN for treatment – he was put on a stretcher and placed in a truck – arriving in BALIKPAPAN on 27 Mar 45. It was decided that it would be better to keep him in TOKKEI instead of being with all the other Jap casualties. He was placed in the TOKKEI and was attended by Lt. YOSHIMURA, who found that the prisoner was in pretty good condition; was able to talk – it was believed that he would be able to recover. For two or three days he was given what possible food YOSHI had – however, at that time the food position was very acute, therefore the only extra thing he could give the prisoner was milk. As his condition improved, he was interrogated by Lt. KAWAI TOKUSHI, at his bedside. The information he gave was transmitted to HQ – believed also transmitted to HQ at SOERBAYA ... However after about ten days the prisoner developed double pneumonia – his wound had been healing, but with the added sickness his condition became worse. On or about the 13th day he died (about 7 May) – he was attended by Lt. ISHIKAWA. (By the way, NAKAMURA died on the 26 Mar.)

Lt. Cmdr. YAMAOKA prepared papers concerning the death of the prisoner, and his body was taken care of in the same way as the other cases mentioned above (Note: CREMATED). According to later information it was said that at least 7 had landed from the rubber boat – they could only account for two, and did not know where the other five had gone. They then tried to get information from the natives, but were unsuccessful. FERGUSON (1) stated the Major Stott was in charge and had gone up the MAHAKAM river.

On the 29 Mar YOSHI went to SAMBODJA with several of his men and together with army, searched for the remaining invaders. YOHSI says they did not succeed in finding them but knew they were around some place, because they saw lights at night and on one occasion a B-24 circled around the MAHAKAM area – river area.

On the 30 Mar it was reported to HQ that an Australian soldier carrying an automatic was confronted by Jap soldiers in the vicinity of DONTAN, and he promptly surrendered. The prisoner was taken to SANGA SANGA, but they wanted to find out how he had escaped after landing, so they thought it best to bring him down to BALIKPAPAN, he was sent by barge from SANGA SANGA on 4 May, arriving in BALIKPAPAN on 5 May. According to the interrogation, men on the mission had left AUSTRALIA in Mar, travelling by submarine, 7 landed in the SAMBODJA area – 4 others in the vacinity of SANGA SANGA. This Cpl. HOUGHTON (2) also revealed that they landed by means of three rubber boats and two smaller folding boats, Major STOTT, another Captain and 2 NCOs, who were in the folding boats, went to the mouth of the MAHAKAM river, also three rubber boats landed in the vicinity of SAMBODJA. The plan for the Australians had been to reconnoitre the position in the SAMBODJA and SANGA SANGA areas. Japs sent searching parties up the MAHAKAM river to look for the two boats, but were unsuccessful. According to the Sgt they landed on Mar 23 in the three rubber boats, they unloaded all the food and equipment, hiding same in the jungle. They then left and went through the jungle and found native village – they also took with them a certain amount of goods. The information concerning the Australians was given by the natives to the Japs in SAMBODJA. According to Sgt HOUGHTON, it was while he and FERGUSON were carrying some goods from the first location to the second that they located the Jap force and after a brief engagement he ran off into the jungle. He also stated that he had a compass and map with him, and that according to the map, if he went east, he would come to a pipe-line leading to DONDANG – he didn't have any food or equipment other than an automatic rifle and when captured by the Japs was in very poor condition. At one time, about 8 May, they received information that suspicious looking persons were in the vicinity of KILO 48 on the BALIKPAPAN to SAMA-RINDA road. They promptly sent search parties but nothing became of it, they also had plenty of information as to their whereabouts, but never succeeded in finding these persons.

They never captured any prisoners after July 1st., before the AUSTRALIAN landing in the area.

[*Correction by Author:* (1) **refers to WO FARQUHARSON AIF and** (2) **refers to WO HOUGHTON NZEF**]
THE ABOVE DOCUMENTS RELATING TO CASUALTIES ARE RECORDED IN THEIR ORIGINAL FORM.

Introduction to Operation Semut –
Borneo, Sarawak & BNB (Sabah)

Semut was originally intended to be a project based on the Baram river (inland, in the interior of Sarawak from Brunei) and to operate in Sarawak, its objective being to collect intelligence data ahead of the AIF coastal landings.

It was expected that Sarawak, Brunei and Labuan Island would be the areas of operational importance by June 1945 and that it would be of great assistance to the Allied General Staff to have an efficient intelligence network built up, capable of passing on information on matters vital to the invasion plan. The cooperation of a sympathetic native population was well schooled by officers especially trained in the creation of an underground resistance organisation, and knowing the area intimately would be of considerable operational value to the invading Allied forces. Further, the establishment of OPs and native CWPs and the submissions of intelligence on suitable beach landing points, coastal batteries and radar sites would be of assistance to the Navy; similarly, reports on the extent of the operational use of Japanese airfields and meteorological conditions would be of value to the Air Force, for which personnel escape routes could also be organised.

The initial planning on Semut started in February 1944 and the preliminary plan was produced and submitted to GHQ in May 1944. It was followed by an outline plan, issued on 16 September 1944. Early approval was not granted due to the low position of the Semut area in GHQ's list of priorities and to difficulties in supplying submarine transport.

The reconnaissance party was scheduled to arrive on the ground in October or November. GHQ's approval was received too late, however, for a submarine insertion to be effected before the break of the north-east monsoon.

Meantime, Brunei had risen to Priority 4 on GHQ's list and Semut planning had therefore to be recast in order to concentrate primarily on this area. Further, Sarawak had become within easy air range of newly acquired Allied bases. Air insertion had always been preferred by both Major Carter (NZ) and Major Harrisson (GB) who considered the coastal Malays unreliable. They were of the opinion that the element of surprise would be lost if quantities of stores had to be carried inland through the coastal regions, which were directly controlled by the Japanese who would soon learn of their locality. By this time, the attachment of 200 Flight RAAF to AIB and its availability for SRD operations made an air insertion practicable.

To meet changing conditions, a revised plan was drawn up on 11 November 1944. It provided for an early insertion by parachute and focused on the initial activities of the party in the hinterland of Brunei Bay. This final plan was submitted to GHQ on 24 November 1944 and eventually approved early in the following month.

Captain Crowther, who had been employed in Sarawak before the war and had an extensive knowledge of the country, joined SRD in February 1944 and took up the appointment of D/H (OC Sarawak Country Section). He was in charge of planning and staff work for Semut from its inception until 27 August 1944 when Major Ednie-Brown (NZ) succeeded him to the appointment. Lieutenant Palmer (NZ) was the staff officer in charge of Semut stores, and took over the Sarawak Country Section when Major Ednie-Brown was transferred to Advance HQ SRD.

Semut had been planned to comprise two parties: a reconnaissance party, and the main body, to follow up after two weeks. The whole operation was to have been controlled by Major Carter from a HQ in the Baram river area but difficulties in intercommunication and the need for decentralising the administration (between the two OCs) of such a large area which at the time included not only Sarawak, but also portions of Dutch and British North Borneo (Sabah), contributed to the subdivision of Semut into three separate commands, later extended to four.

It was decided towards the end of May 1945 that the whole project would be controlled by Group 'A' at Labuan. Each party, thereafter, routed its own signals through the latter HQ and operational directives came under the commander of that group, Lieutenant Colonel J.B. Courtney (GB)

British North Borneo (Sabah)

As the main operations recorded in this manuscript relate to BNB and Sarawak, the reader should be introduced to a little history and knowledge of them to appreciate the conditions that existed 'Within'. On parachuting into the areas during 1945, we operatives were faced with the straight facts that we had jumped back in time a hundred years, similar to the arrival of the British in New Zealand with the indiginous Maori tribes. We were indeed lucky to be able to communicate with them, as the 'Hadjis', the teachers of Islam who had roamed the interior for hundreds of years, were accepted by the tribes, teaching the *Kiai* or the learned ones *bahasa Malayu* which we operatives had been taught at Fraser Island Commando School, north of Brisbane.

The history of Sabah (BNB) is extraordinary – geographically speaking it had existed since time immemorial. Thus the 150 million-year-old 'Virgin Forests' existed with the indiginous tribes of the ULU (interior) roaming and head-hunting the 29,000 square miles within its boarders. Three hundred and fifty different dialects were known to have existed within Borneo. With *bahasa Malayu* being known and taught, the natives could converse in that language.

Before 1881	No overall administration.
	No Government.
	No State Economy.
After 1881	A British Protectorate.
	Approved by the Foreign Office, Colonial Office, and the British Government, with the setting up of an Administration by granting a 'Royal Charter' to the North Borneo Company, with shareholders domiciled in the United Kingdom.
	This existed until the Japanese Invasion in 1942.
1945	Saw the British Borneo Civil Administration Unit, (BBCAU) operating from Labuan Island, Bay of Brunei, administer relief to the indiginous population of the *ulu* (interior), using aircraft drops.
1946	Sale finalised from the Chartered Company to the British Government. Became a Crown Colony.
1963	The States of Sabah and Sarawak formed Western Malaysia.

Sarawak

Under the 'White Rajah's rule (Brooke Regime) the indiginous peoples of the interior were totally protected by various laws instituted by the Government of Sarawak, prohibiting any interference with the tribal customs and lifestyles of these indiginous peoples by outsiders. If the Japanese invaders had treated these people in the correct manner, we, the operatives of Special Operations Australia, would not have succeeded on our missions 'Within'.

Trading Values and Purchasing Power within Borneo whilst we were in Action Against the Japanese

1   SALT   = One day's ordinary work. (That which can be claimed by evaporation from salt springs earthenware trays by one person in one day).

2   SALT   = One *Bareo* (Kampong in Sarawak) type sleeping mat.

4	SALT	= One *Bawang* (Kampong in Dutch area) type sleeping mat.
1	SALT	= One *Par Trap* (Kampong in Sarawak) small E/w pot.
2	SALT	= One *Mada* (Kampong in Sarawak) medium E/W pot.
30	SALT	= One small Chinese pot (2 pint size) traded from the coast.
50	SALT	= One small Chinese gong.
2	Gongs	= Half sized dragon jar. (traded from the coast by Chinese).
2	half sized dragon jars plus salt	= One large dragon jar.

Weighing of Rice

1 Cupak = Half coconut shell in volume.
4 Cupak = One guntang. (5 lbs.)
10 Cupak = One carrying load per person (approx. 50 lb).

Semut Operations – Australian Archives Vol. II

Semut I was originally intended to be part of a project based on the Baram river and to operate in Sarawak. It had been arranged that Major Harrisson would take in the first (Reconnaissance) party to reconnoitre for safety and suitability, and to find other dropping zones for later insertions. For reasons already explained in the introduction Semut I was made a separate project on its own account, working independently of the rest of Semut.

The area in Sarawak originally allocated to Semut was the central Kelabit Plateau and the headwaters of the rivers flowing north into Brunei Bay, namely the Limbang and Terusan. Major Harrisson was able, however, to extend all over the northern section of Sarawak, from Brunei Bay to the Padas river, over southern British North Borneo and into Dutch Borneo as far as the east coast and south to the Kayan river.

Owing to the late start, due to the failure of plans for insertion by submarine, it was not anticipated that Semut could do more than collect and disseminate intelligence data before the AIF landed and took control. The party, however, was able to develop so rapidly that it was given the tasks of organising large-scale guerrilla activities, the medical care and rehabilitation of the natives, and the food distribution in the area.

In company with Squadron Leader Cook (D/Air), Major Harrisson made a reconnaissance of the DZ areas from Morotai in January 1945 by USAAF aircraft. A further reconnaissance was made by Major Harrisson in mid-March with RAAF (200 Flight) to find a more central DZ, which was successfully located. After four unsuccessful sorties, Semut I was inserted by parachute from two B-24s of 200 Flight RAAF at Bareo on the Kelabit Plateau in the mountainous and largely unexplored hinterland of Borneo on 23 March 1945. One of the B-24s (commanded by Squadron Leader Pockley) which transported the party, was lost on the return.

Personnel and stores were scattered over 8 miles of jungle and it took four days to get organised. A considerable portion of the stores were never recovered.

Reinforcements were subsequently inserted on 29 April, 26 May, 11–16, 17–22, 25 June and 10 August. Captain McCullum (Dr.) was inserted with Semut II on 16 April 1945, but worked in the Semut I area for a month prior to moving to the Baram river.

Sergeants Barrie and Hallam asked to be transferred to Semut II upon insertion of that party, whilst Sergeant Long (W/T Op) who dropped with Major Carter was left with Semut I, replacing them.

Phase I

When the party was inserted, it was uncertain whether there were Japanese in the area, and the natives' attitude and probable reception was an unknown factor. However within five minutes of landing, one party was met by natives carrying a white flag. The moment they were recognised as white men, they sent runners to villages for 20 miles around and by nightfall over 500 people had come to help the party find storpedos and other stores.

The natives were delighted to see the party. Though they had no direct experience of war in this remote area, they had felt it indirectly through the stoppage of all trade goods, medicines and commerce. At the same time, they were very nervous about the possible Japanese reprisals if they helped the party. Fourteen natives had already been taken prisoner for helping American airmen who had been shot down in their B-24s whilst attacking the Japanese fleet in the Brunei Bay area.

Major Tom Harrisson immediately assembled all chiefs from an area up to three days' walk around, in order to overcome these fears, and to realise the potential strength of Semut. This conference was successful and from that time on, unlimited native support was received in this area, without any further misgivings on their part.

Phase II

Having established an HQ in the mountains above Bareo at 5,000 feet, and contacted Darwin by W/T, the party prepared for the reception of Phase II. Some days were wasted as Phase II was held up by bad weather. In the early days, when the situation was less secure, four men were left behind to cover the DZ area. In the meantime, Major Harrisson made two trips of five days each – one to the head of the Baram river, the other one over the Dutch border. These missions enabled him to make an appreciation of all approaches to the area, of the potential manpower within, and the future lines of development. The 2I/C, Captain Edmeades, was sent into the Bahu area, to reconnoitre the Kayan Valley. Thus by the time Phase II was inserted, a large area had been surveyed in a preliminary way. Throughout this area, the natives had seen the first white men in four years. Large quantities of medicines had been distributed, and everywhere many conferences were held nightly with chiefs and assembled villagers. The party was able to change the original negative attitude towards the Japanese, and the war in general, into a positive antipathy. The innate native respect for the white man and his form of government helped considerably, and by the end of three weeks the morale of the natives was rising with great rapidity. The preliminary work of preparing an aggressive state of mind had been completed. The insertion of Phase II had further increased the party's prestige and showed that the original landing was not an isolated effort. From then on regular air supply gave the natives themselves an increasing feeling of strength and solidarity.

Within two days, porters and guides had been recruited and the new party had started on its way towards the Baram river. Unfortunately, owing to the high altitude from which storpedos were dropped, a week was lost looking for and locating the original party's own maintenance stores over a radius of 3 miles, and without success. A pig hunter found one in the mountains three months later, totally destroyed and ravished by wild animals.

Semut I was now free to concentrate all of its efforts on the natives and a directive from the Director of SRD dispelled any doubts about the advisability of extending the work into Dutch Territory. The Dutch Christian natives, were more numerous than the Sarawak pagans, and were more violently anti-Japanese, partly for religious reasons. In every respect the Dutch area was most suitable for the extension of the party's activities; it was the centre of all inland routes. By the end of the month, the Kelabit Plateau area of Sarawak had been so consolidated that no Japanese could possibly penetrate it without the party receiving several days' warning. For security reasons, however, an alternative HQ was established on the Plateau at Pa Mudoh, two days' walk southward. This area was also to act as a link with Major Carter (Semut II) as wireless communication with him was unsuccessful from Bareo. (Communications within Borneo were proved at a later date to be good; it all depended on the training and experience of the said W/T operators with tropical conditions. Outstations set up within BNB, Sarawak and Brunei areas were excellent.)

After receiving one further stores drop at Bareo, the main HQ was moved eastwards to the Sarawak-Dutch border, behind Kabak. By now the native deputations were coming in from up to eighteen days walk away, and the party leader was spending approximately eight hours a day talking to these people and conducting interrogations. Everywhere the request was for arms; the time for talking had passed and Semut I was now about to prepare for action. This HQ was in an excellent position, but events were developing so rapidly north and east, that it proved necessary to move forward again in order to be in a position more central to the sub-parties.

Immediately the main party had been shifted over the Dutch border, all the personnel in the main valleys were moved further out, extending the radius of the area and getting nearer to the Japanese at all points. Major Carter having called for him urgently, Captain McCullum left to join Semut II in the Baram area. From then on, Semut I worked without a doctor and the loss of his services was a blow. However, as all personnel had received elementary medical instruction, they continued to give medical assistance to every village visited. This was a major factor in the winning and holding of native goodwill.

Guerrillas

Having consolidated native morale and built up a definite feeling of hostility towards the Japanese, the next step was to begin to satisfy the ever-increasing demand for arms. With the support of SRD HQ, Semut I was able during the latter part of April and May to supply some 300 rifles, and provide instruction in their handling. By the end of July 1,000 men were under arms, some of them equipped with captured Japanese weapons. The new arrival of arms had a further effect in raising the morale of the natives. The main problem as their arming proceeded, was to restrain these people from taking the offensive in an indiscriminate way. They observed excellent discipline in this respect, once the need for coordination with sea landings by the AIF was clearly understood.

Each valley was under the control of one white operative, assisted by Malays and others who had been trained as soldiers by the Dutch and Japanese. Some of these were excellent types and were made NCOs. The main valleys were the Limbang, Terusan, Padas, Sembakong, Mentarang, Semamone and Bahu. Each weapon was issued to a particular native with a specified number of rounds, and his name recorded. He was also instructed that if he neglected his weapon or used the ammunition for other purposes, these would be withdrawn. Arms were not distributed indiscriminately on a village basis. A large quantity was given only to one or two villages in each area, namely those that were at strategic points in the valleys. In some cases as on the Semamone, some dissemination was desirable; then, on receipt of news of enemy penetration all armed men would rally immediately at a central rendezvous, unless otherwise directed. The ordinary guerrillas stayed in their own areas, and were regarded as defensive troops who would kill all Japanese entering their areas, unless the enemy was in force. The regular soldiers moved from place to place. Their numbers increased constantly, but were necessarily dependent on the availability of operative leaders to train and discipline platoons.

These guerrillas were used in a protective roll until 9 June 1945. They killed fourteen Japanese who had penetrated through the jungle into the interior on patrol, but did not go in search of the enemy. They also took forty-eight auxiliary native troops accompanying the Japanese, and captured several notorious collaborators including the Controller of Malinau. This was the situation up to 'D-Day', i.e. 9 June. The party had been in the country for nearly three months and had reconnoitred the whole area behind Brunei Bay, north to the Sapong Estate rubber plantation plus Pensiangan, and east to the Dutch coast.

Having made a reconnaissance of all the rivers in the area, Semut I were unable to find any place for a seaplane landing. The increasing development of operations and the presence of eleven American airmen recovered in the area, made some contact with the outside world essential. Major Harrisson therefore decided to try and build an airstrip for Auster aircraft. He found a site in the Bawang Valley, on a slightly elevated piece of ground, surrounded by irrigated rice fields. More than 300 natives under the supervision of two Australian operatives of the first reinforcement just dropped in, levelled and drained the padi fields. After drying out the land, the runway was made of split bamboos, of which over a thousand were required, each 35ft. in length and 8" to 10" diameter.

On 7 June, nine days after commenceing work, the first two Austers landed from Tarakan. The first plane to take off (containing Major Harrisson) crashed. It overran the strip, just missed a water buffalo and ended up in a padi field. The landing gear struts were broken. It was soon recovered by the multitude of natives on the strip watching the first take-off. In consequence, the runway was extended another 80 yards by the next morning.

The other plane took off with Major Harrisson and returned to Tarakan for a conference with I Australian Corps. A B-24 was flown from Morotai Base HQ to collect Harrisson and return him to that

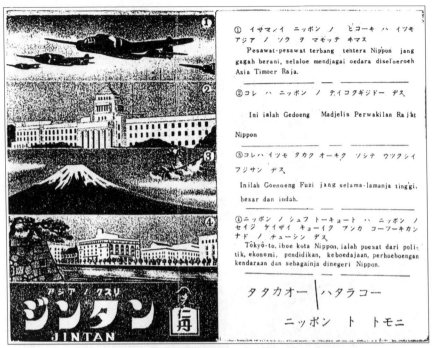

Japanese propaganda among Malay peoples. Postcard.

base. Within two days, he had selected another seven operatives now situated at Morotai and then chuted back into the *ulu* on 9 June 1945. This was the second reinforcement.

Another aspect of this passive work prior to D-Day should be mentioned. At the time of the party's arrival, very large quantities of rice and cattle were being brought down to the Japanese disposed on the coast on both seaboards of Borneo. Semut I soon convinced the natives of the interior that this should be discontinued, and this major source of supply was promptly terminated.

It was some time before the Japanese became suspicious about the reasons for this, due to the cooperation of native administration officers who invented a number of excuses. Eventually, the Japanese sent patrols

Japanese propaganda among Malay peoples. Matchbox labels. 'Tentoe dapat kemenangan' means 'Sure to get Victory'!

Papers found strewn through the house, P. Musa.

to investigate, none of which returned. In the same way, the party was able to terminate the supply of native labour particularly from the Padas river. This seriously hindered the Japanese in their extension of the road to Sindumin and Sipitang and interfered with the gardens supplying the garrisons and railway workers in the Tenom area. An

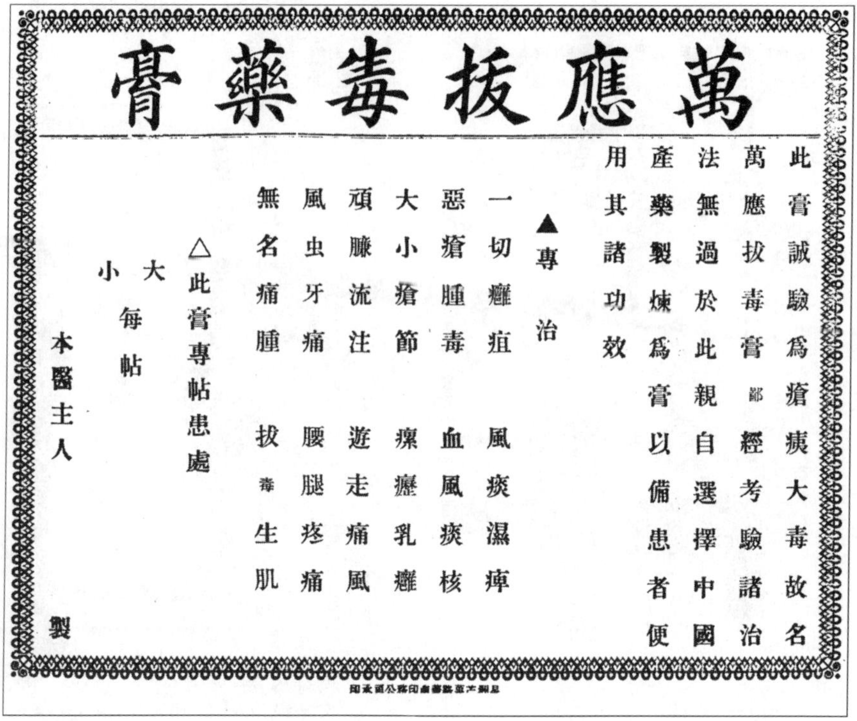

萬應拔毒藥膏

此膏誠驗為瘡痍大毒故名
萬應拔毒膏邨經考驗諸治
法無過於此親自選擇中國
產藥製煉為膏以備患者便
用其諸功效

▲專治

一切癰疽　風痰濕痺
惡瘡腫毒　血風痰核
大小瘡節　瘰癧乳癰
頑癬流注　遊走痛風
風虫牙痛　腰腿疼痛
無名痛腫　拔毒生肌

△此膏專帖患處
大每帖小
本醫主人製

increasing number of auxiliary troops and police were induced to desert the Japanese. Some of these men brought valuable information and a number of them were made NCOs, proving invaluable in training guerrillas. By the end of the operation, nearly 100 of these ex-Japanese personnel were working for Semut I.

D–Day

As a result of the previously mentioned arrangements, when permission was given to take the offensive as from 9 June, Semut I was in a reasonably strong position to do so. On that particular day, all the Japanese in Lawas, Trusan, Sundar, Loembis and Ukong were killed. At the same time, strong patrols hunted out the Japanese along the Limbang river, on the sub-coastal sector from the Limbang to Sipitang, and on the Sembakong river in Dutch Borneo. Considerable Japanese food reserves and prepared hideouts were captured and the enemy plans for moving freely towards the interior were sabotaged.

The Japanese were taken completely by surprise when attacked from inland at the same time as from the coast. This initial surprise enabled the party to keep the upper hand and to maintain the initiative through-out the inland areas within which it was operating. At no time from then on was Semut I ever forced into a defensive roll, except in so far as the dispositions necessarily envisaged the defence of the interior against any very large-scale movement.

The party captured and held given points in the sub-coastal area to protect the periphery of its operations. It was also necessary in order to maintain food supplies and morale, to establish some sort of temporary administration in the area. Ukong, Sipitang, Lawas, Trusan, Malaman, Loembis and Malinau were occupied in this way. These places in the Brunei Bay area were handed over to the AIF when they arrived to take up regular occupation. Malinau and Loembis on the Dutch side and Bole in British North Borneo were held by the party as administrative centres until September 1945.

Soon after the party's arrival approximately 200 Japanese planned to come up the Mentarang river via Malinau into the interior. This was the first of a series of similar attempts to enter the interior, both before and after AIF landings to the east and west. Prior to March 1945, Japanese patrols had only occasionally penetrated into the interior, to make detailed reports on tracks, population and food supplies. Copies of these reports were captured from several groups of enemy moving inland. There seems little doubt that as the situation deteriorated, the enemy planned to move inland into the very rich and rather inaccessible areas, notably the Bawang Valley which was known to them.

In July there were also indications of large-scale enemy movements out from British North Borneo, probably to establish themselves in the interior. In the latter half of July, a strong enemy garrison was established at Pensiangan, the southernmost point on the road from Keningau with a declared intention of forming a bridgehead for a southerly move inland from north and east. In each case these were repulsed. A force of 200 on the Padas was reduced to about eighty before it withdrew. No Japanese force reached within four days' march of the fertile centres from March 1945 onwards, and at no time was there any serious probability of any large force getting inland except at extreme cost to themselves.

One important enemy breakthrough occurred in the Semut I area. This was not an attempt to move inland in the ordinary way, but an attempt to escape overland from Brunei, after the AIF landing, in order to join up with the main Japanese forces in British North Borneo. A force of at least 500 under a general officer made a well-organised trek, crossing the Limbang and keeping about 15 miles inland till they struck the Trusan. From there they moved up the river to the Tengoa tributary, followed this to its headwaters, then crossed the Padas, making for Tenom.

This force was first contacted just before it reached the Trusan, and from then on contact was kept for twenty-one days, during which time at least 320 were accounted for. Through the now well-established wireless communications it became possible for Semut I forces to follow up and pick off stragglers from the rear, as they came up the Trusan, and to meet them head-on from the Padas. Although the enemy was numerically much stronger and better armed than the forces available in the sector, Semut I held the initiative at all times, and those Japanese who were not killed, arrived at the other end starving.

It is probable that very few did reach their destination and that many died of starvation in the jungle without being located. Through the whole operation, only two men (Muruts) were lost. On two occasions Semut I forces were ambushed by the enemy. In neither case was anyone wounded. If it had not been for Semut I activities, it is likely that these forces, which had already evaded the AIF patrols on the coast, would have had no difficulty in reaching Tenom in good order.

By 1 August there were not more than a handful of Japanese known to be alive in Semut I area, i.e. northern Sarawak and Dutch Northern Borneo. On the fringes of this area – the Sapong Estate, Pensiangan and the south of the Kayan river – there were reported to be considerable numbers. The party leader therefore prepared to launch his first full-scale attack on the enemy in their own selected positions which were held in strength.

Seven white operatives with 160 native troops were ready to attack the southern Japanese force on the Sapong Estate, and four whites with 200 guerrillas were to attack the enemy garrison at Pensiangan. Semut I forces were armed with LMGs, SMGs, US Carbines, hand grenades, cup-dischargers and .303 rifles. These attacks were scheduled to take place simultaneously to prevent any easy reinforcement from Keningau, but at this stage the Japanese surrender was announced.

As from 15 August all aggressive action ceased. At the same time it was necessary to maintain the natives offensively armed. In and around Pensiangan, the Japanese took advantage of the party's passive action to send a party of fifty southbound, forcing Semut I detachment to withdraw.

On the Padas the Japanese benefiting from the party's withdrawal to defensive positions advanced to within a mile of Semut I's base at Tomani, stealing food and killing two unarmed natives. On the Limbang Fujino Tai ignored all requests and warnings, and commenced looting and pillaging, raping and burning all kampongs they came across. Our operative-controlled force in that area withdrew four times and did not engage the enemy, but were fired upon on two occasions. On 4 September they finally engaged the enemy in a firefight, but did not sustain any casualties. The Japanese persisted in advancing up the

Limbang, ignoring leaflet-dropping by aircraft of the RAAF and envoys. Three native Dayaks were sent across the river with surrender documents to this Fujino Tai group, but did not return. Captain Fujino executed them, for he did not believe his Emperor would capitulate, and that the leaflets were an Allied ploy to make him surrender his force, which had traversed through the jungle from the Brunei area. Semut I party leader now gave orders to the operatives to prevent Fijino Tai from further advancing into the interior.

By 15 October, Fujino Tai had reached the Trusan river and turned towards Semut I HQ in the Bawang Valley and the bamboo airstrip. As HQ AMF had ordered that SRD personnel must be concentrated in Labuan by this date, Major Harrisson, three officers and four ORs were transferred to HQ 9th Australian Division, who then took over the operation. On 29 October, Major Harrisson's party, having walked through the jungle from the coast into the interior, contacted Fujino Tai. A Japanese envoy with the party armed with letters from the GOC Japanese 37th Army, General Masao Baba, ordered them to surrender. They were disarmed and escorted to Lawas on the coast near Brunei Bay and delivered to the AMF. At the commencement of the march from Kaula Belait area, Fujino Tai mustered 578 personnel – 220 were accounted for directly or indirectly by SRD up to the time of surrender.

At the time of the surrender, Semut I controlled an area stretching

General Maso Baba's aircraft arriving at Labuan Island from Borneo for the surrender of his forces in the Pacific. Note the surrender isignia on the aircraft as ordered by the Allied partners. If not displaying the same, were to be shot down for non-conformance of orders.

Top: General Maso Baba being met by senior officers after the landing of his aircraft at Labuan Island. Officers were from the Japanese surrender camps on the island. 32nd Imperial Force.

Middle: General Baba being escorted into the detention camp by members of the AIF.

Bottom: A Japanese engineer inspects the surrender aircraft after touch down.

AUSTRALIAN MILITARY FORCES

AAF A117(a)
(Introduced Jan (6)
HQ AMF Use Only

RECORD OF MILITARY COURT

R. 176

(JAPANESE WAR CRIMINALS)

AWC No. 294

Accused: Lt-Gen BABA Masao

Aust W.C. List Ser No.................................

Court, Place, RABAUL
Date and 28 May & 2 June 47.
Formation: 8 M.D.

Charge(s)	Plea	Finding
Committing a War Crime, that is to say A Violation of the Laws and Usages of War in that he between December 1944 and September 1945 in BORNEO, while a Commander of Armed Forces of Japan at war with the Commonwealth of Australia and its Allies, unlawfully disregarded and failed to discharge his duty as such Commander to control the conduct of the members of his command whereby they committed brutal atrocities and other high crimes against the people of the Commonwealth of Australia and its Allies.	NOT GUILTY.	GUILTY. TO SUFFER DEATH BY HANGING.

Precis of Evidence: The evidence against the accused consisted mainly of statements from 2 former Australian Prisoners of War, and Japanese officers, which had been used at previous war crime trials.
The substance of the evidence for the prosecution was as follows:- That members of the accused's command pursuant to orders of the accused had conducted on occasions the transfer of a number of Australian and British Prisoners of War, by a route march from Sandakan and Ranau in British North Borneo. The physical condition of the Prisoners of War was so poor that these marches amounted to ill-treatment. Evidence was also given of a number of brutal atrocities and ill-treatment such as insufficient food, failure to provide medical attention, and the failure to provide sufficient clothing and boots, thereby causing many Prisoners of War to march barefooted over the Sandakan, Ranau route a distance of 150 miles. The Prisoners of War encountered such severe hardships on both of these marches that a number of them died on the way. Statements were produced to prove that 2 Japanese Officers under the command of the accused, were directly responsible for the giving of orders which resulted in the shooting and killing of many Prisoners of War during the march from Sandakan to Ranau, and whilst at Ranau.
Over.

Sentence and Date: To suffer: DEATH BY HANGING. 2 June 47.

Confirmation and by Whom: Maj Gen W. M. Anderson Adjutant General A.M.F 17/7/47.

Promulgation: 4/8/47   Executed 7/8/47

Petition: Petition lodged 14 June 47 on behalf of the accused.

J.A.G.'s Report on Petition: Confirm finding and sentence and dismiss petition.

Action on Petition: Dismissed 4/4/47

from the coast of Borneo, westward to the lower Limbang and middle Tutoh, and from a line Malaman – Kemabongio to the vacinity of Pensiangan and southward through the densely populated Bawang, Berang and Balikoe areas to the Kayan river. The controlled area included nearly a quarter of a million population, and approximately 16,000 square miles.

WARRANT OF EXECUTION

WHEREAS Lt-Gen BABA Masao on the 2nd day of June 1947 was sentenced by military court held at RABAUL to death by hanging And whereas the finding and sentence of the said military court have been duly confirmed in accordance with the War Crimes Act 1945, and whereas I have reviewed the said sentence, now therefore I, Warren Melville ANDERSON Adjutant General of the Australian Military Forces, hereby approve of the carrying out of the sentence confirmed as aforesaid.

Dated this *Seventeenth* day of *July.*
One thousand nine hundred and forty-seven.

(SGND) *W. M. ANDERSON*

Major-General,
Adjutant-General,
AUSTRALIAN MILITARY FORCES.

(11)

CERTIFICATE BY OFFICER SUPERVISING THE EXECUTION

I, *FRANCIS JOHN DUVAL* an officer of the AMF certify that I was present at and supervised the execution of the abovenamed Lt-Gen BABA Masao at *Rabaul* at *0800* hrs on the *seventh* day of *August* 1947.

Dated this *seventh* day of *August* 1947.

(SGND) *F. J. DUVAL* (MAJOR)
Signature

(111)

CERTIFICATE BY MEDICAL OFFICER PRESENT AT THE EXECUTION

I, *JAMES MORRIS ELLIS* a legally qualified medical practitioner certify that I examined the body of the person executed in accordance with the above certificate and pronounced life extinct.

Dated this *seventh* day of *August* 1947.

(SGND) *J M ELLIS* CAPT
Signature

The accused gave evidence in his defence and a sworn statement containing such evidence was exhibited by the Court. In substance the accused stated that his command was so extensive that he could not possibly police the actions of his subordinates.

Incidentally, much more geographical information and data on the potential value of the interior was collected and in the course of its duties, Semut I covered and recorded large tracts of land previously unmapped and unexplored. Eleven shot-down American airmen were rescued, five of whom were in a very sad condition when located. Many loyal Malays, Chinese and other government servants, dressers etc., and eighteen natives held in gaol were rescued in attacks on the enemy at Malinau and in the Brunei area.

Enemy Intelligence

From interrogations of Japanese local commanders and the senior Intelligence Officer of the 37th Army HQ, it was evident that local commanders' intelligence of Semut activities was fairly good, but little was ever passed back to 37th Army HQ, with the result that little concerted effort was made to neutralise Semut activities and no appreciation of the effect of growth of native resistance was made until too late.

The knowledge possessed by 37th Army HQ of Semut activities is summarised below.

Semut I

In May 45, it was known that a small party of white men had been inserted by parachute into central Borneo. It was surmised that their role was to gain knowledge of Japanese dispositions prior to an Australian invasion. No action, however, was taken against them as it was considered they would do little harm. Thereafter, no further information on the expansion of Semut I was received.

Semut II and III

In June 1945 it became known that there were parties of white men in the Baram and Rejang areas arming the natives. It was thought that they were from the AIF from Labuan.

Semut IV

No knowledge of this party in their operational area, Makab–Bintalu–Similajav (Sarawak).

Semut I Operations of AKS 173 VNZ 422668 Sergeant F.A. Wigzell

After the arrival of the initial party of Semut in Sarawak on 25 March 1945 on the 'Plains of Bah' at 5,000ft above sea level, communication with Darwin was not established for some time and when it was finally made, Darwin was unable to decode the cypher messages of the party. It was interpreted by HQ that this party had been compromised by the enemy, meaning that the Japanese had captured the group, and someone had broken under torture and related the information to the enemy, enabling them to use the group's W/T and code. Major Toby Carter (a former surveyor and Kiwi working for Shell Oil situated at Brunei) waiting at HQ now at Morotai in the Halmahera group of islands, disbelieved this story of compromisation, advising HQ 'Z' that Phase II of the operation would proceed, and gave the green light for the operatives to drop into Bareo, Borneo. Toby's decision was to be proved correct, and thus Semut was born.

As from the Beginning

At the outbreak of war in 1939, at the age of eighteen years I enlisted for overseas service and entered Trentham Military Camp. Having advanced my age by two years on my application form, my employers, the NZ Government advised Army HQ of my misstatement, and I was immediately transferred under the MS Act to a territorial LAFV squadron in the Waikato area. Here I attained the rank of Sergeant, acting Squadron SM, attended a specialist course for officers and senior NCOs at Waiouru Camp, and was recommended for a commission. As the war in Europe was developing quickly, I dropped most of my rank in order to obtain a posting for overseas service, and subsequently served in the SWPA with Divisional Signals, was based on Guadalcanal, landed on Vella la Vella, Mono and Sterling Islands in the Treasury Group, and Green, also known as Nissan Island, further northwards near Bougainville. I was indeed lucky to have been selected to take part in all of the operations in the Pacific with 3rd NZ Division.

On returning to New Zealand with the main force, was again stationed at Trentham Military Camp, where the morale of the returning troops dropped substantially as nothing was known of their future assignment. Square bashing was certainly no substitute for active service. There appeared on our barracks noticeboard, a request for eight volunteers to be selected for a special assignment, and those with the necessary qualifications were to be interviewed immediately. The interviewing officer was one Major Don Stott DSO and Bar, from the European Theatre of Operations (SOE) but formerly of 2 NZEF, who was captured on Crete, but managed to escape from a POW camp in Greece. After a lengthy consultation I was immediately informed of my selection, was told something of the intended operation in the Pacific, then given the opportunity to withdraw. I would not have been given the above information if he had not been certain of my acceptance to the group. The die had now been cast for my future service in the armed services. On arrival in Australia, Major Stott stated that all

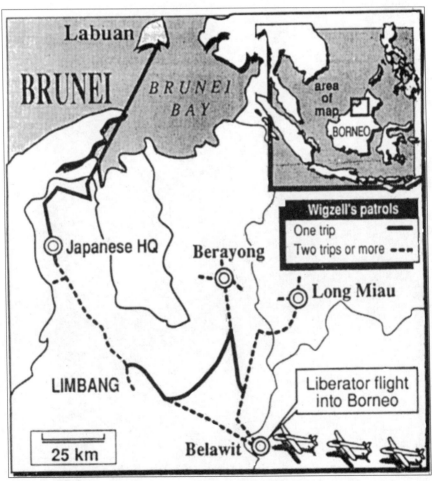

Operation Semut I Borneo 1945. My walk-about inside Borneo.

members were to be given rankings similar to the first party, that of S/Sgt and WO. Consideration in the field was to be given to my previous recommendation.

Ten days' special embarkation leave was granted, and upon returning to camp, the eight, including two infantry officers boarded the US freighter *Waipouri*, a small cargo vessel of about 5,000 ton bound for Australia, with instructions to proceed without escort to Sydney. What an experience! She was certainly an old roller, causing many disturbances and eruptions of the stomach to the landlubbers on board. We

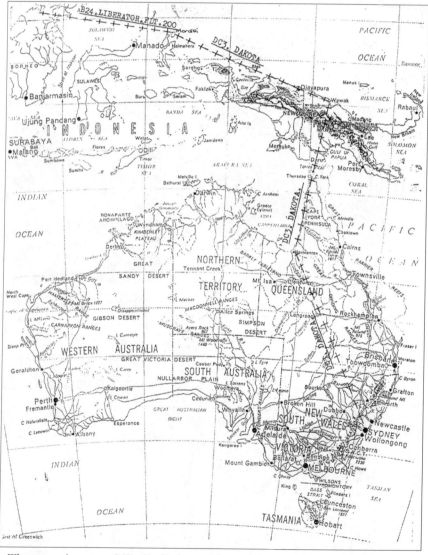

The second party of Kiwi's flight to Morotai from Sydney – then my trip into Central Borneo by 200 Flight.

were instructed to store away all our military clothes, and use civilian ones, and were not permitted topside during daylight hours. We stood to at dawn and dusk, several unexplained sightings were observed, but we finally reached our destination unscathed, travelled overnight by rail to Melbourne and were met by the NZLO. Leave was granted over the Christmas holiday period, and the group was invited to attend a special NZ night at the club, organised by the New Zealand High Commissioner in Melbourne. Later, introductions were made to our new Australian partners for our future theatre of operations – Borneo.

Instructions received early in the New Year informed the party to proceed north and report to Fraser Island Commando Training HQ. This journey was by rail, and a most uncomfortable one to Brisbane. The many troops, including Australians, travelled not in carriages, but in cattle trucks with straw scattered on the floorboards. Something new by NZ standards, but at least we could stretch out and sleep in some comfort. The trip was at a snail's pace, and many of the participants of this method of travel wanting to relieve themselves would hop off the cattle truck, do such where possible, and sprint to catch up with the rear of the train. Many times we were shunted onto a siding to allow a passenger or goods train to pass. Food was non-existent till we reached Brisbane. New Zealand army members travelled better in their own country, and food was also readily available, even if the choice was limited.

In Brisbane being typical Kiwi army types – broke and frustrated in an unknown area – my mate and I noticed a brewery named 'Bulimba' and decided to invade it with the intention of obtaining the necessary soldiers' stimulant at no cost to ourselves. Broke and thirsty, we approached the Manager's office, introduced ourselves, stating that we Kiwis were interested in the Australian method of brewing, and would appreciate it if we were permitted to view it. He smiled and immediately answered our request, 'By all means, you Kiwi types'. Luck was with us, for this man was a New Zealander, and immediately arranged for his foreman of the brewery to give us a complete inspection. We were of the opinion that we were about to quench our thirst with the amber liquid. At the end of the brewing process two hours later, still having not partaken of any, we were informed to hold our horses for about twenty minutes until all the employees had finished their shift, and cleaned up. A hogshead duly arrived on the landing bay and a tap was inserted by one of the staff.

To our surprise several ladies arrived by car, unloading food by the ton, including the Aussies' special fish and chips. Tables were produced and a quantity of glasses appeared from out of the blue! All staff members now arrived and we were both introduced to the group. The

Australians certainly entertained the Kiwis in great style that night, and the ANZAC relationship was again renewed. The party finished in the late hours of the night. We were then taken into their homes, and given a great farewell in the morning. These Brisbane people had a fair idea that something of major importance was happening up Maryborough way!

After arrival at Maryborough, the group travelled to Urangan and then by workboat to the offshore Fraser Island, the largest sand island in the world. The knowledge of specialist training was now to be implanted in us – commando and guerrilla warfare. Without this, our survival rate was approximately nil. Folboat (same as modern kayak) training was strenuous, particularly exercises at sea in extreme conditions, hazardous to the degree that one mistake in navigation off this Australian coastline would be your last.

We progressed to Limpet training (underwater explosive mines with magnetic bodies for attachment to ships' hulls, the same as used by the French on the *Rainbow Warrior* at Auckland NZ forty years later) making many runs at shipping in the harbour. One special tactical operation was to proceed up the Maryborough river during the hours of darkness on an incoming tide, skirt and bypass manned army observation posts (our operation was unknown to them) attacking with 'limpets' shipping and wharf areas, slips and new shipyards where they were building frigates for the RAN. Having completed the exercise we were to await the change of the tide, clear the area, and retire undetected to the coast during darkness. We were then faced with a 7-mile hike against the current at sea back to base at Fraser, a harrowing experience. The command posts along the river were armed with live ammunition. For my folboat partner and I it had its lighter moments. Whilst awaiting for the tide to change, we hid our boat under the wharf and quietly snuck into Maryborough township 200 yards away. We scoffed a delectable meal of fish and chips for which the shop owner charge a ridiculous price of one shilling. This part of the ops we kept to ourselves, for if we had been reported or observed doing so, we would have had to undergo a severe penalty for non-conformity with security instructions relating to the raid.

We later raided the RAAF Station at Bundaberg, taking many prisoners; marching them to the guardroom and presenting them to the surprised Guard Commander. PT was essential, with our early morning runs prior to breakfast being hard and demanding. One of our major fitness runs from the lake situated in the middle of the island to the coast, was given a time limit of 45 minutes. Being a sandy course, it played hell with your leg muscles. If any member did not complete this in the time specified, he had to repeat the run over the next few days until he qualified. During the early part of our training, school instructors played a major part in our learning the *Bahasa Malayu* language. In the mess we were permitted only to receive anything if we conversed in Malay. Our study terminated at 6 p.m., but we were expected to continue until late into the night.

Leave to the mainland was granted on a few occasions; the only method of transport being by folboat, and having to team up with another operative. Thus fishing from the landing became the favourite relaxation period when available. The main self-defence instructor was a top Australian wrestler, who was of the opinion that Kiwi types were fair game and to be shown the Australian supremacy in this section. We did not oblige to his line of thought, and gave as good as we received until the intervention of the camp RSM, WOI Roy Haley, who we were to meet once again after the end of hostilities at Labuan Island in the Bay of Brunei, Borneo.

Explosives was to become one of my favourite subjects, particularly the plastic variety (PE Mk.I) with which we could do so much, and indeed rely upon not to explode prematurely without detonating. Our first introduction to PE was when one of the instructors threw a pound of it to one of our lads, who caught it and hurriedly disposed of it by tossing the bundle into a trench. The clamping of detonators to fuses by the teeth was at first treated with respect and gentleness, until continually handling them it became second nature to crimp in this fashion. Explanation for this procedure was that carrying a metal implement could cause the detonators to explode, or if lost in action some means of clamping would have to be found. Training in the use of time, pull and pressure switches, plus the instantaneous detonating systems, soon gave confidence to all members. We were not given an introduction to the 'Barometric' type of explosive used in aircraft destruction on runways and in the air. Jungle training was not exploited to a great extent, as the majority of the Kiwis had already experienced this in actual combat in the SWPA. We were later to be given the greatest knowledge of this subject, by experts in their own domains – the 'headhunters' of Borneo.

Radio (W/T) and cypher coding was taught to the wireless operators, plus the introduction to one of the greatest sets that I have ever operated, the Boston Mk3 transceiver with field generator. With a range of 3,000 miles it took my fancy, and was supreme in quality and clarity of reception. Being a crystal-operated frequency-operated set, transmissions did not vary. In private life I had studied accountancy, electricity and telegraphy, also as a radio W/T ham operator, and had practised various methods of bounce and skip transmissions in our hilly country with great results. This knowledge could be useful when we finally arrived at our operational destination. Medical training and information was a little skimpy, and more would be needed when we finally started to treat the natives of Borneo who had not received any assistance for three years. The training we received at this base included the most valuable of all – modern weaponry of both British and American design.

We left Fraser Island Commando School knowing that this part of the training was indeed our main survival skill against the Japanese. Richmond NSW was our next appointment for parachute training, one of the main means of entry into Japanese occupied territory to exploit our Fraser training. We were there for two weeks, had finished the instruction on handling the 32-footers, and were preparing for our first jump when an urgent communication was received from the Advanced HQ Morotai in the Halmahera Group, that the majority of us were required at the forward area. Our first Kiwi party under the command of Major Don Stott was reported lost in action or otherwise unaccounted for. This party had been inserted by submarine and folboats near Balikpapan oil fields in the SE region, following which there had been no contact by radio with it. Our party was to set up a search and rescue operation from the most forward base at Morotai, which had just come under the control of the Allies. Not wishing to miss out on several parachute training features, I managed to obtain permission from the chief instructor to use such, provided that I was under the control of an officer.

With Lieutenant Frank Leckie (one of our group) as controller, I negotiated the first obstacle without too much difficulty, this being the 40-ft tower with drop into a sandpit, terminating with a forward or side roll. Advancing to the 45-degree parachute slide and harness drop, which ended with the release at high speed still attached to the harness and into the sandpit, I was slow to adjust the swing and being slightly off centre, rolled and hit my elbow on the side of the pit. My elbow felt slightly numb, with a tingly sensation. Many broken bones had been received on this part of the course, which had been devised for landing and roll control. I reported the injury to the RAP, and received a rub down with an oily ointment on the elbow. I was to find out many years later that the bone had slightly splintered, and I was admitted to a private hospital in NZ for the removal of three pieces. No record of this accident was recorded on my history sheets by the Australians, so consequently I had to cover the cost of the operation myself. It would have been a severe blow if I had been rejected for the Bornean mission with this little complaint, so kept quiet about it prior to leaving by DC3 aircraft for the forward area. It caused a little trouble whilst transmitting for lengthy periods whilst within Japanese-occupied territory.

After twenty-four hours on standby, we travelled north by DC3 to Darwin, then island-hopped to Morotai which was the new consolidated forward base in the Halmahera Group. We encountered a couple of memorable experiences on the way. Flying between two mountain ridges in the Holandia area, we struck a patch of 'no air', and the DC3 dropped 10,000ft before it recovered. Information was given to us that two days earlier two fighter aircraft were lost in this part of the world in the same conditions. We actually observed two tracks in the jungle below us, and were informed by our pilot that these were made by the two unlucky aircraft. On approaching the Morotai Strait, RAAF radio reported that radar had reported and detected an unidentified aircraft following us, and we were within enemy range. Our pilot was instructed to descend to sea level. Here we flew just above masthead height of a convoy, and observed the troops waving to us as we passed by. Fighters were being despatched from Morotai, and if we were attacked we were to knock out the portholes and use our automatic weapons to defend the aircraft. The fighters duly arrived, enemy contact was not encountered, so we once again arrived at our destination in one piece.

The group, now known as Robin II, immediately commenced the selection and assembly of stores and related equipment for the search and rescue mission into Borneo, Balikpapan area. I was given the task of selection of the radio equipment and spares. We all agreed that this operation called for the minimum of weight being transported into the interior, as the group would be travelling at a fast pace, and would encounter enemy patrols if our Robin I mission had fallen into their hands. Two Boston Mk3 sets, three hand generators, two ATR 4s with tropical sealed batteries, cut dual-frequency aerials and plenty of spare parts and testing equipment. Nothing like the 2,300-pound load for our lost party. Two small MCR receiving radios were also included. We rested for a couple of days whilst undergoing intelligence briefing on the area in question, and studying aerial photographs. Everything was now in readiness for our departure, and we were to be inserted by PBY Catalina offshore at night, assembling our folboats and one rubber dinghy for supplies, and proceed to our DZ on the shore. From there on it would be 'take it as it eventuated'. Major Stott's motto was 'Check and double check' and we would certainly follow his advice.

We were called to the briefing room late at night, and given the information that a PBY on a search and rescue mission for a downed fighter off Balikpapan had reported that they had just picked up survivors from a sea-going perahu, and would arrive within an hour. These operatives were from our Robin I party. After arrival they related their experiences at the debriefing, and stated that Major Stott was missing, also Captain McMillan and WO Houghton. WO Farquharson of the AIF was also lost. Apparently the survivors of the party, being hard pressed by the Japanese after being discovered in the area, were able to purchase an old sea-going 16-ft perahu for 1,400 guilders, and under cover of darkness escaped seawards. It was here, on the second day at sea, that the party contacted the Catalina on its search mission. The party's use of the signalling mirror which was an item in the operatives' escape packs was a success, thus bringing about the investigation and their recovery. No contact was ever made with the missing operatives of Robin I, nor were any bodies recovered at the end of hostilities. Robin II, our party, was now to be broken up, as SRD considered the operation was over, from the information supplied by the survivors. As the member of our party with the longest operational overseas service and experience, I was asked to join Major Tom Harrisson's Semut I party in Borneo, Sarawak. He had just been flown out of the interior by Auster aircraft from the party's just-completed bamboo strip to Tarakan, and transported back to Morotai by 200 Flight's B-24 Liberator. I immediately agreed and was advised to proceed to the chute packing and drying shed to select, pack and fit mine. Next morning at 2054 Z (GMT), 0524 a.m. at Morotai, I was on a B-24 Liberator of 200 Flight RAAF, heading for the interior of Borneo, Sarawak – the Bawang Valley just over the Dutch border.

Entry Into Borneo by Parachute

DROP 1	200 FLIGHT		BAREO		
A.1	VB30861	DSO	MAJOR	Harrisson T.H.	GB
A.2	QX11361	DCM	SGT	Sanderson C.F.	AIF
A.4	QX 19872	MM	SGT	Barrie J.K.	AIF
A.3	NX129792		SGT	Bower D.H.	AIF
B.1	SXII095	MC	LT	Edmeades E.A.	AIF
B.2	SX18853	MM	SGT	Tredrea J	AIF
B.3	QX35742	MID	WOI	Cusack R.D.	AIF
B.4	TX16283		SGT	Hallum K.W.	AIF
DROP 1(A)	WXI6705	MID	SGT	Long B.C.	AIF

(W/T operator transferred from the Semut II insertion)

DROP 2	200 FLIGHT		BELAWIT		
A.1	SX22390	MBE	LT	Westley J.	AIF
B.1	NX43707	MC	LT	Pinkerton R.D.	AIF
B.4	NX125429	MM	WOI	McPherson C.W.	AIF
B.3	QX48327		WO2	Hirst H.R.	AIF

A.2	NX91132		CPL	Sterelni I.A.	AIF
A.4	NX88264		CPL	Wheelhouse A.S.	AIF
B.2	NX6086		TPR	Griffiths R.C.	AIF
A.3	NX84226	MID	DVR	Henry P.	AIF

DROP 3	200 FLIGHT		BELAWIT		
A.2 (2)	VB30861	DSO	MAJOR	Harrisson T.H.	GB
A.1	VB257957	MC	LT	Blondeel A.G.	GB
B.1	VB262982		LT	LeBosquet P.G.	GB
B.4	NX110196	MM	SGT	Nibbs W.G.P.	AIF
A.4	NZ422668		SGT	Wigzell F.A.	NZEF
B.2	VX16310	MM	CPL	Griffiths-Marsh C.	AIF
B.3	VX75957		CPL	Hardy McD.	AIF
A.3	NX201131		L/CPL	Darosa	AIF

Having never jumped before, this was to have been the highlight of my military life, but went somewhat sour in the first four hours of the flight. As there were eight members chuting in from the one aircraft, including Major Harrisson, the waist gunners compartment was now jammed full with operatives, and chutes etc. I was ordered to go into the bomb bay for the duration of the flight. Cold, shivering, in shorts and jungle shirt, I was later collected by the observer and taken forward to the observation blimp area, given a hot cup of coffee and a cigarette, whilst watching the progress of the flight across the sea and into the interior.

The Japanese radar apparently did not locate us, for we were not intercepted by fighter aircraft. The observer opened the bomb-bay doors, and at a signal from the navigator, dropped a football through the open bay and watched as it floated down to a cleared area of jungle below. This was from 500ft and the time 0129z – 0929 hrs Borneo time. The location I learned many years later from the log book of RAAF B-24 Liberator A72-183 200 Flight piloted by Flight Lieutenant Les Anderson, was Malinau Hospital in the central Dutch area of Borneo, then under the control of SRD (now Kalimantan, Indonesia). At this point in time Billy Nibbs (AIF, formerly an instructor at Richmond Parachute School NSW), also dropping in, collected me from the observation area stating that Harrisson did not know that I had never exited before, and that I was to be No. 4 in the first stick. I certainly needed a boost in my confidence at this moment and Bill did exactly that, having had previous experience with other first-timer chutists. He helped me don my chute, adjust the web gear and attach the clip on the playline to the short static line of the B-24. Harrisson made a most untimely statement to the despatcher at this point: 'If he

Top: Bario in the Kelabit Highlands Tamabo Mountain region 5000′ above sea level. First landing place of Advance Party Semut I.

Middle: A flight of special duites RAAF 200 Flight B-24 Liberators.

Bottom: Murut girls bamboo flute band led by Paul Batram, Griffiths Airport, bamboo strip, Belawit, 31 August 1945. (Note cut bamboo on runway)

B-24 Liberator 200 Flight RAAF A72–3.

doesn't jump, take him back to base.' How I detested this man's guts for making such a statement at this critical time! I had been previously warned at a send-off party at Morotai a few hours earlier that this GB officer considered that all colonial NCOs were of inferior quality, and treated them as such. This was to be further proved to me and all other operatives of the operation within Borneo. The most consistent thing about him was his sheer inconsistency.

Auster aircraft similar to this were flown into the bamboo airstrip at Be-lawit, Dutch Borneo, on the border of Sarawak, by special duties Auster Squadron, firstly from Tarakan, then from Labuan.

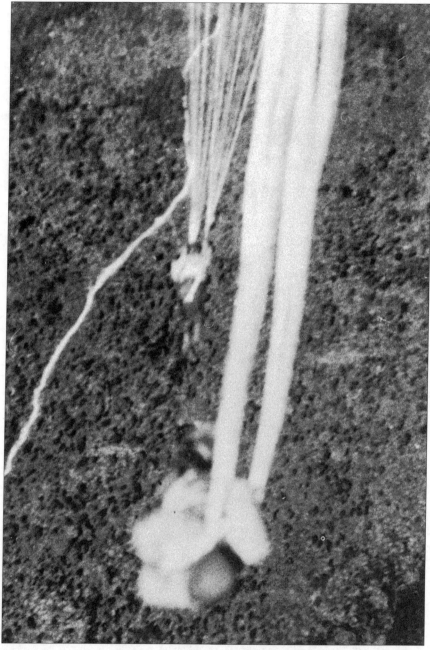

P33. B. Ops Reinforcement Semut I

27 May 1945 – 1002hrs. – 3,000 ft

B-24 Liberator – 200 Flt. – RAAF – A72/187.

W/Cdr. E. Read. Bawang Valley/Borneo.

From F/Lt. Les Andersons Log Book - 200 Flight RAAF -
Attached 'Z' Special Unit - Liberator A72 - 183

hge 1 S/ Anderson missing

-2- *80013/Pc*

RESULTS: 1 personnel dropped on DZ
1 personnel overshot
1 storp dropped on DZ
2 storps overshot.

(17) 10/6/45 MISSION RESUPPLY SEMUT I *Bawang Valley* A/c A72-183
Anderson

10/6/45   Morotai   2054 Z   Airborne
11/6/45   P.Princessa 0523 Z   Landed

ROUTE: Direct to DZ

HEIGHT: En route   10,000

Over DZ   4,000

WEATHER :   En Route   10/10 at 10,000

Over DZ   Scattered on 5/10 base 3000

MALINAU :   One football dropped from 500' at 0129 which fell 30
yards short of Hospital.

DZ   Smoke signals & 100-150 natives were seen on DZ. The air
strip is of bamboo construction approximately 400 yards in length. *Lt Blondeel*
(4)   *Maj Harrison*
First Run: Three personnel dropped from 1000 on heading 020 at 0206 *LKpl Da Rosa*
Sgt Wigzell
Second Run : Seven storps dropped from 1000 on heading 020 at 0214

Third Run : Four personnel dropped from 1000 on heading 020 at 0219 *Lt Le Bosquet*
Cpl Griffiths-Marsh
Fourth Run : Photos taken   at 0225 *Cpl Hardy*
Sgt Nibbs

RESULTS: All men and storps dropped on DZ

(18) 15/6/45 MISSION RE-SUPPLY SEMUT II   *(Long Akah)*   A72-183

15/6/45   Mindere   2130   Airborne
16/6/45   P.Princessa 0525   Landed

HEIGHT: En route   Moderate rain and scattered Cb.

Over DZ   7/10 S/Cu tops to 8000

DZ :   Green Verey fired on arrival and 40-50 natives seen on DZ
Circled DZ trying to make handy talky contact-very weak- ground to
aircraft contact made but aircraft signals could not be picked up by
ground party.Smoke signals were exhibited on each run.   *Maj Wilson*
British Army,
First Run: Two personnel dropped from 1500 on heading of 350 at 0231 *in charge of*
this group
Second Run: Two personnel dropped from 1500 on heading 350 at 0238

Third Run: Nine storps dropped from 1500 on heading 335 at 0 245.

Airborne Morotai 2054 Z plus 0830 GMT Morotai Differential = 0524 a.m.
Chuted Belawit - Borneo 0206 Z plus 0800 Borneo Differential - 1006 a.m
GMT. Differential time (Z) Morotai 8 1/2 hrs. -- Borneo 8 hrs.

From Flt/Lt Les Anderson's Log Book, 200 Flight RAAF, attached
'Z' Special Unit, Liberator A72–183

P.I. Ops. 36–49–55. Resupply Semut I

8 July 1945 – 1138 hrs. – 1,200 ft – SW

200 Flight – RAAF – B-24 Liberator

A72/187 Bawang Valley – Borneo.

Top: Bamboo Airstrip Belawit, taken from 2,000 ft.

Bottom: Two Austers on the strip after the end of the war with members of Semut I and visitors from Labuan Island.

Harrisson, whilst acting as despatcher for the first stick, delayed the jump into a cleared area after the green light appeared, and consequently had the last two in the stick of four overshoot the DZ. The first three slid easily out of the jump chair slide in the waist gunner's compartment aft of the camera hatch, and myself being too eager to follow, was subsequently too quick in position to exit after No. 3. Bill grabbed my arm, held on for only part of a second, then belted me on the helmet. I immediately shot out of the hatch and instantly came in contact with the wash of the B-24, at a dropping speed of about 200 knots. What was only a short duration of time, one second plus, seemed an eternity until I felt the final pluck of the chute from the pack and the breaking away from the playline. Time 0206z – 1006 a.m. Borneo time. We had been en-route from Morotai for five hours, plus the time differential of the two areas (30 minutes). The drop was from 1,000 ft and as I floated down, I said to myself 'Hell man, you did it', and upon looking to my right saw the rest of the party descending. I gave them a wave and they all responded.

On checking my shroud lines I found that they were not tangled or twisted. The swing needed correction and this was done automatically as was taught at Para School in Australia. I was soon totally disillusioned about the peace and tranquillity whilst suspended over this area of Borneo, for upon looking downwards I observed water, and had never experienced or sighted a padi field from the air before. In this locality there were about thirty of them just waiting to oblige with a watery reception for this Kiwi. After coming in contact with the surface after about thirty seconds after exiting, I was ready to operate my release button, when I gently landed in a foot of brownish padi water. My chute collapsed behind me, and becoming completely overcome by the situation that existed at this moment, my body too followed me into the mire; thus I had an early morning bath and swim in a new country.

Kelabits from the nearby longhouses came dashing through the padi fields, laughing and pointing in my direction. They picked me up whilst still bewildered with the experience, and deposited one saturated Kiwi and discarded chute on the new bamboo strip some 30 yards away. These natives of approximately 5' to 5' 6" in height, light olive skinned, were clothed only in loin cloths and some with bark jackets. This was my first introduction to Borneans. Smiling, laughing and talking excitedly to one another in their own dialect, indicating to me my wet condition, they appeared to be a happy and contented people. I immediately rewarded the recoverers with a couple of packets of American 'Old Gold' cigarettes which I had concealed inside my shirt before embarking on this venture at Morotai. Harrisson, who had just jumped with me and landed on the strip, was standing beside the W/T *sulap*.

He observed my gesture to the natives for assistance, and reprimanded me for such practice. He immediately relieved me of the tobacco and cigarettes, stating that they would be shared amongst the rest of the group.

This distribution never eventuated according to my operative friends. Never in my two and a half years of active operational service in the SWPA had I met an officer of such calibre with an offensive attitude towards natives and operatives also. I was to gain further evidence of this at a later date. The information supplied by members of the group at Morotai before my entry was absolutely correct. Bill Nibbs just missed the W/T *sulap* and aerial on the next stick out. Such was my introduction in the *ulu* to Semut I.

As I was a last-minute addition to the party and all storpedos had been packed, I was instructed by Harrisson that I could not bring any of my equipment into Borneo. This included clothes, boots and arms. I duly arrived into enemy-held territory with just what I stood up in, having been told to obtain what I required from those that were there. Nothing according to Harrisson was held in reserve in the local stores *sulap*. Denial was one of our party leader's forte towards his operatives. At least I now had a home, for I was instructed to stay at the W/T *sulap* and assist Bob Long (AIF) transmitting on the link to Morotai. This base station was communicating with the outside world most adequately.

(Before I left Morotai on this mission, Lieutenant Frank Leckie, a member of our Kiwi party, had obtained for use on our Robin I search, several American semi-automatic .45 pistols, to be distributed to the members. I was presented with one and a watch plus compass.) As I had no other weapons, I was instructed by the OC to take a carbine from one of the natives. This I did, much to my disagreeing to do so. Such were the inconsistencies in this place!

Having settled into the *sulap*, Bob gave me a new set of clothing, blanket and towel to dry off with. He advised that I had better get my .45 pistol oiled and cleaned as it had been subjected to immersion in the padi field water when I landed. Next to the W/T *sulap* stood a new hut which was occupied by a captured Japanese construction worker named Ojita. Bob stated 'Give it to Ojita, he will clean it. Leave the mag in.' Hell, what gives in this place? The pistol plus mag and ammunition were promptly returned in polished condition, this being the only time that old 'Gerty' was ever cleaned in Borneo. Two days later I had another run in with our OC. An aircraft was passing over our strip north to south and I contacted it with our walkie-talkie HF radio. These sets were tuned to the same interior frequency as the B-24 Liberators of 200 Flight. It was looking for Semut 2, so I identified our group thus indicating to the pilot that he was off course. Harrisson arrived on the strip from his *rumah besar*, enquiring if we had seen and heard the aircraft. I promptly replied that I had been in communication with it. In answer to his impolite request for method of contact, I had the satisfaction of stating that the HF hand-held set had the same operating frequency as that of the aircraft overhead. He seemed absolutely disgusted with the information so presented to him. 'If I had known that method at the start of this operation, it would have saved a considerable amount of embarrassment.'

He then stalked off in a rage, heading for his private *sulap* in the main village at the northern part of the strip. Perhaps this dumb colonial Kiwi may be of some use to this mission after all! Bob Long informed me that we operatives were not permitted to wander into the main kampong area, but to remain at the W/T *sulap* situated at the southern end of the bamboo airstrip. The following day with our Eureka Rebecca ground-to-air signal beacon not in use, we heard an aircraft in the next valley, approximately a mile away just through the border valley entrance into Sarawak, an area of padi field resembling our HQ at Belawit in the Bawang Valley, Dutch Borneo. I immediately used the HF handset using the vocal R/T transmission of 'Ground to aircraft, come in', and receiving no response, I called again and added, 'You are in the wrong valley, gain height and head due north.' Within seconds the engine noise became louder and louder. A DC3 aircraft came into sight flying low down between the hills at the entrance to our valley, and immediately acknowledged the receipt of our transmitted message with a magnificent waggle of its shiny silver wings as it passed close to our *sulap* at the southern end of the strip. A delightful present from the outer world, as we in this situation were now the meat in the centre of the sandwich, being surrounded and hemmed in by the Japanese from the north, south, east and west. Was this to be our resting place for time immemorial? 'Only time would tell'.

It was on this strip that I first met one of the recovered eleven USAAF airmen, Sergeant Dan Illerich. They had been hidden by the indiginous peoples of the interior from the Japanese, and after the arrival of our group were brought into contact with us. Dan, who was not too badly affected with his forced stay in the interior, remained at Belawit with Bob Long to assist him with the radio, as this was his trade in the Air Force. At the end of June he was flown out to Labuan in the Bay of Brunei by Auster from the bamboo strip. In late 1945, Dan was awarded the BEM as recommended by Major Harrisson, and with special consent from the US Congress was permitted to accept and wear it.

On the fourth day a runner arrived at the W/T *sulap*, summoning me to report to our OC's HQ in the main kampong. Major Harrisson questioned me on my experience and service in the Pacific, and previous history. He was surprised at my lengthy time on operations and landings with the 3rd Division 2 NZEF in the Pacific theatre. He immediately informed me of my future with his Semut party, that of being a roving W/T operator and operative, to set up a new network of outstations with a 'Base Station' situated at Ba Kelalan area. This new base was to be in operation in a few days time, after the arrival of Captain Gordon Richter AIF by Auster aircraft. My orders were brief and as follows:

(1) Select 10 guerrillas from the Belawit area. Arm them with .303 rifles, US carbines and Owen SMGs.

(2) Obtain an ATR 4 radio set from the W/T sulap on the strip.

(3) Move to Ba Kelalan, Pa Pala and Long Belayu in the Padas area. Continue northwards to Long Miau and contact Major Ian Lloyd of the ATIS AIF, who is deciphering Japanese documents there. He will then return to HQ Belawit.

(4) You will set up radio communication with Ba Kelalan, relaying runners' messages from WO Colin McPherson situated in the Ebaru or Bole area. You will not disclose your being in the Long Miau area, and not be permitted to join any other party of 'Z'.

(5) Further instructions will be related to you at a later date.

So ended my stay with Bob Long and the American Dan Illerich at the 'Bob Griffith's Airport, Belawit, Bawang Valley' just over the border of Sarawak in the Dutch sector of Borneo.

On the first part of the operation northwards, I arrived at the small kampong of Ba Kelalan and then continued onward to the area of Pa Pala. Slept in a *rumah besar* with my guerrillas, awaking next morning with a high temperature and feverish, immediately forming the opinion that I had contracted malaria, presumably at Belawit whilst living in the W/T *sulap* next to the padi fields. This malady was caused by my own neglect at not following and observing the standard procedures in this infected part of Borneo. Prevention was readily available to all operatives. I had failed to take Atebrin, and thus suffered the consequences of non-conformity. I stayed at the former missionary, an evacuated two-storied, brick house, now taken over by the Kelabits as communal sleeping quarters. The missionaries had long been gone, having been captured and marched to the coast. Their fate was unknown. The *Kiai* or learned one of the kampong noticing my condition prescribed my taking of the native medicine for this illness, that of boiled bark water, tasting similar to quinine. Next morning I had recovered sufficiently enough to recommence my walkabout northwards to Long Miau. You learn from your mistakes, and I had certainly paid for my error this time. Conform at all costs in this heavily diseased and infected location. It was here at Pa Pala that the first native court was held under tribal customs for trials against collaborators and informers to the Japanese. Major Harrisson and Lieutenant Bob Pinkerton (AIF) were in the area a few days before I had reached here and witnessed part of the procedure. Several major offenders were dealt with by the native court.

Punishments were handed out according to tribal law, consistent with the severeness of the crime, which were related to each individual on trial. These included severe reprimand, loss of tribal rights and death by parang or shooting in major instances where information so supplied to the Japanese caused reprisals of death and destruction against the population.

Long Miau, BNB, Sabah

After trekking through Ba Kelalan and Pa Pala and the malarial attack, I finally reached Long Pa Sia, stayed the night there and crossed the river heading northwards. I finally reached my location contact area with Major Ian Lloyd of the ATIS at Long Miau. He had been in the area translating captured Japanese documents supplied by our operatives, seeking intelligence information about retreating forces into the interior and intended destinations. This information was requested by RAAF for bombing and softening-up operations against the HQ areas of the Japanese 37th Army controlled by General Masao Baba. Major Lloyd was out on reconnaissance in the area on my arrival, and did not arrive back until nightfall. He was indeed pleased to meet another English-speaking person, as he did not speak Malay. He had managed sufficiently with sign language so far, and the Muruts of this locality had cooperated magnificently. We stayed the night at the temporary *rumah besar* on the eastern side of the river. The main longhouse on the western bank had been vacated with the approach of the Japanese heading for the Sapong Estate, after the invasion by the AIF on the coastline.

That night, after consuming a meal of rice wrapped in a banana leaf, I had a session in *bahasa Malayu* with these tribespeople informing them of the impending arrival of a very large party of Japanese from the Brunei region, approximately 2,000 strong under the command of a General Haragushi. This party had been attacked in the Limbang river region on 7 June at Ukong. They had then retired downriver to Bukit Malu, crossed the river in force and cut a new track 15 miles inland from the coast towards Lawas, so as to evade the invasion forces in that area of the 9th Australian Division. The Japanese escape route was

Semut I Resupply, 17 July 1945, 2,000′.

via Lawas, Trusan and Tenom, making for the Sapong Rubber Estate in Sabah. It was here that this force plus others escaping into the interior were to make a last stand against the Allied forces. I advised the kampong *kepala* that for the safety of the tribe they should, immediately prior to the arrival of this force, vacate the area, using our denial strategy for removal of all food stocks, salt and containers to a safe place in the jungle. Also there would be no porters to conscript or guide the enemy northwards. A safe and secure location was known to exist in the dense jungle not too far distance away (one day), and the *kepala* would guide his members of the tribe there at the designated time; our denial program was in place.

A *sulap* which had been built in the jungle approximately 150 yards from the longhouse for Colin McPherson and his guerrillas, now became my sleeping and radio station HQ. I set up my equipment and slung a DF aerial between two 100-ft trees, and contact was immediately made with the new central W/T sub-station at Ba Kelalan, using my own 10x10 hundred square formulated code for this area of operations (01 = Long Miau, 02 = ammunition, 03 = supply drop, 04 = McPherson,

Typical of the type of rain-forest near the coast of British North Borneo.

00 = operator's identification etc.). Major Lloyd now returned to Base HQ at Belawit for return to his unit now at Labuan Island in Brunei Bay, by Auster aircraft from our bamboo airstrip. He had failed to contact our operative McPherson, due to the fact that the old *kepala* of the area was not inclined to send a search party into the Tagal tribal domain up north in Sabah BNB. Tagals were an untrustworthy tribe, having surrendered two USAAF airmen to the Japanese, who rewarded them with the decapitated heads of these men to be shared amongst the tribespeople. Such were the devious tactics of the Japanese.

My first introduction to headhunting was whilst travelling through the many kampongs, seeing bleached skulls hanging from the rafters of the *rumah besars*. Each area was known in importance for the numbers so displayed in this manner for all to see. I had noticed several new wicker and reed baskets woven out of the local vines, hanging above the smoky fireplaces. On inquiring, much to the delight of these people, was informed that these were new additions of the younger generation who were following the customs and rituals of their forefathers. Without native or government control over these last three years, they had reverted to their old customs. Many small parties of the enemy had been totally annihilated and completely eradicated in this area, having travelled into the *ulu* demanding that the natives cooperate by sending food supplies to the coast for Japanese troops. These patrols were fed and then entertained by the tribes, supplying the unsuspecting soldiers

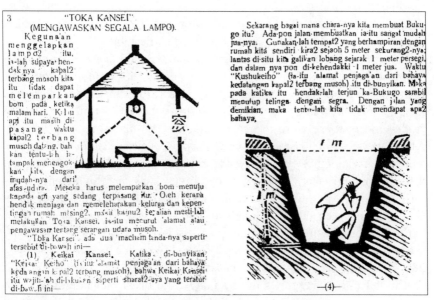

Japanese instructions for the building of air-raid shelters and lighting control at night

with their local brew Borak (rice wine) and the distilled version, Arak. When intoxicated, they were then despatched by parang.

Now with the supply and distribution of arms from their friends from the sky (Z), vengeance was being extracted on the Japanese for their treatment of all tribes within Borneo over the last three years. I was glad I was on the right side of the fence at this point in time. To be confronted by these well-built, strong, muscular-figured native warriors was menacing indeed, with earlobes pierced, large hornbill carvings and leopard teeth adorning same, and heavy ornaments hanging from them to the shoulders. Under each knee reposed twenty or thirty *unus*, bands of a special species of creeper, twisted and secured in place and of many colours. On their wrists a few more of the same, plus a little bangle made of some material – copper or aluminium probably traded from the coastal Malays or Chinese. Arm these warriors with a *sumpitan* (blow-pipe with spear attached), parang, automatic or US carbine rifle and fighting in their own domains, the Japanese had much to fear. Provided that these warriors were under a controlling influence of an operative from the beginning, it was hard to make them understand that until our guerrillas were equipped with a substantial number of weapons and knowing just how to use them, the Japanese were still in command of the situation. The headhunters soon learned the skills of the outer world and modern methods of warfare.

The womanfolk of these warriors wore only a black sarong to their ankles, and were bare above the waistline, sporting the same adornments as their male partners. Hair was cut to shoulder length, and they wore conical skull bead-head hats. Beads were small, multi coloured and of great age and value. Being young and from the modern world, I could only but admire these beautiful young maidens, for if we transgressed, I am sure that our heads would soon adorn the main positions and contained within reed boxes, hanging from rafters in the longhouses! I first gave away panels of my parachute, but soon found out that as trade objects these were in great demand. The materials of green and white became much respected sarongs for special occasions, and hidden from roving enemy eyes. Material from the coastal regions had not filtered through from that area for three years, as the Japanese had forbidden such practice. The males only wore loin cloths, made from about three yards of black material, and changed to a clean one after bathing, and washing the one just discarded. Such were now my guerrillas – Ibans, Kelabits, Dayaks and lowland Muruts. My *Bahasa Malayu* was improving with everyday contact with the natives, and not speaking English. At times my friends would break out laughing when I uttered a strong word trying to make myself understood, and heard many of my bad expressions repeated. All I could do was smile. It certainly was great to be accepted by these tribes people living in conditions a hundred years behind the times.

This leech-invested country of the lower Padas area was indeed a heavily diseased and infected part of British North Borneo, Sabah. Even the slightest cut immediately became septic. My supply of drugs in the first aid kit was limited to Aspro, Sulphaguanadine, Sulphamerazine, Atebrin, iodine, bandages and a few Benzedrine tablets. Sulphadiazine was also included. Many of the locals were badly affected by leech bites gone septic, so each morning I held a sick parade which was well attended. Many received aspirins, for all they wanted was to be taken notice of. Malaria was rife in this area, and my supplies were running low and were insufficient in this situation. I had grown a beard, mainly as a protection against mosquitoes which heavily infested the Padas area, and my skin was turning yellow with continual use of the Atebrine.

Runners were now appearing from the northern area of Ebaru and other locations from the west also. Each day further information was being received from tribesmen, bearing news of the slowly advancing Japanese force from the Brunei Bay area. The local inhabitants knew of my W/T station at Long Miau, so all messages passing through, and runners, were diverted to my *sulap*.

After a week of transmissions, there appeared a Japanese Betty bomber recce plane from the NW at about 10,000 ft every time I transmitted. It homed in on my signals, and flew in a direct line towards our kampong, returning again and again when I went on the air to HQ. I came to the conclusion that it was operating in direct contact with the Japanese force below, trying to locate for them the exact location of this radio station in the interior. Perhaps the enemy were now of the opinion that a party from the invasion force was stationed in this sector and waiting for them. It continued to patrol for another two days, and the next morning at dawn (5 a.m.), when we were just awakening in the *sulap*, we heard the approach from the NW of two aircraft, low, and heading directly for our kampong. We in the jungle *sulap* did not move, so I gave the order to my guerrilla force, '*Tinggal disana, Japan kapal terbang*', pointing towards the floor! We all hit the deck as two fighter-bombers made a 180-degree turn behind us, and headed towards the longhouse, each dropping two bombs from approximately 200 ft.

Their accuracy was somewhat astray and ineffective, as no damage or casualties were sustained by anyone. These aircraft did not return and strafe the area, but continued on their return NW from whence they appeared. I came to the conclusion that the Japanese, being short on fuel, had lightened the aircraft by discarding the guns and ammunition to enable the flight to reach its objective and return. I now sent off patrols to search the area opposite our kampong for any sign of enemy advanced patrols in our immediate area, but nothing was observed to indicate such was the case. An Iban arrived across the river, and was quickly transported to this side. He stated that he had observed the Japanese main force of great strength on the trail westwards at 11 a.m. He had circled around them using his skills and in the protection of the jungle. It now being 1.30 p.m. this force, allowing for the time factor relating to the arrival of the Iban from that contact point, was approximately 1½ hrs. away.

On contacting base I was immediately ordered to clear the area. The Japanese Betty once again appeared, so I hurriedly terminated the transmission, packing the W/T set and other equipment. Five minutes in all! We were fortunate that we cleared immediately, for we missed confrontation with the enemy by the skin of our teeth. The *kepala* and the whole tribe also headed for the eastern interior of the jungle, heading for their safe and secure hideout, and denial of food and labour to the enemy. We crossed the river by perahu and just missed the forward patrols of the enemy, whom we observed whilst still in the cover of the jungle, advancing cautiously upon the unoccupied longhouse on the hill. My team moved unseen immediately to the south trail, and had gone some 300 yards when a terrific crashing sound commenced from the secondary undergrowth on the side of the hill above us, and the vacated kampong area.

A water buffalo came thundering downhill and passed us on the track, heading for the safety of the jungle below. We all formed the immediate opinion that the disturbance of the beast was caused by the Japanese advance patrols above, who were searching for the W/T station in this area. We all jumped off the track and followed the downward crushed trail of the buffalo, this to cover our tracks, and headed towards the Miau river. We must have been observed by these patrols, who had been informed by the Betty reconnaissance aircraft of our location. The leading Kelabit, who knew the area well, led us to an old disused trail which my group followed silently and cautiously, for the next hour travelling southwards. We now stopped, and all ears were finely tuned to listening for any sound or movement from above and along the river path. After waiting in silence for about ten minutes, I produced a roll of tape from the W/T set, and set up each member with a two-magazine method of action. This involved taping the magazines together in a reverse way. With a twist of the wrist, after emptying the first mag, in two or maybe three seconds the second was in operation. In a firefight, rapid fire from SMGs and US carbines would certainly tell the Nips not to venture into this barrage of fire, and that it came from a fairly large force.

We approached the main track again, searched the ground for any sign of recent enemy movement on the surface, and not finding any, immediately set up our standard patrol procedure of scout in advance and rear protection. We rapidly retired across rivers and valleys, arriving at the Ba Kelalan W/T base after about fifteen hours continuous walking time, instead of the usual two days for the journey. I was encouraged along the way to keep up with my guerrillas, with a little help from a couple of tablets from my medical kit – Benzedrine!

One of the most interesting forms of native clothing in this region that I encountered was a patch of deer hide of about 14″ × 14″ attached to the loin cloth at the rear of some tribesmen. Its use soon became clear and obvious during the wet periods when we stopped on the side of a track. The majority of the natives just squatted, whilst those wearing the hide patches in the rear sat in comfort, not receiving a wet backside! My operative friend in this northern area in front of me at Long Miau arranged to meet a Tagal *penghulu* on the trackside approaching Ibaru. After they had conversed, it commenced raining in pure tropical style, just falling out of the blue sky on a clear bright day. One of the visiting party immediately approached the group, unfurled a large black umbrella and held it over his *penghulu*, protecting him from the rain. 'One never knew just what to expect, or what waited around the corner "Within". It was an experience that very few would encounter in their lifetime.' Special Force operatives within occupied territories were volunteers, given a code number and disposable!

Another Location and Encounter

Totally exhausted, covered with mud from the wet tracks, this was an example of what we could expect in this interior section of Borneo. We arrived at our destination with the vital information of the Japanese force and their slow movement on the tracks in this area. We were given a warm welcome, and a cup of hot coffee, the very first drink other than water (*ayer minum*) since leaving Belawit airstrip and Bob Long. The guerrillas and myself totally collapsed for a short period of time before recovering completely, and relating that which had transpired at Long Miau. Gordon Richter remarked that it was hoped that I would follow this group at Long Miau up north to the Sapong Estate. I informed him that we were not equipped to do so, as no food existed in this area. Without food and with no chance of being supplied with it, we were prevented from such action. I took over the Boston radio link with HQ Belawit, and worked a couple of lengthy skeds. Reception was great, and it was good to relax and converse in English again with members of our Semut party.

Major Harrisson arrived a few days later – a sight one would not readily forget – wearing a cap with a major's crown attached, sarong, bare above the waistline, and not carrying a weapon for protection. He had about twelve headhunters in his party and presented me with a colourful badge to be worn on the shirt lapel, this being in the form of a shield with the 'Sarawak Coat of Arms'. Approximately 1½ cm in length and width, in blue and gold, Harrisson stated that this badge gave us the equivalent rank of Major in the Sarawak Armed Forces of the Rajah Brooke Government. I disbelieved this information as he had previously told one of the group that he had been promoted to Lieutenant and to place a couple of bottle tops on his shoulder tabs. (I never saw a bottle all the time I was 'Within', but was informed at a later date that many existed in the stores and in his *sulap* at Belawit.) The motto on these shields I was to learn about many years later from one of my friends, was 'Dum Spiro Spero', when translated means 'While I breathe [live] I hope'. Fully recovered and with two additional carriers for the wireless equipment, my guerrilla group were ordered to Lawas in the NW, to report to Lieutenant Bob Pinkerton AIF who had requested my help. I had previously met and worked with him on exercises at Fraser Commando School when he was in the same intake B19 group. He was located with his group near Lawas and was experiencing communication problems there. Our trek was through a new area to Pa Berayong, four days' walk to the west.

My guerrillas and carriers travelled at a slow pace on these wet and slippery uphill tracks, finally reaching a small kampong of fifteen families, to be greeted with the information that rice and other foods and fruit were exceedingly scarce. These Murut villagers were good gardeners, but with supplying the enemy with food they were deprived of that which was necessary to keep the tribes people in good health. Just observing their bodies told of the conditions that they were submitted to over these last three years of occupation. I was guided around the kampong and garden areas, and noticed the extent of their plantings. The maize crop would take another month before maturing, picking and harvesting. The rice padi fields were empty, and no planting seed was held. At about dusk a runner from the garden area arrived and gave the information that a small herd of sika or sambar deer had arrived in the area and at that moment were attacking the green crop, deer having been scare in this area since the occupation of the Japanese. My assistance was urgently sought to bag one for the kampong. With two of the local tribe members, we silently approached the gardens, crossed over a small stream and nearly fell over a hind that was devouring the unripened crop. 'Hell, I missed that one,' I thought. It immediately bolted for the cover in the centre of the garden. 'Tidah apa' ('Never mind') the nearest Murut to me stated.

The light was still fairly good, so the native led me to the slight hill towards the jungle. Here the tree-lined fence was broken, thus allowing entry of these animals to the crop. He plucked a leaf from one of the trees, folded it in half, and proceeded to blow through it. The sound produced resembled that of a fawn calling for its mother. Immediately there was a response and commotion from the centre of the garden, and my Murut friend called out, 'Nampang kijang, tuan? Disana,' ('See the deer, tuan? There') indicating with his hand the location. In the failing light I got away a telling shot from 30-40 yards, immediately reloaded and fired a second shot into the same area hoping that if I had missed, it might hit the target. I had been given a trusty old SMLE rifle by one of the home guardsmen of the area, a reliable and accurate weapon. Two tribesmen immediately dashed into the maize patch from the cover of the riverbank, and yelled and screamed in delight as they held their next meal high above their heads in triumph. Soon several other members arrived to assist with the carrying to the longhouse. Amazing – by the light of the family fires they were all chattering excitedly and indicating one to another the two holes that appeared in the neck of the deer. 'Baik tembak, tuan' ('Good shot, tuan') and many slaps on the back which were now my reward from these people. Meat had not been partaken of in this area for many months.

It only took a moment to skin the deer, and portions were distributed to everyone. I was given the choice of the meat and selected the kidneys. The cooking was done in old woks, really aged types, probably traded from the Chinese from the coastal areas. The meat I had eaten on a few occasions was exceedingly tough, being cut with the grain and not across it. The reason for such practice was that when in plentiful supply from hunting, it was cut in this manner and hung out to dry in the sun to be consumed at a later date. About half an hour later I was presented with a delightful change of menu for the day wrapped in banana leaf, plus the usual rice. This was washed down with a couple of half coconut shell cups of the amber liquid, Borak. I was soon at peace with the world, and slept amongst the bodies of my guerrillas for body warmth on mats, on the bamboo flooring during these cold nights.

Living off the land and eating rice continually was proving somewhat difficult, for I was eating less and less of this diet, but more frequently and in small amounts. Salt I missed, and it was not available in all of the kampongs, being a priceless and scarce commodity in this central part of Borneo which I now considered my home. Survival was my own concern, being given no support of food, clothing and medicine replacement. Most operatives received nothing from our store at Belawit, although much was recorded to have been chuted into Belawit. With the mangy kampong dogs running loose within the longhouses at night, I took the precaution of hanging all of my equipment out of reach, as they chewed up anything that contained salt. Some of our operatives had lost considerable amounts of possessions to them. At this kampong I was approached by a likeable Kelabit named Jon, about sixteen years of age, who had followed me around ever since my arrival in the area (native sixteen, our equivalent age twenty-five).

This young warrior finally plucked up enough courage to seek my permission to join our party, expressing utmost loyalty and willingness to show his bravery in attacks against the hated Japoon. He was to prove soon that this was no understatement. I agreed, giving him the only spare weapon in the party, this being my second choice and reserve, the Owen SMG, web gear, ammunition and magazines. I retained my special weapon, the .30 cal. US carbine which in my estimation was the most suitable for close infighting in the dense jungle conditions, being semi-automatic and with a mag of 20 rounds.

I slept long and loudly that night until woken for a quick morning meal of the usual rice. We then prepared to continue the movement to the north. On this walk we were to encounter many trials and tribulations whilst moving through the virgin rain forests of Borneo. Whilst ascending a steep portion of the track, the advanced scout indicated that we had trouble ahead. Jon informed me in sign language and Malay that red bull ants (never encountered by me before) were falling from the 100-foot trees along the track directly in front of us. These could inflict severe pain to anyone who was unfortunate to come in contact with them. The guerrillas and carriers, one at a time, did a hasty dash over a thirty-yard portion so affected, and three were bitten. I was last to run the gauntlet and received a single attack. I hurriedly bashed the ant off my knee area, and uttered a typical Kiwi expression that was not understood by my companions. The sting had the equivalent feeling of being touched by a red-hot poker. A guerrilla cut a vine at the side of the track, and the juices were applied to the affected area. Within minutes the pain subsided. Such were the native medicines from the jungle resources.

The journey resumed northwards, climbing the steady incline and hill areas of Sarawak. Within an hour we encountered the second experience of the day. The jungle trail took a fairly new turn to the left and was marked by an upright forked stick and a directional horizontal one. This indicated, according to native customs, 'beware of this closed-off part of the track'. Jon explained that an unknown monster lurked in this defined place and superstition prevented anyone entering such places when marked in the manner we had just sighted. On informing my lads that I intended to investigate this area, a reply was fast coming. 'Tidak, Tuan Prank' (they could not pronounce the letter 'F') – No Frank! I immediately advanced onto the old track, with Jon and two others cautiously following close behind, searching for movement of any mysterious monster lurking on both sides of the track. After walking thirty or forty yards, I was alerted and directed to a section of the jungle canopy in front of us. Here on a branch overhanging the trail, motionless and in strike position was a python – large, green with black stripes and perfectly camouflaged in its natural environment. I immediately froze dead in my tracks, somewhat astounded by this new experience. My guerrillas were silent and unmoving. I slowly lifted my carbine, sighting just behind the head on the neck area, fired two shots in rapid succession from the semi-automatic, and watched as the reptile slithered and fell onto the track in front of us. Courage now returned to the natives, for they immediately flourished their parangs and beheaded the monster. It was cut into four sections and disposed of jungle-side. We all now returned to the junction of the two trails, and destroyed the forked native message, then proceeded on our way accompanied with much banter and laughter from the delighted members of the party. Jon was still of the opinion that local superstitions of the tribe domiciled in the area should have been respected and observed in this case. All I wanted to do was to show my guerrillas that they could rely on me in any situation that might occur during the encounters which were to follow against the Japanese. Contact within this area would be a certainty at any moment of the day or night. My old boy scout motto certainly applied now: 'Be prepared'.

In the afternoon, whilst continuing to climb the hills towards Pa Berayong, the forward scout reported that there were tribesmen and whites immediately ahead of us. We did a reconnaissance of the area to substantiate the information, and contacted the rear guards of this party. We all walked into a warm welcome from two members of my group who had parachuted into Belawit with me. The Japanese had just taken over Pa Berayong to the north about 5 miles across the mountains. Bill Nibbs and Joe da Costa (both AIF) with their force had just returned to this base from a reconnaissance of the area, and were pleased that I could transmit the information to HQ. The jungle we were now based in was an elevated hillside area overlooking a deserted kampong next to a small stream on a flat valley floor. About 300 yards north of the communal cleared area was the track leading over the range to Pa Berayong. It was not known if the Japanese force intended continuing up the Tengoa Valley heading for the security of the interior, or

Resupply Semut I
P12. 27 May 1945. 0945 hrs. 3,000ft. – 200 Flt. RAAF – A72/187.

proceeding southwards to the more known productive areas of the Sarawak rice and padi fields.

I set up my ATR 4 radio, and immediately contacted the Pa Kelalan Base HQ substation. As food was short and ammunition low, we required an immediate drop of our requirements; I was advised that it would take place at first light. An attack by the RAAF was requested and the information and details relayed by cypher. At 0800 hrs we heard the sound of slowly approaching aircraft. They appeared to be searching the ground closely. Not knowing if they were friend or foe, we remained in the confines and security of the jungle. The flight commander, when he flew over the intervening hillside, observed the kampong and immediately dived upon it, releasing one of his 50-lb A/P bombs. When this exploded we were able to sight the aircraft, and immediately identified ourselves with a hand-held signalling mirror. A note was dropped attached to an ammunition clip asking directions to the enemy force. We were at this point in time in an unmapped area of Sarawak. On the deserted kampong ground clearing, with a roll of toilet paper produced by Bill Nibbs, I traced out a hill, a square box indicating a long-house, a river running westwards, X indicating Japanese positions, an arrow in the direction of travel plus direction of travel to the target. It took but a few moments to complete this sign,

A group of young Kayan headhunters Semut I guerrillas, Sarawak, Borneo, August 1945.

Top: Young Kelabit mother and child from the Belawit Region.

Middle: Young Nabawan Murut girls, interior of Sabah (North), in traditional costumes.

Bottom: Ibans from the Limbang who came across to Labuan Island.

Top: A Lundayeh girl from Tenom.

Middle: Young Dayak lass who lived in Tuan Sanderson's location on the Sungai Limbang.

Bottom: Muruts from the interior of north Sabah.

and the aircraft acknowledged it and flew off in a direct line over the mountains to their objective, Pa Berayong. The message also included information that the supply aircraft had been sent back to base as it had not located our HQ. So once again no supplies or equipment were received. Oh, the thought of something different once in a while?

Late in the afternoon of no sighting of the enemy, we decided to do a reconnaissance over the mountain after the RAAF attack, and ascertain if the enemy had remained in the area, or sought the security of the dense jungle confines whilst moving into the interior. Our total force would now be used jointly on this operation. The members of the Pa Berayong tribe – women, children and the elderly people who had sought refuge in this area – were escorted into the thick jungle nearby, and were to remain there until they were contacted by their guerrilla friends. We now cautiously approached the jungle track over the mountain, and prior to entering it, three scouts did a reconnaissance of the immediate jungle to confirm the non-existence of enemy troops within. Negative report. We now commenced our patrol over the mountain pass track with three scouts in advance, followed closely by Jon and myself plus my Bren gun carrier with ammunition. The rest of the guerrillas followed, putting into place the rear protection policy. The track was in good condition and dry, but progress was slow and unnerving. We finally reached the top of this mountain track unmolested, and then started the downward decline to the kampong below. Jon beckoned to me to advance and approach the scouts ahead silently and quickly. He indicated that five Japanese were immediately in front of them on the trail.

Just around the bend of the track, on a thirty-yard straight section of the trail stood the Japanese, in earnest conversation and with their backs to us. Jon and I immediately took two steps out into the centre of the track, and the Nips must have heard us or detected our movement. They immediately faced us and prepared to defend themselves. Then the silence of the jungle was broken by the deadly sound of Jon's SMG and my carbine. Three of the enemy fell to the ground mortally wounded and the other two dived over the embankment when they first sighted us. Two seconds, perhaps three, and it was all over. Close warfare is such – instantaneous – and those who hesitate endanger not only themselves but their party members. Our three scouts immediately gave pursuit but lost their quarry in the dense trackside jungle. Several of our guerrillas advanced thirty yards down the track for security reasons, and set up a holding position in case of attack. We inspected for intelligence information, the contents of the dead Japanese soldiers' equipment. The packs contained little food, reasonable clothing and in their web-gear 20 rounds of ammunition.

Having now blown our advance into the area and informed the enemy of our presence, we now returned back over the mountain and set up an ambush near our recently relinquished resting area in the jungle heights. We would soon know if the enemy were withdrawing south to the Bawang area, or westwards following the river through the Tengoa Valley towards the Sapong Estate in Sabah, BNB. I informed Base HQ of our attack and the results, received a reply in code and then signed off. On deciphering the text for Sgt Bill Nibbs from our OC, I was utterly shocked by its contents. It read 'Kill or be killed'. Bill had delayed his attack on this major force of 2,000 until he had the situation where he could succeed when conditions were advantageous to his force, and not lose too many of his guerrillas. The above message received was not in conformity with the standard practices and principles of Special Operations Australia. Most of all, the operatives in the field were becoming less and less dependent on our OC, for his denial and attitude towards them was just too unbelievable. At my debriefing at Labuan at the end of the war, I reported the above 'Kill' message to Lieutenant Colonel Jumbo Courtney, OC 'A' section Borneo (SOE, GB) who informed me at a later date that Major Harrisson firmly denied having ever sent that message, although others confirmed in their manuscripts after being released from the Official Secrets Act, that they too had received similar messages. This was the reason I received nothing at the end of the operation.

Next morning, as we were preparing to cross the mountain again, we observed from the OP site a party of natives appearing from out of the jungle beside the jungle track. We soon identified the group which contained three whites. On focusing my binoculars on the party, I was utterly and pleasantly surprised to find that the white members were none other than the three Kiwi members of my party, having left them at Morotai when I chuted in to Borneo – Frank Leckie, Jack Butt and George Edlin. We made contact with this group, and immediately held a conference relating to the Japanese who had just vacated Pa Berayong. It was decided that we would retrace our steps back to this kampong and follow the Nips along the river into the interior. We passed the three dead enemy soldiers on the trackside where we had had the contact. On reaching Pa Berayong from the confines of the surrounding jungle, three of our guerrillas conducted a 360-degree search of the area, but could not find any trace of the enemy. We now took control of the area, setting up observation and defensive positions. From inside the longhouse I slung my dual-frequency W/T aerial and advised Base of the relevant situation in the area. Having now settled in, with guards posted, we went in three parties searching for the retreating 2,000 enemy force, clearing the stragglers and rear patrols as we went. At this point in time, the Japanese commander did not set a trap or major ambush for our group.

Frank Leckie took the bottom trail following the river eastwards into the interior, and my guerrillas the top trail heading in the same direction, about 500 yards separating both by jungle. We sighted nothing, but noticed enemy activity had been in this part of the world by the boot indentations, easily identified as Nippon, on the soft earth of the track. The sound of a short burst from a LMG came clearly through the jungle directly below us, easily recognised as from a Bren gun. Frank later related that they had approached two rear guards, and as the patrol had not been detected, he and two Kelabits with parangs drawn went forward hoping to take them without causing a disturbance, thus protecting the advance towards the main force. This was not to be, for they were observed and the Japanese went for their weapons. Jack Butt, who had set up his Bren to cover the party, immediately took the rear guards in one short burst.

My guerrillas, following the Japanese marked track, were approaching a small jungle clearing. We advanced slowly and cautiously, till the forward scouts in front of me indicated to halt. Jon was quickly by my side informing me that in the clearing was a small *sulap* built on the ground for coolness. Scouts would investigate the area. Soon my young friend was beside me with the information reporting 'Tuan, Japoon tinggal dalam *sulap* di-sana' (Sir, there are Japs in the *sulap* over there). As the door was closed and the large shutters were drawn, the patrol approached with the utmost caution. (The only noisy one in the party was always myself in rubber jungle boots and not bare feet.) The lads covered the doorway in a semi-circle from the confines of the jungle, and three went up the trail ahead just in case we had further visitors from that area if firing broke out. The scouts and Jon, when approaching the *sulap* on the first occasion, had noticed a Nippon rifle leaning against the side of it, and with their keen hearing heard foreign voices emanating from within. I swapped my carbine for an Owen and two mags with a member of my guerrillas, and made for the doorway with Jon. I indicated to him that I would kick the left side hung door open as it was partly ajar a few inches, not use a grenade, but both spray left and right. I took the right and Jon the left, the easier. We immediately did this, and I cannot remember much of the action, purely reflex and Fraser training. Bodies slumped to the floor as we continued to expend the 28 rounds in the magazines. Slightly sickened by the sight of blood and death I retired outside with Jon into the fresh jungle air, and gave the order to my lads, 'Ambil orang Japoon di-sini dari *sulap*.' I wasn't prepared for the next event that took place.

On the order to bring out the Japanese from the *sulap*, there was a rush to comply, so I walked back to the other waiting guerrillas at the edge of the jungle and returned the Owen to its owner plus the empty magazine. I then retrieved my carbine. With the chanting of 'Baik, baik, baik' and the raising of the arms in the air as though holding weapons of ancient times and customs, I was greeted with the sight of four Muruts holding high in the air trophies of the hunt, the decapitated heads of the unfortunate Japanese. All I could do with these smiling and laughing guerrillas was to comply with the known ritual of long ago. I too therefore held my firearm aloft and gave the chant. Unbelievingly, I just shook my head and thought, 'Ye gods, Frank! Just what have you got yourself into?' My face must have turned completely green at this point in time. The rest of the action is better not to be recorded.

We all now returned to Pa Berayong, our new base, as our whereabouts were known to the enemy plus the fact that they were being followed into the interior, after hearing bursts from a LMG. We placed a circle of Muruts, Kelabits and Ibans around the fringes of the jungle adjacent to the longhouse and *sulaps*, for our own security and defence against the possible return of the enemy. Frank Leckie, being the senior (Lieutenant) member, now took control of our combined group. He had carried into the interior with his group a small army mortar, and as my allotted defensive position was the protection of the escape route over the mountains, being elevated with a commanding view of the area, I was given this weapon to control. I decided to have one practice shot with it. Laying and sighting on a tree stump 150 yards in an old disused garden area, I fired a phosphorus bomb at the target. When it hit the tree stump and exploded, the locals were absolutely astounded for they had never experienced or sighted warfare of this nature before.

Contact with Pa Kelalan was made and information transmitted relating to the patrols in the area. An incoming message stated that an RAAF fighter had been lost somewhere due east of the kampong heading up the Tengoa Valley. It had gone down in the jungle whist operating against the enemy in our area, and had not been located by searching members of the strike force which we had requested.

The third patrol was undertaken by Sergeant Bill Nibbs AIF, who took the trail towards Lawas via Pa Tengoa to see if the area was now clear, disposing of all stragglers encountered. On the second day out on the track, and so far no contact with the enemy force, Bill, whilst being in the advanced position of the patrol with a Murut named Sabal and negotiating a thirty-yard straight section of the trail, came under fire from a Japanese LMG on a fixed mount which had been incorrectly set in position, being elevated too high. The first burst was above the operatives' heads. If the Nippon gunner had waited for a couple of seconds longer he would have liquidated the whole patrol, who for some reason had become too overconfident. Unscathed, both Nibbs and Sabal dived off the track, plunged into a small ravine and went jungle-side. The rest of the group engaged the enemy, then returned to Pa Berayong. After two days I advised HQ by radio that we were of the opinion that the two members were considered lost in action, our first operative casualty of Semut I. We immediately sent out patrols in this specific area to locate the enemy party, but they had apparently gone back into the dense jungle and were never sighted again. After the fourth day in the thick forest, and with Sabal's knowledge of the conditions that existed in this part of Borneo, he located an area he recognised. They quickly returned to our base at Pa Berayong and received a great reception on arrival.

The two Japanese who had eluded us on our first patrol towards this area were finally captured by our guerrillas. The Muruts actually brought them alive to the kampong and after our interrogation of the pair, awaited for orders as to just what was to be done with them. In halting Malay these Nips actually requested us to deliver them to their medical officer, for they were stricken with malaria and beri-beri. They were undernourished, had lost considerable weight since leaving Brunei in the south, and had moved via the new jungle track into this area having escaped attention by the Australian attacking force. We had instructions not to keep prisoners within Borneo in the initial stages of the operation, for if they escaped we would soon be detected and our native guerrillas and tribes people helpers would be executed for their assistance to us. These two Japanese went for the long walk into the dense jungle.

On the third day at this new base, with the encirclement of the kampong with native outstations, George Edlin and myself were allocated the task of security on the outer river bank, for it was bad practice for all operatives to be in the same place during the night if attacked. We selected a round visitor's *sulap*, built on poles about 8 ft above ground level for cooling purposes, thus ensuring the occupants a good night's rest in these conditions. Unbeknown to us, a mangy, flee-ridden *anjing* (dog) considered the ground below as its favourite sleeping quarters. It whined and whimpered all night and about 2 a.m. we had endured enough and tried to chase the animal away several times, but it returned on each occasion. George got slightly irritated with this performance and handed me a . 32 cal Welman silenced, single-shot pistol. He requested my assistance to dispose of the nuisance, claiming that as the senior member of the party it was my duty to do the necessary. This I did and we dumped the flee-ridden mongrel into the river below; sleep was proclaimed the order of next importance. George sarcastically remarked that I needed night glasses, for three shots to terminate a mongrel was not considered good marksmanship under these conditions!

In the event of attack we had our location to defend, and if the situation warranted we were to encircle the attacking party from the rear. Whilst in action using my carbine, I found it most advantageous to use the W/T tape and strap two magazines together. Upon expending the first it was fast and simple to remove it and insert the second with a simple movement of the wrist, thus giving me plenty of firepower with little or no loss of time. With forty rounds from a semi-automatic against a bolt-action rifle, it was a major factor for our survival in these jungle conditions. Having greater firepower gave the enemy the impression of a larger party in front of them.

Late on the fourth afternoon rifle fire was heard coming from the direction of the river upstream, and as I was transmitting at that moment I immediately terminated using the 'Q' emergency sign. I hastily picked up my carbine and web gear and headed at pace for my escape route protection site. Jon and my lads followed close behind with my Bren and ammunition. We located the mortar in the jungle beside our position plus carrying packs of its ammunition, setting up its position covering the lower reaches from which the enemy might appear. Minutes ticked by – nothing moved below and no more shots were fired. Finally we sighted Frank Leckie emerging from the secondary growth accompanied by several Muruts carrying a body. Frank reported that the natives saw an unidentified person approaching from upriver and were fired upon. They immediately returned the fire and killed him. At the kampong the victim was identified when we did a body search, finding in the pockets several pieces of information. It was Flying Officer George of the RAAF who had gone missing and crashed in the jungle near the river, whilst on the mission we had called for a few days earlier. He had survived the crash, receiving multiple bruising to the body and head. All his morphia injections from his survival kit had been used. Having survived to this point, he was indeed unlucky and unfortunate to end his life in these circumstances, being so close to recovery and help. His pistol, a S & W .38, had fired three shots. At the time of his death he was wearing a WO's flying jacket.

We sent the natives back upstream and found several items that had been discarded by this pilot; his aircraft was never located. I was allocated the task of making a headboard for his grave and traced details on a piece of local timber. My lads then copied the pencil marks with a red-hot iron, thus burning his identification onto the board to provide a lasting record until the War Graves Commission recovered the body from this area. He was buried in the kampong communal grounds, a sad moment indeed of my time in central Borneo. Major Harrisson was immediately advised by radio of this incident and arrived smartly in the area two days later, having been in the forward area of the Padas when the signal was received at Base HQ Ba Kelalan. He advised the RAAF at Labuan Island of the sad incident, with our deepest regrets from all operatives.

Another Slog and Encounter

On the arrival of our OC, as had happened on all occasions, morale dropped substantially. His treatment of the natives and sharpness of his tongue left much to be desired, also causing as much disharmony amongst the operatives as he could possibly inflict. He talked to all the operatives about the shooting, and stated that he was going to inflict punishment on those who had killed Flying Officer George. We all remarked that the natives were fired upon, and the mistake and action was not of their making in the first instant. Punishing them, under the circumstances, would put us at risk with our guerrillas who would not respond to our leadership as previously given. He finally agreed with our finding on the situation. As had happened on three previous occasions, I was again given my marching instructions for another long walk. I think he really enjoyed playing with us. He told me he had plans for me to trek up north to the Sapong Estate and set up communications with Base under the noses of the Japanese at their 37th Army HQ, but as we were about to be invaded in the Limbang area, from the Brunei region, by a substantial force, my group was immediately to move southwards to this area and meet up with another operative for W/T communication and intelligence purposes.

The AIF sergeant known to me as Fred, was on his second mission to the Limbang river. This part of Borneo was in an isolated, unmapped region and had never been traversed or explored by a white man. He had originally walked into this location from Base HQ at Belawit, and attacked General Haragushi and his personal bodyguards when they ventured up the Limbang river by motorboat on 9 June. He was recalled into the interior at the end of June. Being so far from interior HQ and runners being used to deliver intelligence information, the period of four days till the receipt of the documents caused them to became outdated by the time of their arrival.

Within the hour my group was back on the trail for the rendezvous with Fred's large force moving into the Limbang, and it would take a lengthy time travelling at a fast pace to arrive at the designated meeting place on time. George Edlin was now left without a radio set, so I agreed with Frank Leckie to part with mine so that they could continue skeds with Base at Ba Kelalan. My group arrived at the cross-trails early in the afternoon of the second day, having quickly covered the distance without carrying much equipment. I observed George's discarded Boston Mk 3 set at the rear of the longhouse. It appeared to have been well handled and not damaged, although he had stated it would not transmit and had not received any instruction at Fraser on it. Just why I do not comprehend, for it was certainly on our training schedule. The Australian operative Fred, and his group, duly arrived just before nightfall. A W/T set was not in their equipment. Another slog was now pointed in my direction – back to the Belawit strip!

At first light next morning we left the hillside *sulap* and headed for the Bawang Valley, Dutch Borneo, to obtain and collect the necessary equipment required for the Limbang operation. This took four and a half days to complete, and it was mostly all downhill travel. I again met up with Bob Long who was still at the W/T *sulap* situated at the end of the bamboo runway. Dan Illerich, the American, was there also, and was soon to be flown out to Labuan by Auster aircraft and thence to his homeland with the rest of the recovered airmen. They had been previously reported as missing to their relatives, whilst in action over Borneo in a B–24 Liberator bomber. Ojita, the captured Japanese construction worker, was now the trusty cook for the W/T *sulap* occupants. An Auster aircraft had arrived from Labuan Island that morning carrying, as part of its cargo, a Boston Mk3 set with all necessary spares included in a repair box. Bob stated that it was not necessary to be tested before I retraced my steps to the west, as it would have received a major check prior to insertion into our area. Also Major Harrisson had just arrived back from Pa Berayong.

I now went in search of my OC and sought permission to re-equip my guerrillas with clothing and ammunition from the store *sulap*. This was denied, and I was not permitted to go near it. Whilst Harrisson was away from base, a senior Malay policeman living in the kampong, who served with the group, had possession of the store's key. He had been instructed that operatives were not permitted to enter this sacred area, or demand anything from within. I urgently required clothes, boots, trade money and ammunition, but got nothing. This officer was certainly living up to his reputation as told to me by those whom I met and had known him in Borneo. This was his first active service encounter of the war, previously being with the Green Howards and a member of the King's Royal Rifle Corps stationed in Northern Ireland. Perhaps, as many of the lads of the group thought, he was preparing for the end of the war, being now in possession of money and stores and thinking of setting up residence at Bareo in the Kelabit Heights of the interior. My group was to go into the Limbang area and needed effective automatic weapons when and if we encountered this Japanese force from the Brunei and Tutoh area. We were now out on a limb, having insufficient firepower and ammunition.

I could not help but notice the changes that had taken place during my short absence. The northern end of the main kampong had increased in the number of buildings – a medical *sulap* with an attendant Chinese dresser, recovery hut for operatives (?) needing relaxation from stress and duties in the field, and a private *sulap* for the OC. The latter was a most palatial residence, and considered by all who sighted it, as a magnificent home in this interior part of Borneo. It contained native-built beds, chairs, tables and everything imaginable for comfort. I even noticed a case of beer. He had six young Kelabit maiden servants in attendance all the time. Denial forte was certainly this man's mode of thought to us 'colonials'. Known as Tuan Rajah Tom to all the Kelabit and other tribes of the area, they believed that only a king or rajah would wear a crown on their shoulders or hat. Harrisson had advised all operatives, in their operational instructions, that there was to be no fraternisation with the womenfolk of Borneo. But just who should break this order firstly, none other than himself. The operatives kept to themselves and were much respected by the tribes people, who were prepared to share everything they owned with their 'friends from the skies'.

Before I left Belawit after collecting the Boston radio and spares, Harrisson asked why I had returned to Base HQ after meeting Fred at the cross-trails eastward. I informed him that Pa Berayong was now an operational base, requiring W/T communication with HQ. George Edlin, having disposed of his useless set, had no means to continue the flow of information required from this area. Hence my return to base after meeting my new partner and finding that they did not carry a radio. He accepted my line of thought, as he now had another operational W/T party on the network of outstations.

Feeling completely devastated with the non-supply of necessary equipment to defend ourselves against a major enemy force, we decided that the advance into the Limbang was to be exceptionally fast. Severe caution was now to be observed and undertaken upon entering the unknown area past Pa Brunot, and the kampong just below the de-manding climb over the mountain to the Limbang river. My party was now increased to eighteen members, with carriers now for the W/T Boston and hand generator. A new addition to the fighting guerrillas was Jon's friend named Ranu. He was always full of life and the joys of living, a welcome addition to our group. Also requesting to travel with us was a Chinese-Malay, a former Sarawak Government employee of about thirty years of age, a stroke of luck, for he spoke fluent English. Oh my, this was a magnificent addition to the group. It seemed to me that 'The old Master up above' had taken pity on me, presenting me with a companion to converse with and boost my morale at my moment of need. Morale down one moment, then suddenly a surge upwards the next. One never knew what to expect in any situation inside this enemy-occupied country.

Information received just prior to the commencement of our movement into the unknown was that the enemy force was reported to be moving towards the Limbang area in fairly large numbers. They were travelling from the Semut II area controlled by Major Toby Carter (NZ) in the Baram river area. Our trails were saturated, slippery and treacherous, making conditions for fast movement impossible. We crossed six medium-sized streams and decided to stay at a kampong just beside a larger but fairly shallow river. An amazing settlement this turned out to be. All the longhouses and *sulaps* were built on the ground, and slightly elevated above the level of the river when in flood. It was totally closed off from the jungle by a ringed fence, being 8 ft high and made of bamboo with the tops sharpened to a fine point. Wild animals in large numbers were causing trouble in this area, hence the barricade for protection.

Next morning we discussed whether we would cross this swollen river, for it apparently had been raining heavily upstream during the night. The decision was to proceed forthwith. Using a 6-ft staff to assist and taking the pressure of the flow against our bodies and legs, we just managed the crossing. We should not have put the group at risk but awaited until the river had subsided a little before attempting it, but time was not on our side just now. At our meeting place on the cross-trails, Fred had informed me that near this kampong on a junction of the trails, was a hidden native-built store of equipment. He had sighted it and its contents, which included eight SMLE rifles and six 4-gal tins of 03 Field Rations. He had opened one of these and taken half of its contents. (I was to learn in later years from group members that many of these dumps were in their areas unbeknown to them.)

We managed to locate the jungle store, and unofficially secreted the rifles out of the area. These would be an asset in the Limbang. We would never admit to having removed them, although it was released from HQ that the store had been 'rifled'. An amazing term that! Kiwis had practiced it in many theatres of operation. We had need for these weapons, although I did not know it then that we would never receive a supply drop in the Limbang when confronted by a formidable Japanese force of approximately 500–600. We should have taken part of the 03 rations as food was going to be short in this region.

At the junction of the two tracks where George had disposed of his Boston W/T, I assembled the new set and tried to operate it, finding that it would transmit but not receive. It must have received a knock in transit to Belawit or on the track to this location. I learnt from this experience never to trust anything – try it first before accepting delivery of the unit. On checking the radio, I withdrew the bottom slide-out tray with all the component parts visible, and after testing was unable to locate the fault. I then resorted to the only related method that was available to me in this circumstance. I exchanged the tray with that of the one in the *sulap* left by George, felt the fingers set into place and reassembled the unit. With Jon propelling the handle of the generator, I switched on and immediately realised that it was now in working order. I tested reception around the dial, and was completely satisfied with the result. I had been instructed by Major Harrisson that if contact was not made with Base Ba Kelalan, I was to do the long walk back to the Bawang. The Australians down at Ukong on the Limbang river were unable to contact anyone from their location, and if I experienced the same, I was to return immediately to the interior as I was wanted in other areas of importance. Experienced operators in SOA were in demand and low in numbers.

I arrived at Pa Brunot wet and exhausted, totally devoid of any energy within my young frame. The tracks were hazardous and slippery, plus travelling on slightly uphill trails. This was a great kampong to arrive at – clean, tidy and in a cool valley beside a wide river. A restful area to recover from the ordeal just encountered. Being a Sunday, all the Christian Muruts were going to their church *sulap* down by the river. I joined them after changing and having a clean-up, and was given a seat of importance being reserved for visitors on the platform beside the officiating minister, a native *Kiai*. I was requested to read the bible in Malay to the assembly, made a few errors, but was well received. The *Kiai* stated that it was the first time since the missionary had left that someone other than himself had read the lesson. He had no knowledge as to the fate of the missionary who had surrendered to the Japanese.

All the women and young girls were clothed in pure white dresses for the service, presumably made during the time the missionary was in their midst, prior to the invasion. Men wore shorts and white shirts. It was certainly back to civilisation once again, but immediately after the service the females reverted to their standard type of clothing – sarongs and topless. The temperature in this valley was a 100 degrees plus in the shade at this time of the day. About twenty families lived within this kampong – clean, tidy, well educated and excellent gardeners. I was given a conducted tour of the area, accompanied by Jon and Ranu who had several of the light-skinned young maidens of the longhouse chattering excitedly to them both. On being invited to accompany the tribe down to the river for a swim, I immediately accepted the offer and made for the bathing area. Much to the delight of this group, I stripped off, taking the necessary precautions of the tribe before entering the water in my now naked condition. Perhaps the invitation was extended to me owing to my body odour, which I had obtained through hard slogging and sweat whilst travelling in this area of 'Within'. My beard was now turning white with the mosquito repellent I used on it, and needed a trim. One of the tribesmen produced a hunting knife and did the job. One slip of that knife and I would be hanging from the rafters in one of those reed boxes, above the smoky fireplaces! It was amazing that after having a clean-up and swim after so long since the last one, my skin, which was dark brown from travelling the tracks during daylight not wearing a shirt, immediately turned white. The tan completely vanished – washed off – much to the delight of the natives. Many had never encountered a white person, and wondered at the change of colour having seen me prior to the river dip. That night sleeping on the hard bamboo flooring on a mat, I missed Jon and Ranu. I enquired of their whereabouts and received a smiling reply from one of the elders, that they were being entertained by their young maidens. It was customary in these tribes that visitors of tribal importance were offered such recreation.

The next move to the Limbang was the most demanding that I ever encountered whilst in Borneo. In the early-morning mist, we all crossed the river and started to climb the mountain range, about 3 to 4,000 ft high. This took all day from early dawn at 0430, arriving at the top at 2000 hrs. The incline was so steep that in places we were at a crawl gaining only inches at a time. The bearers and my guerrillas were exhausted when reaching the summit. Before the climb one of the natives from the kampong relieved me of my arms and equipment, stating I would need his assistance and not to carry it. I was truly thankful that this happened, for I am of the opinion I would never have made the top, fit as I was at that point in time. It was at this location that I sighted the most amazing scene that I had ever encountered whilst in Borneo. For miles along this mountain ridge, as far as I could see, there was a huge crack in the earth's surface, giving the impression that it had been created by an earthquake of great magnitude thousands of years before.

The natives had formed a clearing at this spot, and the void of 20–25ft was bridged by two large trees about 40 ft in length. My guerrillas and bearers just ran across, but the one carrying the Boston, who was the last of the group, had an extremely narrow escape. He partly overbalanced and slipped on the rounded surface of the bridge of trees, recovered well and cleared the obstacle. I was told to wait and be last across, being instructed by Jon, 'Jangan nampak di-sana' (don't look down), indicating the bottomless void. With all the encouragement given to football teams when in action in my own country, I too, thankfully made the crossing by lying prone on the two trees, and pulling myself across the void. Hell, I could never have done the running balancing act. We camped in the clearing for the night, and Jon cooked me a well-received meal of rice. Oh, the things we do in the Army, we would never accomplish in civilian circumstances!

About midnight the natives reported that a runner was approaching on the uphill track leading from the *rumah besar* below on the Limbang river. A Murut duly arrived from that area stating he was on his way home, for he had finished his portering for my new partner in this unknown and unmapped portion of remote *ulu* Sarawak. Fred and his force were now located just below my team, and were preparing to perahu down the Limbang river from Kepala Tamabo Sarawak's long-house (his name means 'Great Mountain of Sarawak') to whatever awaited them downstream. At dawn we moved down the mountainside and reached our objective by mid-morning. The news we received there was that Fred's group had taken to the river at dawn. I should have sent a runner during the night to contact them to await our arrival. One learns fast when experiencing situations of this nature. 'Act now – delaying could cost you substantially in the end result.' It would take Fred's group a full day to travel to the Iban longhouse of Kepala Bilong, situated just upriver from the major *rumah besar* of the area controlled by Penghulu Kadu.

Japanese troops had not been reported in the immediate vacinity of this kampong where we were now located. My party had progressed rapidly to the river, having made up the lost seven days required to return to Belawit for a W/T set. We certainly needed a rest after this latest slog uphill. Next morning I set up the Boston and rigged the aerial with the help of the locals, who slung it between two 60-ft trees close to the *sulap*. We were now situated between two large mountain ridges with the river running between. I put into practice my theory of being able to transmit in such circumstances – bounce the signals. I received no response from the first call seeking receipt and signal strength from our Ba Kelalan base, so I considered the implications of the cut, duel-frequency, slung aerial, and decided to try the secondary part by pulling the cord and breaking the contacts in the middle. This brass finger joint could be unstable, having been subjected to climatic conditions that existed in this theatre of operations. I had experienced this operating fault during my service in the Pacific at Guadalcanal and other islands over the last few years, being caused by humidity and moisture. My next transmission was immediately answered, giving a strength of five-plus, and I was requested in plain language to advise the location of my group. For security sake, I encoded in cipher 'Limbang area', and received 'Congrats first ever trans from this area. Where is Fred?'. I replied that he was now one day ahead of me, and I was awaiting return of the boats. Harrisson must have been in the W/T *sulap* there, for an immediate reply stated 'Get walking'. I replied that the only method of travel in this remote spot was by perahu and I would await the return of them in two days' time. I received no reply to this, so presumed that the answer had satisfied the receiver, transmitted the close sign and received an acknowledgement.

It was at this kampong that I received a severe dose of amoebic dysentery, which could have been avoided if Fred had informed me of the circumstances that had occurred at this longhouse recently. The *kepala* and three members of his family had died from the same complaint being caused by the seeping of urine into the well beside the building, the water becoming contaminated. Modern hygiene was not practised and was completely unknown in this primitive world of the indiginous natives of the interior of Borneo. From my medical kit I partook of a heavy dosage of sulphaguanadine, gradually increasing the amount taken over two days, then decreasing it as it came under control. My physical condition was still holding at this point in time, although salt was sadly missed and non-existent in this area. Whilst passing large quantities of blood, and becoming weak from this malady, my guerrillas built a seat and dug a hole beside a tree close to the longhouse. During the night, a rope was tied around my waist and secured to the tree to support me. My body was now covered with a blanket for protection against the heavy mosquito population which existed in the area. These beasties were as big as DC3 Dakota aircraft, flew down, refuelled then took off trying to take me with them (hallucinations that I would rather forget). Members of my guerrilla force including Jon and Ranu took turns at standing guard over me during the night, just in case a Japanese of the advancing force infiltrated into the area unnoticed. The free flow from my bowels during the first two days was a most excruciating feeling, similar to the anus being burnt with a blow torch, a complaint which was also endured by many of my operative friends within this heavily diseased and infected island of Borneo.

With the close experience of the near contact with the Japanese at Long Miau in the Padas, I now had sewn into the lapel of my shirt the cyanide capsule, for one never knew just what the morrow might bring, as this was a completely unknown area. It had only been penetrated and traversed by my new operative companion for a period of three weeks in early June to coincide with the invasion of the Australian 9th Division. Our assistance within this area was requested by Kepala Bilong who had walked into the interior, having heard that our force was now in control of it. Crocodiles, large pythons and piranha fish in the rivers were our main worry in this Ulu Limbang operation. Thank our lucky stars, for behind us we had finally left the diseased 'Valleys of the Padas', and the ever-lurking leeches waiting for a meal. A wonderous thought indeed.

Whilst in this locality I took a walk to fill in time until the return of the perahus downriver, and with Jon and Ranu visited a small kampong located on flat ground above the river. We were introduced to one of the worst native living areas that I ever saw in Borneo, consisting of about ten families, lazy hill Muruts, heavy Borak drinkers for most of the year till stocks became exhausted. They were unhealthy and undernourished. Hygiene conditions were extremely bad, and the gardens neglected. No wonder sickness was rife in this area, being also the main contributing factor in my dysentery encounter.

After recovering from my bout of sickness, and having no inclination to eat rice, Jon and Ranu went into the jungle in search of game. They sighted a hornbill (*burong besar*) and finally tracked it down, sitting on a top branch of a 100-ft high tree. With my carbine they managed to bag it. After being dressed it weighed about 5–6 lb. It was then placed

Drawing of an Iban visitors' round *sulap* situated on the Libang river, Borneo. Accommodates six people. Spent a night in one of these, whilst awaiting an attack at dawn from the Fujino Tai.

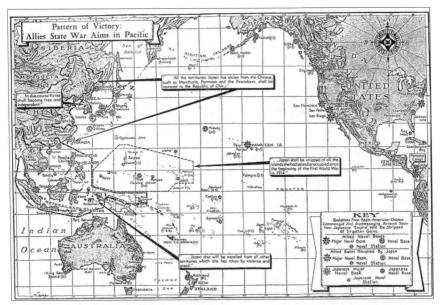

An official communiqué issued in Cairo on 1 December 1943 announced
that President Roosevelt, Generalissimo Chiang Kai-shek, and Mr Churchill
had completed a conference in North Africa. This map, reproduced from
the *Christian Science Monitor*, is based on those sections of the communiqué
stating the aims of the three allies in the Pacific.

Photo taken in the Baram river area where this box of Japanese skulls are
a local attraction for tourists (S.E. of Brunei)

SURRENDER OF JAPANESE FORCES

Address Delivered by

COMMANDER - in - CHIEF, AUSTRALIAN MILITARY FORCES
GENERAL SIR THOMAS BLAMEY

to

Lt - General Teshima, Commander Second Japanese Army
On the occasion of the signing of their Surrender

MOROTAI, 9th SEPTEMBER, 1945

LIEUT.-GENERAL TESHIMA, COMMANDER, SECOND JAPANESE ARMY :

"The Japanese Navy has been destroyed. The Japanese Merchant Fleet has been reduced to a mere fraction. The Japanese Air Force has been driven from the sky. The Japanese armies have been defeated everywhere and all that remained for them was to await their inevitable total destruction. Japanese cities lie in waste and Japanese industry has been destroyed. Never before in history has so numerous a nation been so completely defeated.

"To escape the complete destruction of the nation, the Emperor of Japan has yielded to the Allied Forces and an instrument of total surrender has been signed in his name. He has charged you to obey the orders which I shall give you.

"In carrying out these orders, the Japanese Army and Navy organisation will be retained for convenience. Instructions will be issued by the designated Australian Commanders to the Commanders of the respective Japanese Forces, placing upon you and your subordinate Commanders the responsibility for carrying out your Emperor's direction to obey all orders given to you by me.

"You will ensure that all Allied personnel, prisoners of war or internees in Japanese hands are safeguarded and nourished and delivered over to the Allied Commanders.

"You will collect, lay down and safeguard all arms, ammunition and instruments of war until such time as they are taken over by the designated Commanders. You will be given adequate time to carry this out. An official date will be named and any Japanese found in possession after that date of any arms, ammunition or instrument of war of any kind will be dealt with summarily by the Australian Commander on the spot.

"Orders will be given for these and other matters as I consider necessary and you will ensure the obedience to all such orders without delay.

"In receiving your surrender I do not recognise you as an honourable and gallant foe, but you will be treated with due but severe courtesy in all matters.

"I recall the treacherous attack upon our ally, China, in 1938. I recall the treacherous attack made upon the British Empire and upon the United States of America in December, 1941, at a time when your authorities were making the pretence of ensuring peace.

"I recall the atrocities inflicted upon the persons of our nationals as prisoners of war and internees, designed to reduce them by punishment and starvation to slavery.

"In the light of these evils, I will enforce most rigorously all orders issued to you, so let there be no delay or hesitation in their fulfilment at your peril."

Above and opposite page: Surrender documents signed at Morotai.

Instrument of Surrender

In accordance with General Order Number One issued by the Japanese Imperial General Headquarters by direction of the Supreme Commander of the Allied Powers we hereby:—

A. **Proclaim** the Unconditional Surrender to the Commander in Chief, Australian Military Forces of all Japanese Armed Forces and all Armed Forces under Japanese control in the Netherlands East Indies, East of and exclusive of Lombok, and in Borneo.

B. **Command** all Commanders and members of the Japanese Armed Forces and Controlled Forces within the Territories, Islands and Areas aforesaid to cease hostilities immediately, lay down their arms, remain in their present localities and do all such acts and things as may be required of them by the Commander in Chief, Australian Military Forces or his authorised Representative or Representatives.

C. **Command** all Civil, Military and Navy officials and all members of the Japanese Armed Forces to obey and enforce all Proclamations, Orders and Directions issued by the Commander in Chief, Australian Military Forces, or his authorised Representative or Representatives.

Signed at Morotai on the Ninth day of September 1945.

小 外   Commander Second Japanese Army.

山 山   By command and on behalf of

Japanese Imperial General Headquarters.

Accepted at Morotai on the Ninth day of September 1945.

T.A. Blamey General

into a large fireside pot within the longhouse, and I ultimately enjoyed a tasty drop of fresh soup, exceedingly nourishing and a welcome meal to first enjoy after these last few days of non-consumption of food. Later I ravenously ate the flesh and did not become ill again. The native perahus returned to Ulu Limbang on the fourth day, and the next morning we commenced our journey downriver. After the torrential tropical rain which we had endured over the last few days, the Limbang was in heavy flood, flowing at about 7–8 knots. None of the Muruts paddled, but the stern member controlled it with the sweep of his oar.

Keeping close to the southern bank on this downward trip of the river, Jon was in the leading perahu to observe and kill any game along the river bank but he missed two wild pigs. The natives immediately placed my perahu in the lead position, and we silently drifted and observed the foreshore. Seeing a pig asleep on a ledge, we approached and I shot it with my carbine. It continued to struggle, so using a second to finish the job, it fell the 20 ft to the bank beside our perahu. From here on I used one of the SMLE 303s which was far more effective. With the quiet approach of the perahus the game were easy victims. The natives now fished from the moving boat and caught many varieties that I had never encountered before. Fred, my new operative friend, had arrived at Kepala Bilong's temporary small longhouse on the northern side of the river on 11 July, myself following on the 15th.

I first sighted the Ibans on the river about a mile upstream, when a youngster in a small perahu suddenly appeared from around a bend of the river. He was light-olive skinned, in good physical condition, and gave us a loud welcome. He then increased his paddling and headed for the kampong a little downriver. On arrival we were greeted by Kepala Bilong, who explained that Fred was twenty minutes downstream at Penghulu Kadu's main *rumah besar* and would send a member to advise him of our arrival. Bilong had recently vacated his dwelling on the southern side of the Limbang to avoid unheralded contact with the Japanese forces that were now roaming the interior after the Australian 9th Division invasion on the coast. These Ibans, plus those of Penghulu Badak's near the confluence of Sungai Limbang and Madalam, were of the Tabon Tribe – Rajah Brooke's favourite tribespeople. Well built, light-olive skinned and fighters supreme! Fred stayed with the two families at Bilong's *sulap* on the northern side of the river, while I was to be housed at the main longhouse of Rumah Kadu.

We now travelled by perahu to my new home of thirty-odd families for the duration of my operation in Borneo. Orders were immediately given for the building of a *sulap* near the main longhouse to house the W/T and generator. These builders of *sulaps* in this area were a sight to observe. Within six hours the twenty-odd natives had completed the job, firstly having to cut and collect all the necessary timber from the nearby jungle. The only tool that was used was the parang, similar to a jungle knife (manufactured by themselves from metals obtained by trading with the Chinese on the coast) with a carved handle and adornments attached to it – a deadly fighting instrument. A table for the W/T set plus a stool were soon manufactured. In front of the table they had built a lift-up shutter on the wall of the *sulap* to allow the breeze to filter through the area. Several sleeping mats were laid on the floor, and thus my home and radio station were complete. Our location was now about 50 ft above river level on a flat side of the hillside, being close to the jungle and 60 yds downwards to the water's edge. The track leading to Bilong's longhouse went past my *sulap*. These Tabon tribes people were great supporters of the original eight members of 'Z' who had chuted into the interior.

The natives slung my aerial in a north-south direction, I made the final adjustments to the set and fitted the crystal frequency unit. With Jon and Ranu taking turns with the hand generator, I contacted Ba Kelalan HQ on the first call and was given a strength five-plus recording. My Boston MkIII was living up to its name, having been transported carefully by the carriers since leaving Belawit to Pa Brunot and over the mountain to the Limbang area. My conclusion after contacting base within the interior was that W/T transmissions from this area were not to be as formerly expected, a hit or miss affair. The quality in reception was exceptional, and transmissions great. It had been presumed that contact would not be effected from this location on the Limbang, as the Australians downriver at Ukong could not transmit or receive messages from the close proximity of their HQ, now situated at Labuan Island in the Bay of Brunei.

I sought the assistance of tribal members to help with the hand generator for the Boston. They complied, and there was always a replacement when one needed a rest. I took over on one occasion to do the donkey work, having firstly tuned to an American Forces station broadcasting jazz music. The receiver was set to maximum output to allow all those assembled in the *sulap*, plus outside, to hear the trans-mission. The Ohs and Ahs from the group who were experiencing for the first time *Orang Puteh* music from the outside world, showed amazement and wonderment at just what instrument could make those sounds. I had now proved my point as to my needing their help in providing the necessary turning of the generator handles. My new native name from here on was 'Tuan Pukal Wireless Prank' (*pukul* means the striker of, beat or knock – the 'F' in my name could not be pronounced, thus I was known as Prank). When future musical sessions were announced I could not accommodate them all in the *sulap*, and the last to arrive sat outside on a mat. This period of contact with the Tabon tribes people was indeed enjoyable, relaxing and coming to terms with myself. For four and a half years of my young life, I had missed growing up in a situation surrounded by people of my own age 20–21. I was now accepted as one of the family, and the pressure of living within an occupied country was somewhat relieved.

This *rumah besar* situated on the northern bank of the Limbang river, was built on poles about 10 ft above the ground, 80–90 m in length, and 45 ft in width. It was divided into three sections. Along the right-hand side were small rooms, closed off with a door, for the elderly or senior members of the tribe. Amazing to see the doors were actually hung with rough hinges probably forged by the Tabon tribes people. The middle part, with the bamboo floor, was the communal section with fireplaces every 10 ft, sufficient room for a family and surrounded by sleeping mats. Large old Chinese cast-iron woks were evident, having been traded to them many years before the war. From the doorway to the rear of the longhouse, the families were placed in position of importance in the tribe. On the side wall were benches made from thinly cut bamboo, making sleeping quarters for visitors. These sections were covered by an atap roof covering, the third section being an open veranda. The smoke from the fireplaces seemed to have a detrimental effect on the mosquito population in the area for they did not seem to exist within. Entrance to this *rumah besar* was by climbing a tree log, set at about 45 degrees angle to the ground, with steps having been hacked out with the usual parangs, slippery indeed when being negotiated during the wet weather and when having muddy boots and feet. Beside each fireplace was a trap door of about 10″ × 10″ set in the floor. After darkness nobody ventured outside the structure until dawn. The tribespeople just squatted over these openings when necessity arose, so there was no need to go out into the darkness. Underneath the longhouse roamed the household pigs who kept the area clean – no pork for me, unless I managed to bag a feral one. I had eaten the native pork and it tasted like that which they fed on! This Tobon tribe was exceedingly clean and their hygiene far more advanced than the tribes of the interior. Warriors from this locality had been selected and trained as bodyguards for the Rajahs of Sarawak.

At this moment in time, little movement was being reported by bush telegraphy about the Japanese retreating into the interior. Relaxing at this kampong certainly made a difference to my health, and after the strenuous period over the last few weeks, my young body was recovering rapidly even though the main diet was only rice, with fruit in the area being non-existent.

It was now about a week since we had left Pa Brunot, and noticing the Ibans moving down to the riverside, I too immediately moved in that direction as I certainly needed a wash and clean up. In this humidity and heat, one soon became high with body odour, although the native population did not seem to sweat as much as we whites did. Following the customs of the Bornean peoples, I undressed on the river bank (leaving my carbine and web gear handy in case of emergency) covering the vital parts of the body with my hands until immersed up to the waistline – the water felt magnificent. I had managed to scrounge a cake of soap from Bob at the Belawit airstrip and proceeded to enjoy the feeling of a good wash, rare indeed in that part of the world. Oh, the luxurious thought of a bath and shower back in civilisation when one dreams of times at home, family, and mostly of one's own young lady. Mine, I had tucked away fairly close to me, for inside of the plastic handle of old 'Girty', my .45 pistol, was her photograph.

To the chanting and laughter of the fifty-odd Ibans, old and young, pointing their arms in my direction and shouting 'Orang puteh, Orang puteh' (White man, white man) I now became the main attraction to these people. Really hilarious at this point in time, and with the chatter, laughter and singing one could almost believe that the war was non-existent. Several young maidens of the kampong in a nearby group beside my position in the water (aged between thirteen and fifteen years of age, of marriageable status, as this is the norm in Borneo) called to me 'Tuan Prank, boleh kasi sayah awak kamu punya sabun, mahu itu' (Frank please give me your soap, I want it). Upon hearing this I immediately replied, 'Mahu ini sabun? Fikir kita boleh ambil itu dari sayah!' (Want my soap? Think you can take it from me!) Immediately I was tackled by many slithering and naked bodies, and dumped below the surface of the river and gently held there by two of them. (No protesting from this lad, for I had certainly asked for that and enjoyed it too.) The soap now being in their possession, my head and beard were given a substantial scrub by many of the group. The yelling and screams of utter delight by all and sundry in the vicinity should have been witnessed to be really believed. The tumultuous uproar would have carried far into the jungle. Many little pranks were played on us during our life in this area with the Ibans.

The Tabon tribespeople were just children at heart, loving and caring, but what magnificent warriors were the menfolk. I was soon to find out that on returning to my *sulap* after a patrol or ambush, all my clothes (threadbare at this point, having never received a food drop, clothing, medicine or ammunition) were washed and dried, neatly laid out on my sleeping mat in the W/T *sulap*. It was at this time in our stay at Kadu that I noticed I had three warriors at my side twenty-four hours a day. Where I went, they went. They were changed regularly and were responsible to the *penghulu* for my safety. When we were on patrol or in action they were but an arm's length away.

As it was a quiet period in this locality for a few days, and Japanese were not reported in the vicinity, I was invited to attend a mouse deer hunt in the cornfields area close by. These deer are a small animal of approximately 18″ in height and a dead replica of the larger animals, even to the antlers and hoofs. They lived in the cornfields, inquisitive creatures who were attracted to light during darkness, and when exposed to this they ventured out into the open areas surrounding the fields. The natives built fires during the night, and when the deer came within 30 yds of the warriors, they were shot with the *sumpitans* (blowpipes) using paralysing poisonous darts. To make them edible, the natives immediately cut their throats releasing the blood and the poison contained within. Using the *sumpitan* and being noiseless when operated, other animals were soon to appear having not been disturbed by noise.

This method was used to good effect on Japanese patrols, silently picking off the end members, and not giving any warning to the main advancing patrol or column. Small parties of the enemy were being ambushed and killed in the area continually, so there was a shortage of all types of ammunition caused by the non-supply and receipt of stores, which had been requested by W/T for our Limbang operation. The native bush telegraphy was working constantly, providing knowledge of enemy infiltration long before they were in the close proximity of our well-defended area. It was now becoming a question who was going to spring the ambush and erase these parties? The enemy had no chance of survival in small groups as ambush positions were set up well in advance of their arrival, from positions beneficial and specially selected for our operations. Our denial of food and porters to the enemy was always a major part in preparation against the Japanese, plus clearing of the native population from the line of advance.

The one thing needed by the Ibans of this area was PATIENCE, and they were well conditioned in this subject by Fred and myself. In jungle encounters with the enemy we were advised well in advance of their location. With the Ibans' strong sense of smell, pin-pointing the enemy was of great benefit to us. Many times only a parang was used, for such was the silent approach and cautious movement within their 'jungle domains'. The Japanese did not realise the immediate danger and presence of these warriors until it was too late. It was at Rumah Kadu that I first encountered the first case of cerebal malaria whilst in Borneo. The Limbang river was located in the 'Seria 25 Malarial District' east of Brunei Bay, known as being a potentially heavily infected zone. The young Iban concerned developed the usual symptoms of the malady –

hot and cold periods, increased temperature over the next two days and gradually becoming uncontrollable and raving, necessitating him being restrained. Finally death on or about the seventh day. This type of malaria affects the brain, and gradually drowns it with fluid.

Small parties of the enemy were now appearing regularly in the area and were quickly disposed of, much to the delight of the Ibans. They all wanted a trophy to hang from the rafters and copy the customs of their forefathers, which had been discontinued not too many years before by order of the 'White Rajah Brooke' of Sarawak. My Boston now became overloaded with messages from the interior informing us of the breakout from the perimeter of Major Toby Carter's Semut II (GB-NZ) area SE of Brunei in the Barum river area, and of a large force of the enemy. The estimated strength was given at approximately 500–600 strong, heading for the interior via the Belait and Tutoh areas, following the river system northwards to our Limbang river HQ. Great elation in the kampong, as the guerrilla warriors anticipated the coming arrival in their midst of this substantial force.

Patrols were sent out into the jungle across the river, and downstream to the confluence of the Madamit and Limbang rivers. Nothing was sighted, and it was now thought that the party was travelling through the interior at a snail's pace.

We were soon to learn from the natives escaping from the area to our base that the enemy were destroying, raping and killing everything that they came upon on their advance into the interior whilst avoiding the Australian invading force, plus our own operatives. A small party was observed at the confluence of the two rivers, building a raft. They quickly dispersed into the jungle and I awaited their return to complete the raft, but they must have changed their minds on sighting my guerrillas. I fired a burst from my Bren into the jungle close to the waters' edge where they were building the raft, just to warn them of what might happen on their journey into the interior. We continued with our patrols keeping a close watch on the situation, but nothing eventuated for several days. Fred, with seventeen perahus containing 120 guerrillas, Ibans and Muruts, journeyed down the Limbang and headed up the Madalam River to locate this force, thus defining the direction of travel so we could put our denial programme into practice.

After advancing up this river for about a mile, with scouts on each side of the river bank observing and tracking under cover of the jungle canopy, the patrol was lucky to return to base alive. With the perahus following close behind the advanced trackers, a scout sighted a Japanese soldier on the opposite bank with a raised rifle pointing directly towards the perahus. The Iban's shout must have unnerved the firer, for the round aimed at the European in the first perahu (Fred) missed its mark and lodged two inches behind his seat. (Standing joke with Fred. 'Rectum! No, bloody near killed him.') Our guerrillas immediately vacated the perahus, took to the dense confines of the riverside jungle and engaged the enemy. The Japanese sustained casualties and withdrew a little way from the river bank to consolidate, under unexpected automatic fire. Our automatic and semi-automatic weapons certainly could cause havoc against the enemy. As ammunition was short at our HQ, Fred now broke contact with this force and recovered thirteen of the perahus, the remaining four being destroyed and sunk preventing their recovery and use by the enemy.

The Last Entounter with Fujino

The patrol now commenced to return downriver to the junction of the Limbang, and then to our HQ at Kadu. Many a tale was told around the fireplaces that night of their good luck and fortune in not sustaining any casualties in this close encounter. One never knew in this environment 'Within' where or when it would happen.

The enemy crossed to the eastern side of the Madalam and started to slowly trek up into the interior heading for Kadu, cutting a new track as they advanced. We both reported down below the Madalam to the maximum penetration line of the 9th Australian Division, 2/17th Battalion, who had travelled upriver by LCI landing craft. They received our latest intelligence report and information relating to the contact with the Japanese. This unit was not permitted to travel east of this point to engage the enemy as the area was the direct responsibility allocated to us. The CO of the 2/17th did not believe that such a large party of the enemy existed and were proceeding upriver heading for the interior. As mere NCOs, our credibility was questioned. We were given a small amount of .303 ammunition, but not 9mm. They were restricted in doing so, but the lads of the 2/17th, when informed, were just itching for a contact with the advancing Japanese. Having walked down the northern side of the Limbang river, and for safety sake not using perahus, many of the light-skinned young maidens of the kampong accompanied the patrol. These young ladies of the Tabon tribe wanted to observe the many orang puteh soldiers in the LCIs, their first encounter with so many of us whites. They stood at the riverside and watched proceedings. Amazed and envious, young and old, Aussie soldiers watched these beautiful bare-breasted maidens, clad only in their special occasions sarongs, as they silently walked around the landing barges. Thankfully none of Fred's or my favourite expressions were voiced by them! How the Aussies envied us both, for we were subjected to many pertinent questions about our life in the interior. We received many packets of cigarettes from the lads, who were totally surprised to meet a Kiwi in their operational zone. Cigarettes were a luxury in the interior, and of late we had been smoking native weed rolled in a dried, split–banana leaf. Little did these men dream of the discomforts of being in the interior, living off the land and being denied many things, for if they had it might have changed their opinions substantially. Our position relating to food, ammunition and clothing, plus medical requirements, had been causing extreme anxiety.

Instructions in writing from the Divisional HQ, which were received from this LCI patrol on the 1 August, were that the Australians at Ukong were under a temporary ceasefire order and nothing was to be supplied to us. The surrender order had not yet been signed. In the event of being attacked by the Japanese we were to retire to the safety of downriver, and not be involved in a firefight. Once again we were in a situation upriver where we could not sustain a heavy attack against our guerrilla supporters and tribespeople. We were just Special Force coded personnel (mine, AKS 173) and dispensable, having been cut off from our own interior force and forward base at Morotai and Labuan Island. We had little clothing, food, ammunition, trade money and medication was nearly exhausted. We felt deserted, and the same feeling has remained ever since by extant members of our NZ group. Both of us agreed that we would never desert our guerrilla tribes people.

Allied aircraft were now appearing over the area containing this Japanese force, dropping pamphlets stating that a ceasefire was in operation, and when presenting this notice to the Allied forces when surrendering, they would be well treated. Nothing was heard from their commander, later identified as Captain Fujino of the Imperial Army. We decided to send four Ibans across the river to contact the Japanese, known as Fujino Tai. The pamphlets signed by the Emperor of Japan instructed that they surrender to the Allied forces. Our Iban carriers on delivering the documents were put to the sword, and a wounded native held by this group was sent back to us with a reply, 'Come out and fight you White B's'. Their officer was later to admit he was of the opinion that his Emperor would never surrender, thus the non-belief of the information contained in the pamphlets. Also he believed the news of an atomic bomb on his country was only an army ploy to force his surrender, plus the Emperor's chop (seal) appended thereto was not the correct one. Incoming reports from the roving Ponans (pigmy tribes people) in this dense jungle location, indicated that the Fujino Tai were moving up the Limbang to our immediate area of Rumah Kadu. Our request for the necessities of war by W/T – food, equipment etc. – was once again declined by our OC in the interior, who stated that the instructions from the 9th Division included the non-distribution of further arms and ammunition to his operatives.

The situation in this location was now horrendous. We could not turn our backs on these indigenous Tabon people who had supported the operation from the beginning of the mission to this point in time. Without them 'Z' would never have succeeded within Sarawak and Borneo. We both decided to remain with the headhunters, to lead and control them the best we could. I informed Base of our decision by W/T in cipher, that we would not retire to Ukong and the 2/17th Battalion HQ. I immediately signed off not waiting for a reply, completely shutting down the Boston W/T net. Hit and run tactics were now our order of the day, plus our denial programme and the movement of all tribal members not involved to a secure hiding place in this dense jungle. We would now take what arms and ammunition from the enemy which could be recovered when we sprung our ambushes. *Sumpitans* (blowpipes) were numerous and would be extremely useful under these circumstances.

With the enemy now in close proximity of our HQ at Rumah Kadu, we operatives decided that we would not sleep in the longhouse or W/T *sulap* for security reasons and selected a visitor's round *sulap*, one of several near the river bank. With the Limbang at its lowest level for many a day, we were of the opinion that the enemy would mount an attack from across the river that night. If it did eventuate, I was to dump the W/T and already weighted code book into a deep hole in the *sungei*. We would then split up and attack the engaging patrol from two directions with automatic fire, assembling any of our guerrillas who under cover of darkness had managed to retire in our direction. Outposts consiting of three headhunters were positioned at likely spots along the river bank after dark. If placed corectly, these could give the necessary warning in advance of the attack. That night it did not eventuate, but it was necessary in this situation to be prepared for anything. Movement could be heard directly opposite our area. Being totally exhausted we finally went to sleep in the company of our mutual friends the mosquitoes and ants, on the hard bamboo flooring of the open *sulap*. Oh, for a soft bed and not a sleeping mat on the ground or bamboo flooring.

Next morning at 1000 hrs when tuning the Boston W/T set for our prearranged listening hour (as it had been previously disconnected), I broke into a transmittion from one of the new outstations requesting under the 'Q' sign code for immediate use of this channel. It was denied to me, so in a high-speed transmission keyed in plain language to our Signals Officer, named Captain Gordon Richter who tried to pull his rank on me, I told him in plain outback language to conform with known practices and procedures as related in Army manuals under such conditions. My informative message left no doubt of my intentions at a later date if we survived this situation, for without help of an immediate air drop, we were both condemned to the earth and the Ibans would starve. This was now a pure case of being criminally neglected by our own people! The episode was reported to OC 'A' Division 'Z' controlled by Lieutenant Colonel Jumbo Courtney (GB, SOE), Labuan. This confrontation was to cost me substantially after the end of hostilities with the Japanese in our area. If we were disposed of by the enemy, perhaps the above information would be available to the NZDF Intelligence (see Top Secret document recorded).

After completing the sked and getting nowhere, we both decided to deceive the Fujino Kai into believing that a battalion of Australians were at Kadu. We put on a display in our best regimental voices, drilling an imaginary force in rifle drill and inspection, to broadcast to the ears and watchers of the Fujino Tai that they could expect heavy opposition in this area. They could not observe the action that was taking place on the hillside, as the flat communal area we were occupying was situated inland about 40 yds and approximately 50–60 ft above them. The headhunting Iban guerrillas and families enjoyed these tactics and helped with voices and stamping of feet around the kampong square. We set up two Brens overlooking the river, placing logs in position as protection for the gunners against incoming fire. The enemy could observe these items of warfare, plus guards in attendance ... Protruding from the log barriers were the muzzles of .303 rifles. Ibans patrolled this position, allowing themselves to be sighted behind these hurriedly constructed fortifications and not be subjected to direct fire from the enemy. These could be a major factor in the non-attack that night from across the fordable Limbang river. We had apparently fooled the Japanese. Confidence by all the Tabon tribespeople was certainly extended to us both on this occasion, and at night, with the guards scattered all around the river jungle-side, we celebrated our success in preventing a direct attack on the kampong, with a couple of half coconut shells of the native brew, Arak.

Major Toby Carter (NZer seconded to the British Forces in the SWPA and now a member of 'Z'), our next-door neighbour of Semut II situated in the Barum river district SE of Brunei, intercepted part of my plain language heated transmission with the interior base W/T HQ. Knowing the full extent of our position, as this force had broken out of his encirclement in the Barum, he totally disregarded all orders from the 9th Australian Division and AIB, not to supply us with the essentials of warfare. He immediately despatched two operatives and four carriers with a bounteous supply of ammunition plus a few luxuries for our group. This relief party encountered the rear protection group of the Japanese, engaging them, then skirted around their area without sustaining any casualties. The Iban tracker led them to a known contact area downriver, where they were observed and transported across to safety on the northern side.

On arrival at Kadu, we fed them and under cover of darkness took the group down the Limbang river and deposited them on a safe track for their return to Semut II. The turning point in this location had now been reached, and we owed Major Toby Carter our sincere appreciation for assistance. (Before Toby died at Rotorua (NZ) in August 1988, it was my pleasure to shake his hand and relate the events that had eventuated with this Japanese force.) The Australians still at the Ukong were not prepared to assist in any form, but were awaiting their surrender. We were still being requested to track the enemy and advise them, but if attacked not to engage, only retire and observe. As we had not experienced any tropical downpours for a considerable period of time in the upper Limbang, fording of the river upstream of Kadu would be easily completed at several points without too much effort. Scouts were now placed at all these known crossings for observation and protection against entry into the northern sector.

At this point in time the Ibans at Kadu decided to make a tribal offering to their gods in the customary manner, praying for rain. I was lucky to have been included in this ritual and witnessed the proceedings instituted many hundreds of years before by their headhunting fore-fathers. The *rumah besar* was cleared of all obstructions. Warlike instruments including guns, ammunition, *sumpitans*, poisonous darts and arrows, parangs and knives or anything that could cause or inflict damage to a person, were piled into the centre of the floor. This area was now declared sacred. All the fighting Ibans and their elderly tribes people, plus our own guerrillas, sat in a circle around the pile of weapons. The children and young girls were sent into the closed rooms and forbidden to enter the main area until permitted. Each woman, sitting and positioned at the rear of her family group or fireplace in the longhouse, now went to her area and produced a coconut half-shell filled with Arak (distilled rice wine) and gave it to the senior member of the sitting group (*penghulu*). After drinking a small portion of the contents it was passed on to the next warrior seated in the circle until it was all consumed (the inner circle contained only the fighting warriors). The next woman behind her family then carried out the same procedure as the first until all had done so.

At the conclusion of this ritual, all the participants were well and truly primed up, including Fred and myself. Then silence reigned for a little while as the group prayed to their 'rain god' in the heavens, seeking his help in their time of need. From a banana palm leaf one of the elders fashioned a perahu with outriggers and sail, filling the interior with jungle fruit, nuts and rice. We all now tramped down the jungle trail to the river bank in the darkness of the night, watched the small craft being launched and swing out into the current, then disappearing downriver. Quietness was the order of the night during these proceedings. Within twenty-four hours torrential rain that I had never encountered in the tropics during the previous two and a half years, just fell from the skies. The Limbang river, within a few hours, was uncrossable by foot. We could now recall our scouts and observers and increase our main holding guerrilla force. Just before nightfall on the second day the rain subsided so I accompanied the Ibans downriver in a large perahu to Rumah Badak, another Iban settlement. Contact by this means had not been possible over the last few weeks. Nothing happened, as the Japanese group had apparently gone inland away from the river for their own security after seeing and hearing the Allied aircraft in their immediate vicinity. Another Arak session now took place to celebrate and thank the 'Gods' for their timely help and deliverance on this occasion. Oh, my poor head. One never learns, but forgets and continues!

After the fermentation of the rice wine (Borak) the ingredients that were used to produce it were fed to the kampong pigs. To see these animals drunkenly running around the area was a sight to behold. The ingredients from the stills (large chinese dragon jars) were rapidly disposed of, and they fought among themselves, protecting their share of it. Arak was distilled from Borak, and had a high alcohol content with a kick like a mule. One never drank more than a half spirit glass at one session. If a larger portion was consumed, the taker would soon succumb to its potency. This latter effect was the downfall of many Japanese soldiers in the area. Large and small dragon jars were traded from the coast by the Chinese hundreds of years ago, carried into the interior on the shoulders of the purchasers to their destinations. Tribes people of the various kampongs were known in importance for the number of jars owned, and they were also used in their bridal agreements and settlements.

Further aircraft came into the area from Labuan Island, now only about an hour's flight time away, requesting the location of the retreating Japanese force, which was travelling slowly up the Limbang into the interior. The flight leader dropped a note requesting information to their whereabouts. The natives carried a lengthy log of wood onto the communal square, forming an arrowhead with other pieces of timber. This now pin-pointed the direction of the enemy. I used the bodies of the warriors in the prone position to form a figure 5, indicating the distance in kilometres to the enemy. The flight leader again approached the kampong square, flying extremely low to observe the signs, saw them and flew off in that direction. All the aircraft acknowledged our information with a rapid waggle of their wings and headed upriver. My Ibans, Muruts and Kelabits had never experienced or sighted such a show in their lives before, thinking we had arranged this especially for their benefit.

Fred, my partner, now ventured upstream to the small Rumah Bilong location twenty minutes upstream by perahu. I was left to contact Base by W/T, and then follow with my group. On completion of the sked, with Jon and Ranu carrying the Bren and ammunition, we followed the trail taken by my partner towards the Nipponese force. We had been travelling the jungle track for an hour, when an Iban suddenly appeared in front of the scouts. He was from the Madalam area and informed us that the Japanese were exceedingly close, and he was lucky to have avoided them. Questioned if he had seen a white man and his guerrillas, or heard weapons being discharged, he answered in the negative. A precarious situation was now developing, for my partner may have bypassed the enemy who would now arrive in the perahu dispersal area of Bilong before his return.

My immediate reaction to this information was to return to the river, hurriedly retracing our steps. The instruction to my lads was to take the sixteen-odd perahus to the opposite northern bank beside Bilong's *sulap*. For the first time in Borneo I took control of a perahu and single handed successfully crossed the swollen Limbang. The guerrillas paddled the remaining boats to safety. I climbed the high ground at this location for an observation point overlooking the deserted old longhouse on the southern side, then placed my patrol along the riverside in defensive positions. Fred's group was sighted about an hour later emerging from the jungle into the open area of the disused kampong. At the river bank they were astonished and astounded to observe that all their craft were missing. We immediately fired a shot to inform them that we were on the opposite bank and for the second time I paddled a perahu across the river, much to the pleasure of all the waiting guerrillas. I certainly made a few extra friends on this occasion. The group reported that they had not encountered the enemy, or seen the Iban who was now with us. The main trail heading to the interior in an easterly direction to Kepala Tamabo's Limbang area showed that it had not been used by troops or natives for a considerable time. We were now of the opinion that the Japanese were cutting a new track.

The following day the BBCAU (British Borneo Civil Administration Unit) situated at Labuan Island who had undertaken the responsibility of supplying the natives of Sarawak and BNB (Sabah) when the surrender

Natives in colourful dress.

Dancing floor in longhouse.

Souvenir distributed to troops in the Pacific on VJ Day.

of the Japanese forces was imminent, flew over the area. We were now to sight another first on this day, for a Catalina PBY appeared from downriver and commenced a free drop of food supplies from a height of 500 ft to the cleared grounds of the kampong below. Amazing! Everything was immediately collected and taken to a spare room in the longhouse. On inspection it was found that 80 per cent or more of the supplies were lost through damaged, broken or bulged tins. The rice in bags, being of a brown variety, was not well received by all the population, and only a small portion of the drop was recovered due to being spilt all over the ground.

I saw many small tins with the 'Planters Peanut' label attached. On opening one, to my utter surprise it contained fifty 'Old Gold' American cigarettes. Oh, the magnificence, the aroma emanating from that small container brought a sigh of relief and contact with the outside world for the first time in months – years it seemed! This was indeed heaven, for I had been smoking native weed and having a dry and sore throat in the mornings. Nothing was included in the drop from our unit, giving us further proof and notification that we were still abandoned and left to fend for ourselves. Clothing was now a little threadbare and jungle boots needed repairs. Socks were non-existent. Perhaps our 'superiors' at Labuan and the interior, sleeping in tents and consuming large amounts of army rations plus tea and coffee, were of the opinion that the wearing of a native loin cloth by the pair of us suited the situation.

It was now past 15 August, the surrender date. That morning dawned bright and clear – a typical cloudless tropical morning. For five years we had awaited this moment, but with the non-surrender of the Japanese in our area, we were of the opinion that we would not survive the ordeal, but if we did, we would certainly record it!

Further drops of pamphlets by air onto the Fujino Tai produced a negative result. The surrender had been in operation for two weeks., and our observation patrols were still being sniped at upriver. A W/T message from the interior informed us that a party from the Semut II area was following the Japanese trails through the Tutoh from Belait, with instructions to help us turn this force towards the east and into the arms of the 2/17th Australians, who still did not believe that this group was 500-plus.

Heading up into the interior from our HQ at Kadu, we entered the Ponan jungle domains. These were nomadic natives, who hunted and completely killed an area out, then moved to another location nearby. They consumed the flesh of their kills raw, were 4'6" to 5' tall, immensely shy and did not wear any clothing or loin cloths. Hunting was by *sumpitan* and poisonous darts, and they were experts in their jungle domains. When warriors from other tribes were venturing through these areas, visitors would observe the friendship ritual of cutting a twig and feather cutting one side of it, placing it in their hair or hat. We in this party were now friends and not on the warpath. On one occasion, noticing that the Ibans had a stranger with them, they came out into the open from the confines of the jungle to investigate. Most of the conversation was in sign language, for they only used tribal utterings which were not understood by my guerrillas. I was thoroughly inspected, skin colour pointed at, beard causing some laughter amongst the group. I provided a few cigarettes for them to smoke, which produced smiles and acknowledgement for the gift. The children also smoked. We were soon on our way again, silently probing and searching for movement in the jungle on the southern bank of the Limbang.

Feral game in our area was becoming scarce. Deer (*kejang*) in most cases had gone jungle-side due to the discharge of weapons in various areas. The kampong pigs, after they had been killed, tasted like the matter they fed on. Yuk! Wild pork when available once in awhile was totally appreciated., but without salt being available something was missing when consumed. Monkey was quite edible when roasted on the fireplaces. Snakes were oily but palatable – crocodile was reported to be delicious but never encountered by myself. Poultry was scrawny and fleshless. Many years later I was to find out from those who had lived on the interior strip that ducks were imported into their area to provide eggs and meat for local consumption.

Two days later our guerrilla patrol was attacked at a deserted kampong about four kilometres upriver. We managed to elude the Japanese, not engaging them in a firefight, or sustaining any casualties. The enemy were still keeping to the river bank and had not located the track leading to Tamabo's longhouse at Ulu Limbang. Late the following evening two advanced scouts arrived at Kadu with the information that the Nips were now camped right on the river bank, in a patch of totally cleared jungle. The group appeared to be relaxed, unconcerned and confident we would not approach them due to their numbers, and our continuous non-aggressiveness to engage them in a firefight.

We had not approached the Fujino Tai as directed or engaged them in a scrap. Now with the instructions received, we were to try and head them towards the coast, with the help of the Semut II patrol. This was an opportune time to execute this action. Having been attacked on four occasions, it was time for us to show our strength and not turn away. With luck they might turn westwards towards the coastline, and be contacted by the 2/17th and the 9th Division who now controlled the whole of Borneo. The 'brass hats' were not prepared to assist in any way relating to the interior. Pity a little plastic explosive could not be used to wake them up, for this mob continued their burning, raping and pillaging all the food supplies as it went. We were to learn later what the 'brass hats' stated about this force: 'Well, they have to eat and live'. One wonders about this statement! Our guerrillas should have been permitted to stop them.

The time had now arrived to give a little back to these advancing Japanese – we had had enough from them. The surrender had long been in force yet they were still disobeying it and killing the natives as they went. The Ibans, Kelabits, and Muruts sniffed a fight in the offing, noticing both our attitudes towards the previous instructions. They anticipated the order before it was given to prepare for a long night's walk. 'Mahu luan Japoon? Bagus – besok' (Want to fight Japanese? Good, tomorrow). All hell broke out within the *rumah besar*.

From his kampong room, Penghulu Kadu presented me with a carrying bamboo tube of rice cooked in coconut juice, with a vine sling attached for carrying from the shoulders. This he informed me, would be sufficient to support a person in the field for two or three days. The cooked rice, green in colour, jellied in form, would not spill out from its container if dropped or unbalanced and contained moisture which was essential.

With about 100 hungry guerrillas spoiling for a firefight, plus Jon and Ranu acting as Bren gun and ammo carriers, we walked all night up past Rumah Bilong into the *ulu*. Just before dawn we arrived at the spot where the scouts were awaiting our arrival. Under cover of the darkness the guerrillas were now located on the northern bank of the Limbang directly opposite the Japanese camp site. In the security of the jungle we now relaxed and consumed part of our rice from within the bamboo tubes which were approximately 18″ in length and 5″ in diameter. Smoking was totally prohibited, for being only 150 yards away from the enemy, a wind change could drift the odour across the intervening distance to them. This would certainly have cooked our goose if it had happened.

At dawn we moved into position along the river bank, with the overhanging jungle foliage protecting our approach from observers across the water. This location turned out to be to our advantage. From previous flooding of the Limbang, it had formed a ditch similar to a trench close to the bank – protection indeed for this encounter with 'Tojo's Sons from Heaven'. A pistol shot was fired just on daybreak by the Nips to awaken their troops, women nurses and camp followers who were classified as 'Comfort Girls' for the troops.

Fred had gone upriver about 30 yds to a slightly elevated area to observe the action, and I was to open the engagement when my guerrillas were settled in and ready to strike. A terrific chattering emanated from across the intervening space as the group of Japanese prepared to ready themselves for the coming day. Many were walking down to the river for morning ablutions, prior to having what food was available to them under these jungle conditions in the interior. I certainly held my breath and prayed that some of the light-fingered members of my group did not squeeze a trigger, and discharge a round prior to my use of the Bren. Time went slowly by, and you could feel the tension mounting amongst them all. I slowly eased back the Bren bolt and let it clatter forward, this to inform all of the group that action was imminent; hastily I pulled back the bolt reloading and slapped into place the magazine.

Reflex was immediate with the pulling of the Bren's trigger mechanism, and with a hundred vengeful indigenous headhunters' hearts pounding, the thunderous small arms plus automatic fire disturbed the cool, calm quietness of this tropical dawn. I emptied ten magazines during the short period of the ambush, stopping at times to control the fire of the natives, and changing the barrel of the Bren once. Hell, was it hot (I still have a burn mark on the left hand today to prove it). The action lasted about five minutes, but seemed a lifetime. We expended about a thousand rounds of various types of ammunition (thanks to Toby Carter's contribution). Incoming fire was slight, as the enemy were unable to locate our exact positions.

One smiling, happy, old headhunter stood up beside me, indicating with his hands the height above my head that a projectile had come singing by. They had no fear of anything during a firefight, and laughed and joked with me all the time. Perhaps they thought that we whites needed some encouragement whilst in action, but I had recently been informed that the youngest member (twenty years old) of my eight-member NZ group into Australia had been killed. He had parachuted into Balikpapan, Semoi area, was captured, tortured and beheaded. As I pulled the trigger on my LMG I thought, 'This is for young Ernie', and let fly with a whole magazine.

Fred arrived from his observation post, and travelled to us under the protection of the rear thick confines of the area's tropical forest, suggesting that we vacate immediately before we got roasted. Rumah Badak, Bilong, Kadu and our own guerrillas had given their all, for the four brothers that had been executed by the Fujino Tai. An eye for an eye was the tribal law. Being the last to leave and with Jon and my other trusty friend Ranu, we heard the Japanese climbing the trees across the river searching for us. I set up the Bren again, deciding to give these types over the river one more tickle up. The rest of our force now being in the protection of the jungle a little to the rear, we sprayed the area from which the voices were coming. One of the enemy who was tree-bound, screamed when we fired directly at him. The three of us now smartly sought the protection of the rear jungle cover. The rest of the attacking party had awaited our arrival a little downriver, then proceeded on the track leading back to Rumah Kadu and Bilong.

On arrival at our base Fred and I discussed the action, and what he had seen from the OP in advance of the ambush position. 'On the release of the Bren's bolt warning the natives of immediate action, deadly silence reigned from the direction of the opposite bank. It was only one second-plus, but you could have heard a pin drop. With the opening salvo the Nips broke into a rush for the nearest protection of the Jungle.' They had been completely taken by surprise, for the first time en-countering action in Borneo. Asked if he had got many rounds away, as the enemy were in the open directly in front of the OP, he replied that he had withheld as he did not want to put himself at risk!

The sequel to this encounter with the Japanese was that under cover of night, the Ibans crossed the river by perahu downstream from the target and inspected the area. Dead were seen scattered in the jungle near the river; one Malay woman who was wounded and abandoned by the enemy was recovered.

On returning to the main longhouse downriver after the attack on the Fujino Tai, we all rested for part of the afternoon, then cleaned and overhauled all equipment used. We both decided to remain here for the night and sleep in the main communal section on the bamboo structures. About 2100 hrs the returning Iban party entered the front of the longhouse by the steps carrying the wounded Malay woman on the back of one member. The commotion that eventually awoke us both was the shouting of 'Japoon, Japoon!' We immediately vacated our sleeping benches and quickly donned our fighting equipment and jungle boots from above our heads. From the clamour that was eventuating directly in front of us in semi-darkness, both of us formed the opinion that the Japanese had crossed the river and were deadly intent to extract a reprisal on those who had dared to ambush their party. Fred said, 'I knew that this would happen some time. We should have taken precautions and posted sentries around the perimeters of the kampong and the rock pass into the area from Bilong upriver.' We soon found an answer to the commotion, for it taught us a hasty lesson in security under such conditions.

When questioning the Malay woman, we gained the information that many of the enemy were wounded or had been killed. The attack was totally unexpected and our scouts had not been observed across the river. I inspected the wound on her leg and dressed it. In our hands she must have been relaxed and at ease, for she asked for a meal of chicken and rice. We now learned the full particulars of the Fujino Tai, their strength, arms, ammunition, food, medical and woman followers, the exact information that the AIF downriver had previously received and disbelieved.

I coded this action report and transmitted it to Base HQ at the airstrip, learning later that this information was well received there. As Major Harrisson was at Labuan Island the message was forwarded

KENYATAAN

Ashkar-ashkar Kerajaan Nippon memberi tahu ia-itu semua orang-orang yang ada tinggal di-dalam daerah-daerah yang sudah di-dudukki oleh ashkar-ashkar Nippon mahu-lah menurut larangan-larangan yang tersebut di-bawah ini :—

(1) Berpakat atau mangasut-asut orang-orang menyuroh buat derhaka kapada Ashkar-ashkar Nippon.

(2) Berkerja menchari rahasia yang berkenaan dengan hal ihwal ashkar-ashkar Nippon.

(3) Merosakkan atau menyebabkan ka-hilangan kapada tempat-tempat yang ada keluar minyak, lombong-lombong, dan ladang-ladang yang ada termasok segala harta benda dan barang-barang keluaran daripada tempat-tempat yang tersebut yang ada sangat berguna sekali.

(4) Merosakkan atau memotong perkakas-perkakas telephone, telegraph atau kereta api ; dan juga menutop jalan-jalan raya, terusan-terusan ayer atau-pun jalan-jalanan di-laut yang berguna kapada ashkar-ashkar ia-itu oleh sebab ka-rasokkan yang akan di-lakukan itu boleh mengganggu ka-senangan fasal jalan mengirim atau mengantar perkhabaran atau lain-lain-nya pada masa di-dalam kuasaan Nippon.

(5) Membuat susah kapada pegawei-pegawei, ashkar-ashkar dan orang-orang priman yang ada berkerja dengan ashkar-ashkar Nippon, dan juga menchuri atau mengasi rosak senjata-senjata dan peluru-peluru yang di-punya-I oleh ashkar-ashkar Nippon.

(6) Mengasi tabor barang-barang yang ada rachun atau-pun ulat-ulat yang membawa rachun dengan niat hendak mengasi rosak kapada ashkar-ashkar Nippon.

(7) Menyebabkan orang-orang menjadi haru-biru atau mengachau hal perniagaan sa-hingga boleh jadi tidak tentu atau mengambil ka-untongan berlebih-lebih.

(8) Menutop jalan memberi ka-senangan fasal barang tumboh-tumbohan dan juga fasal mengeluarkan barang-barang tumbohan yang berlainan dengan maksud Penguasa-penguasa Nippon.

(9) Menchuba hendak membuat atau-pun membikin sa-barang perkerjaan yang akan merosakkan ka-selamatan ashkar-ashkar Nippon.

(10) Berpakat atau-pun menolong atau mengasut di-dalam apa-apa perkerjaan yang saperti sudah di-sebutkan di-atas ini.

Hukuman-nya kapada sa-siapa yang sudah melanggar atoran-atoran yang sudah di-sebutkan di-atas ini ia-lah HUKUM MATI atau KENA HUKUM YANG BERAT SEKALI oleh MARTIAL LAW.

THE COMMANDER OF THE IMPERIAL JAPANESE ARMY FORCES.

PROCLAMATION

The Imperial Japanese Army hereafter call the strict attention of the citizens or residents in those districts occupied by the Japanese Forces to observe the following restrictions :

(1) To plot or excite a rebellion among the people against the Japanese Forces.

(2) To engage in espionage concerning the movements of the Japanese Forces.

(3) To demolish or cause any loss whatsoever to oil-fields, mines, farms including their annexed property and resources of any importance or description.

(4) To destroy or cut off the equipment of the telephone, telegraph or railway systems and to block up the passage of roads, canals and sea-routes of military use, thus disturbing the smoothness of communication and traffic under Japanese control.

(5) To do injury or harm to officers, soldiers and civilians attached to the Japanese Forces, and to steal or damage the ammunitions or munitions possessed by the Japanese Forces.

(6) To spread poisonous stuffs or bacterium with the purpose of inflicting damage to the Japanese Forces.

(7) To cause public confusion, to throw the economic and financial circles into disorder, or to make excessive or un justifiable profits.

(8) To obstruct the smooth production and circulation of commodities contrary to the policy of the Japanese Authorities.

(9) To commit or attempt any actions that may menace in any manner the safety of the Japanese Forces.

(10) To plot, aid or incite any such activity as set forth in the above mentioned sections.

Any violation of the afore-mentioned provisions is liable to DEATH or SEVERE PUNISHMENT by MARTIAL LAW.

THE COMMANDER OF THE IMPERIAL JAPANESE ARMY FORCES

佈告

西海州長官

西海州居住之華僑，印度人，馬尼拉人，白人及其混血兒，必須在其所住之家宅，照左列方式貼一氏名票：

一、氏名票得使用木板及白紙，該木（或紙）之廣大約二十珊（即約八吋）之標準，每名直寫以一珊（即約半寸）爲標準，在姓名之橫面，並須寫馬來語。

二、氏名票由家主或包租人爲首，順序而至於子女，傭人，使女，或店員，記明其姓名，性別，年齡於氏名票之上。

三、該氏名票須貼於其居住家宅顯明之處。如一家之內，有數戶間居者，則各戶須各寫其氏名票，（濶度相同）在同一地點，順序貼之。

四、氏名票之內容，如有異動時，例如出生與死亡及移居之亦，但此必須通知鄰組長及向附近之警察署訂正方可。

本佈告即日施行，亞庇市內在十日期間內，即須完結。其他各地域之終結日期，由各縣知事加以通知。

如有違犯本佈告所定者，或有異動時怠於通知者，則必受責罰。

本佈告所言「氏名票」之方式，如有不明者，可向縣顧，郡顧及各警察署詢問，彼等當加以說明。

昭和十八年十一月八日

KENYATAAN.

Orang2 yang tinggal di-dalam Jajahan Pantai Batat, ia-lah bangsa2: China, India, Manila, European dan juga peranakan bangsa2 yang tersebut, mau-lah taroh satu Papan Nama (sign board) di-rumah tempat tinggal masing2 saperti di-nyatakan di-bawah ini:—

(1) Papan Nama mau-lah di-buat daripada kayu atau kertas yang puteh, besar-nya: panjang 8 inchi lebar-nya ka-bawah tiap2 sa-orang kurang lebeh ½ inchi dan nama2 itu di-tuliskan dengan tulisan Rumi.

(2) Di-atas Papan Nama itu hendak-lah di-tuliskan: ketua rumah, bini, anak, saudara (sebutkan perhubongan-nya) dan orang2 gaji, kemudian nama masing2, laki2 atau perampuan dan umor, menurut susunan saperti di-bawah:—

KETUA RUMAH	(NAMA).....................LAKI/PERAMPUAN		UMOR
Bini	?	?	?
Anak	?	?	?
Saudara (chuchu, abang dll.)	?	?	?
Boy	?	?	?
Babu	?	?	?

(3) Papan Nama itu hendak-lah di-lekatkan di-dinding hadapan rumah, terutama sa-kali letak-nya pada tempat yang lebeh senang kelihatan. Di-dalam sa-buah rumah jikalau ada lebeh daripada satu family tinggal, maka papan Nama-nya hendak-lah di-susun bertingkat, satu family satu Papan Nama.

(4) Jikalau ahli2 isi rumah ada perubahan-nya, mithal-nya beranak, mati atau mengambil orang2 baharu dan sa-bagai-nya, hendak-lah hal ini di-beri tau kapada Ketua Kampong atau Ketua Kedai, kemudian baharu di-hadapkan pada Police Station, lepas itu baharu-lah kenyataan di-Papan Nama itu boleh di-ubahkan.

Pekerjaan ini mesti-lah di-buat dengan sa-berapa lekas-nya, dan bagi orang2 yang tinggal di-Bandar Api mesti membuat-nya di-dalam tempoh 10 hari daripada kenyataan ini di-keluarkan.

Di-lain2 Ken yang lain daripada Api Ken, ketetapan tempoh2 membuat-nya akan di-putuskan oleh Kenchiji masing2.

Barang siapa melanggar akan Undang-Undang ini, ia-itu saperti tidak mau atau malas menulis Papan Nama-nya, atau pun tidak mau atau malas memberi tahu akan perubahan ahli2 isi rumah-nya, akan terkena denda. Form Pepereksaan ahli2 Rumah di-dalam Undang-Undang ini telah di-serahkan kapada Kencho (ketua pejabat), Guncho dan Police Station, maka orang2 semua boleh dapat tahu lebeh terang daripada tuan2 yang tersebut.

to that destination, and the 9th Div AIF was given information of the action. The 'brass hats' at HQ considered the action as a breach of the 'cease fire' order that was in operation, though the Fujino Tai were killing, raping, burning and destroying everything as they went through the various areas directly in their path, on their forced march into the interior of Sarawak. Our 2 i/c of Semut I was ordered by 9th Division, who were now in control of the whole of Borneo, to enter our area of the Limbang and establish just what the situation was and report back to them. Two days later he arrived at Rumah Kadu by perahu from the coast, stayed the night and in the early dawn commenced his trip up into the Ulu Limbang river area. We warned him of what was waiting for him.

He returned a few hours later, stating that he and the crew members of the perahu were lucky to be alive, for they were fired upon by a LMG and rifle fire. Being close to shore on the opposite side of the river from the enemy, all in the perahu dived overboard and took refuge in the riverside jungle cover. During this contact with the Japanese he lost his automatic in the river. 'I can see just what you are up against. They are in a nasty mood,' he stated. Under cover of darkness he left for the coast and Divisional HQ to report his findings and contact with the enemy. At this stage the Semut II group had not arrived in the immediate area from Belait and via the Tutoh. Enemy movement was observed and heard from across the river from Rumah Kadu, giving us an indication that they were trying to cross the swollen river to engage and encircle our position. A new station answered my next sked transmission to the interior, giving my strength of receipt at that station as QSA-5. I immediately answered and requested identification with the old WU operator's talk. The reply was 'Base Labuan, have urgent message for you in P/L' (My 10×10 private code was not held by them). They required a helping hand as the AIF downriver at Ukong could not receive or transmit any messages by W/T to and from Base at Labuan. Why? They would certainly have more efficient and powerful transceivers than our little organisation.

The message in plain language read as follows, 'Lieutenant X? [I have forgotten his name] and two perahu loads of captured Japanese are on their way up the Limbang to contact the enemy force moving into the interior. You will advise them to return to base immediately, as the enemy will now be contacted by "Z" people in the interior.' This message was received in a severe thunderstorm in our immediate vicinity, and one that I will always remember. With the interference by lightning and thunderclaps, it was indeed a session with the rise and fall of incoming signal strength. I acknowledged receipt of the message with CU–LTR. It is amazing to record that after four or five years of continually transmitting and receiving coded messages in figures, taking one in straight plain language really shocks the old memory and concentration. Ten figures against twenty-six of the alphabet. Rusty – I'll say. Must be the humidity? Dampness!

Ten hours later, a strange sight appeared on our doorstep. My guerrillas had been informed of what to expect, and had fully armed themselves, expecting trouble from these well-dressed, well-fed Japanese in their native perahus. I was immediately called to the river bank when they were first sighted and I signalled the Lieutenant in the middle of the first boat to pull ashore beside the kampong. I repeated the message to him, and was immediately requested that the order be given to him in writing before they would leave. This officer was advised verbally that written orders were not the order of the day in jungle locations, and that he should comply. He was also instructed that this area was under our control not his. Seeing the hostile appearance of the Ibans and the arrival of Jon and Ranu with my Bren, the Nips in the perahus armed with British SMLE .303s became a little jumpy. The Australian officer now indicated to them to turn about and head downriver. Three fully laden perahus with armed Dyaks and Ibans accompanied them out of their territory. I could read the guerrillas' minds. 'Why do the orang puteh fraternise with the hated Japoon – they armed them after the war was over, but would not do the same for us?' An exceptionally good comment this!

Next day an unexpected development occurred at Kadu. The natives noticed a Japanese on the opposite bank of the river waving a pamphlet that had been dropped by RAAF aircraft in the area a few days earlier. This document stated in Japanese that the bearer would be given food when surrendering to the AIF. A small three-man perahu was sent across the river as a security measure if the enemy were trying to lure us across. It was not the case, for the perahu returned with a surrendering Nip. Not a normal practice during the war! He had become detached from his unit and the main Fujino Tai. On finding one of the pamphlets near the river, he decided to surrender for he was completely lost and without food. We could not obtain much information from him, as he spoke little Malay nor understood English.

That afternoon a thunderstorm of great intensity struck the kampong area. If you have ever encountered a fireball you will fully appreciate what happened. With the storm directly above, the electrical display was dangerous. A fireball struck the aerial which was still connected to the Boston, proceeded to slowly move along the wire to the lead-in, then halfway down, fizzling like a fireworks sparkler, it terminated its downward path. From that point in time all my efforts to transmit or receive were totally unsuccessful. I came to the hurried conclusion on inspecting the set, that the operating frequency crystal was burnt out plus the generator. It was now an unserviceable unit, worthless! Two days later a twin-engined aircraft appeared overhead, and released a storpedo from 1,000 ft. The green chute failed to open and crashed into the jungle beside the longhouse, half a mile away. After recovery by our tribes people, I unpacked its contents which included an ATR 4 radio. Everything was totally destroyed except the instruction on paper which read, 'Please get on the air'. A physical impossibility with this lot of junk. Base must have realised that I had lost contact because of the storm we had encountered in the interior.

Just prior to our loss of communications, we signalled base at Ba Kelalan to stop our overland resupply of stores, weaponry, ammunition and radio equipment (if they kept their promise to do so) rather than airdrop. This method of supply would now come in direct contact with the Fujino Tai mob. The reply was forthcoming informing us that this was impossible as the supply group was now out of range and could not be contacted. We had been advised just a few days earlier that we were finally going to get help, but had not been given any idea of when and by what method. This signal was signed by a new member of the group at Belawit airstrip as 2 i/c. Major Harrisson was now out of the area and situated at Labuan Island. We were later to learn that the whole party was totally wiped out in an ambush, and the Japanese were supplemented with these supplies including medical. Usop, one of our guerrillas, was lost in this action. What a tragic blunder trying to supply this outstation through enemy lines, when an air drop was only an hour plus away. This attempt was the first since our arrival in the Limbang area.

Lieutenant Middleton now arrived from the Semut II area via the Tutoh and Madalam rivers, having followed the Japanese tracks which had originated from their location at Labi, inland from Miri and Marudi on the Barum river HQ. This Nippon group had travelled slowly through the area to our defensive position. At this point in time, the enemy had delegated part of their force to try and encircle Rumah Kadu for reprisal reasons, after being attacked and receiving their first baptism of warfare and casualties within Borneo. On 22 September a party of forty detected by our forward patrol, managed to cross the Limbang and were travelling through dense virgin jungle in the direction of Kadu. It would take them three days. They never arrived at our location, so we presumed they had become lost in transit or continued their trek into the interior.

On 25 September, Lieutenant Middleton and I went downstream by perahu accompanied by six of our guerrillas to pick up another member of his party from Rumah Badak. Having travelled half the way downstream, the natives at Rumah Lasong contacted us, stating that thirty or forty odd Nips were on the opposite bank of the river near them. They appeared to be completing the encirclement of Kadu. We all disembarked and travelled through the secondary growth unobserved, and attacked the enemy party with automatic fire. After a rapid engagement they disengaged and withdrew into the jungle interior. The firefight was not to their liking – bolt-action rifles against our modern weapons.

After picking up our operative at Badak, we commenced the return journey upstream to Kadu. Near the confluence of the Limbang and Madalam rivers we were in a shallow part of the estuary when we were fired on by the enemy again. Luck was certainly with us this day, for we were caught in the open. Being close to a small island we beached the perahu on the protected northern side, and engaged the Japanese for the second time that day. Apparently this party had in their possession Australian .303 SMLE rifles captured at Singapore, plus grenade cup dischargers. We came under fire from these, and one grenade slightly wounded Corporal Graham on the hand and myself a slight cut above the left eye, caused by a piece of wood or stone. We gave these Nips hell with heaps to worry about with our semi and automatic weapons. I had the pleasure to see one cartwheel from the trees when concentrating on one firing position. We were of the opinion we had accounted for five of the enemy who soon retired into the depths of the jungle for protection. We continued on our way home, and further upriver became the target once more of a small group. Three times in one day is three times too many to experience being caught out in the open. Why we did not sustain any casualties cannot be answered. Perhaps we had someone special on our side?

My operative partner Fred was experiencing a little traumatic condition since the Sungei Madalam escapade, and with this encounter and Lieutenant Middleton's takeover from him in the Limbang, a form of mental psychosis developed rapidly. At the end of the war he was returned to Australia on the hospital ship *Manunda*, entering the repat hospital there for psychiatry treatment, and was unlucky to have it repeated during his lifetime. This war had been over since the signing of the 'surrender' treaty on 15 August, and I was now of the opinion I would never leave Borneo.

The small Japanese patrols now disappeared into the interior and headed towards their main Fujino Tai group upriver heading further into the *ulu* of Sarawak, and in the near future were to become a nuisance 'Within'. Travelling over the same route that I had advanced into the Limbang, they duly reached Long Belayu undetected and headed for the rich harvest area of Belawit and Bawang Valley – our HQ and airstrip. Lieutenant Frank Leckie (a member who was in my party from NZ) and Flight Lieutenant Paul Bartrum (AIF), the latter now our 2 i/c whilst Major Harrisson was in Labuan, were just preparing to leave for Lawas and return to base at Labuan with the last party as instructed by 9th Australian Division who now had the total control of Borneo. They had cleared up the area and collected most of the arms and equipment, as the war had officially been over since mid-August.

It was now 22 October, and the Fujino Tai had not been sighted since leaving the Limbang on 26 September. On this day a native hunter arrived at HQ stating that he had encountered a large Japanese party slowly making their way towards Long Belayu. Frank hurriedly reissued arms and ammunition to the local guerrilla force at Belawit, and headed for the area to set up an ambush. The enemy walked into this area and fired on the natives, but received the worst of the argument when the tribes people replied killing five of them. They stayed in this area overnight, unsuspecting that a reception was awaiting them once they left the kampong. Next morning the trap was sprung after all the Fujino Tai emerged out into the open valley heading for Ba Kelalan. Sulalong, one of our guerrillas handling the Bren, killed many with the opening burst. The Nips retreated to the confines of Ba Kelalan to lick their wounds, taking with them their dead and wounded. The guerrillas witnessed the Japanese dispose of their deceased members by cremation.

Major Harrisson who had been co-opted by the 9th Australian Division to re-enter Borneo with two Japanese envoys to contact this force, made a hurried trip into the interior from Lawas on the coast accompanied by many armed Iban warriors. With the delayed departure from Long Belayu of the Japanese, Harrisson's surrender party finally reached the outskirts of the ambush area. The envoy was sent in to contact Captain Fujino, who initially refused to negotiate with his own people. He finally did so, after being informed by his 2 i/c that he knew the bearer of the document from General Masao Baba to immediately surrender. This happened on 28 October 1945.

I was ordered out of the Limbang on 26 September, whilst my operative 'partner in crime' remained in the area to collect all the weapons, leaving only a few .303 rifles for Penghulu Kadu to use for his tribespeople, much to his disgust. Lieutenant Middleton, from the Semut II area, now returned via the Tutoh and Madalam to the Barum on 27 September, taking only enough rations for one day.

On my downward trip to the coast by perahu I was instructed to call at the HQ of 2/17th Battalion AIF at Ukong and report to Lieutenant Colonel Lawrence. The reason given was to try and assist the W/T section there regarding their failure to transmit or receive from this location. The equipment at this battalion was exceedingly sophisticated, equivalent to a small ZB station in NZ, its performance 'Nil'. The main features of their failure seemed attributable to aerial direction, faulty connections and climatic conditioning of their equipment not being sealed or tropical proofed. I was firstly greeted on arrival by perahu with, 'Oh! Another one of those "headhunters" from upriver?' I gave as good as I received from the junior officer that I first encountered. My reply shook him a little, for I explained in broad Kiwi language that I was not an Australian but one of five NZ Special Force personnel serving within Sarawak interior, and did not appreciate his comments. As I was the first NZer they had encountered in the SWPA, I was well treated after this encounter. One of our Boston MkIIIs could have served them well, for it had a range of over 3,000 miles and it was but 50 miles to Labuan Island.

The 'Z' workboat arrived at the 2/17th bamboo jetty in the afternoon of the 27th, and immediately proceeded downriver to the coastal town of Limbang. A fresh meal had been cooked by the unit at Labuan and kept fresh in the boat's refrigerator. After heating, I thoroughly enjoyed a sumptuous banquet, a taste of things to come! I had at last made it away from the confines of the jungle, ants, mosquitoes, leeches, pythons and the many awaiting diseases of this heavily infected island of Borneo. I would certainly miss my friends, the indigenous peoples of the interior, when returning to the future of modern-day life. Within minutes of finishing the meal, I immediately lost all overboard as my young stomach rebelled at the intake of high-class food. Hell, rice was better, no reaction! It was going to take a little while to re-accustom oneself to these new conditions, even if it was only normal army food.

I arrived late in the afternoon at Labuan Island in the Bay of Brunei by the workboat, presented the skipper with my 'coolie' hat that Penghulu Kadu had given to me and was immediately whisked off for debriefing at 'Z' Special HQ. OC 'A' Division, Lieutenant Colonel Jumbo Courtney, conducted the interview; every phase of my action in the interior was discussed including the W/T session, plus the report I had filed on receiving the coded message to Sergeant Bill Nibbs stating 'Kill or be killed'. I was to pay for the latter severely, for Major Harrisson totally denied sending it, therefore no recommendations were received for this part of my army service whilst attached to SOA. In later years, after being cleared by the Official Secrets Act many of the operatives recorded the same in their manuscripts, including three members' statements that they were going to liquidate him for his treatment 'Within'! After interrogation I was taken to the Australian General Hospital for a complete check-up including the endemic dysentery after-effects. I had an enjoyable three days in hospital plus many great showers. The thought of things to come. Oh, to become human again.

On returning to our HQ camp I was informed that information from NZ confirmed that I had completed three years of active service, and under the instruction just issued to all units, was to be returned to Australia. Within forty-eight hours of island-hopping I duly arrived in Melbourne and was taken to 39 Akland Street and thence to Mt Martha to collect my NZ army kit bag. I was given two weeks leave and upon the arrival of the English aircraft carrier in Sydney, the *Indefatigable*, I travelled by train to connect with it prior to its departure for New Zealand. There were five army personnel boarding, and our accommodation was on the first aircraft flight deck. We slung a hammock between two supports and prepared for the journey, arriving in home waters after about three days and just before Christmas. The carrier was approached off the lighthouse on Rangitoto Island by a pilot launch from Auckland, which off-loaded four people onto it. A call came over the loudspeaker system that all NZ personnel were to report to the flight deck immediately. Awaiting our arrival were three well-dressed civilians from the RSA, Army – and none other than Tom Skinner. He was introduced to us all and he took me aside, saying that my parents were on the dockside awaiting my arrival. I was to be driven home to Hamilton, and never enter a military camp again. Great news! I was finally discharged in March 1946, after spending several unwanted trips to hospital with malaria. This malady continued for another twelve months off and on, until my doctor friend contacted 'Z' in Australia, who forwarded my request for medical assistance to Darwin. From there I was sent a new drug which was being tested – 'Paludrine' – and I became a guinea pig taking such medication. Reaction to this – 100 per cent effectiveness, but in the meantime a medical board pronounced that I was 'medically unfit' to resume duty in my vacated government position prior to entering the Army Service!

Epilogue

My encounter with the Ibans, Dayaks, Dusans, Ponans, Kelabits, Tagals, Muruts and the Orang Sungai people of Borneo, as trackers, friends, and natural guerrilla fighters has given me the greatest experience of my life. Money could not buy it. My knowledge of their customs, loyalty and community working togetherness leaves me with the thought that they could teach us outsiders many things that we could put into practice in this modern world we live in.

We, the surviving members of Special Operations Australia, cover named 'Z' Special Unit and Services Reconnaissance Department, have been sadly disillusioned on receiving and reading our New Zealand Army base records. Nothing has ever been recorded on these files indicating our volunteer service to the Special Forces, or seconding to the Australian Army. The following entries on my records relate to the above: 'Re-embarked 12/44 – No unit stated. Returned to NZ ex leave Australia. Disembarked NZ 12/45.' Completely devoid of any information between these two periods. One small entry at the end of the service record will need some explaining in the years to come. 'Para pay nine pounds six shillings'.

Australia did not issue a service medal for the Borneo operations, but in 1989 'Z' Special Unit advised the extant Kiwis that they were entitled to receive the 'Front-Line Medal' for services in Borneo, by operating in the enemy-occupied zones. This medal was struck by the 2/12th Australian Infantry Battalion, and approval was given to 'Z' to recommend members to receive this on the basis of being 'further in front' of them. Sixty-two were issued to SOA – three coming to New Zealand (George Edlin, Invercargill, Bob Tapper, Pukekohe and myself).

Before leaving the Limbang river in Borneo, I was summoned to the main room of Rumah Kadu to partake of a farewell meal with Penghulu Kadu. This consisted of boiled rice and Arak. The latter I drank freely, but made a resolution immediately afterwards, 'Never, never ever touch a drop of rice for the rest of my lifetime!' For the next thirty-odd years I did exactly that. To my friendly young companion and 'brother warrior' Jon of Kelabit parentage, who showed me his loyalty, bravery and willingness to be in my company at all times and in dangerous circumstances, I presented him with my trusty old US carbine, web-gear, ammunition and magazines, plus all the army gear I possessed, including a blanket. I also wrote a letter addressed 'To whom it may concern', giving a reference for his use in years to come. I certainly hope he used it and did well!

I came into Borneo with nothing and did the same going out, with the exception that I carried a couple of souvenirs to remind me of this adventure – not that I needed the latter. This manuscript may be read in the years to come, and may inform the public of New Zealand that our group of twenty-two seconded to the AIF did really exist, and was the first Para Commando NZ Unit to have some members chute into enemy-held territory, before the formation of the NZ SAS in the mid-1950s.

Nothing has ever been released by the Government or the NZDF that such a group existed in the Second World War. In 1990 the *NZ Herald* published a full-page report that I released, plus action photographs from the operations. Further coverage in 1990 was given by

IN BRIEF 1945

The dates shown in these diaries are those on which the news referred to was first published in New Zealand, and are not necessarily the actual dates upon which the events themselves took place. Events have been listed up to the latest practicable date before publication. Those which took place after the last date shown will be tabulated in the next issue.

JUNE, 1945

June 1—British intervene in Franco-Levant unrest. Americans take Shuri, Okinawa (south of Japan). New war criminal list of 1000 names compiled.

June 2—Four hundred and fifty Superforts raid Osaka (Japan). U.S. doubling army. British restore order in the Levant.

June 3-4—French withdraw from Levant under British supervision.

June 5—Allies assault Borneo. Japs attempt to escape from Okinawa in small boats.

June 6—Allies announce German zones ; controlled by Britain, Russia, France and U.S. Goering to be tried as a war criminal.

June 7—Moscow announces Demarcation Zone, about half of Germany under Russian control. Japanese abandon big towns on China coast.

June 8—France proposes Five Power talks to settle Levant dispute. Superforts raid Osaka.

June 9—Japs trapped in South-East Asia corridor. Petain's trial in progress

June 10-11—French refuse leave Aosta Valley (Italy). Allied generals meet at Frankfurt-on-Oder. Australians advance on Bougainville (Solomons),

June 12—Australians take town and airfield on Labuan Island and land in Borneo. Nine killed in Damascus ; Levant position deteriorates.

June 13-15—General Eisenhower accorded Freedom of London. Australians take Muara Island and Brunei town and airstrip in eight-mile advance (Borneo).

June 16—Timbalai airstrip taken by Australians (Borneo). British repulse Japs east of Prome (Burma). Ribbentrop captured in Hamburg.

June 17-18—Allied representatives invited to Poles' trial in Moscow. Tarakan Island captured (Dutch Borneo).

June 19—Trial of 16 Poles begins, 15 plead guilty. William Joyce (Lord Haw Haw) charged with treason. Lieutenant-General Buckner killed on Okinawa. Chinese take Wenchow.

June 20—Superforts bomb Shizouka, Toyohashi and Fukuoka (Japan). General Eisenhower reaches New York.

June 21—Chinese three miles from Liuchow. Two thousand Japs holding out on Okinawa.

June 22—Okinawa falls to Americans. Trial of Poles ends ; General Okulicki sentenced to 10 years imprisonment. British ships repulse Jap suicide planes.

June 23—Chinese at gates of Liuchow. Capture of Aparri, last Jap-held port on Luzon (Phillipines). Superforts raid Kure (Japan).

June 24-25—Indians cross River Slelanguchaung (Burma). H.M.A.S. *Australia* damaged by suicide planes. Graziani on trial for collaboration and treason.

June 26—Australians nearing Sarawak oilfields (Borneo). Chinese approach Kweilin.

June 27—President Truman reaches San Francisco for World Peace Conference. Superforts raid Nagoya, Osaka, Akashi and Gifu (Japan). Australians take Mt. Tazaki (New Guinea) and Miri oilfields, 300 wells (Borneo).

June 28-29—Darnand, ex-Vichyite, captured by British, handed over to French.

June 30—Americans land on Kume Island (west of Okinawa). Superforts attack Kudamatsu oil refinery (Japan). Chinese take main Liuchow airfield.

The events of June 1945.

EDITION — *FREE TO THE TROOP* — **ABLE TOPS**

Daily By The Australian Military Forces Abroad — Mon., 17 September 1945

Princess Elizabeth Thrown By Horse

LONDON, Sun.—Princess Elizabeth, heir presumptive to the Throne, was thrown from her horse recently, says a statement issued from Buckingham Palace. She severely bruised both legs but her injuries were not serious. She has been ordered to rest.

Appalling PW Death Toll In Borneo

LABUAN, Sun.—The tragic story of Australian and British PWs at Sandakan (NE Borneo) shows that as malnutrition and disease took toll the mortality rate gained appalling momentum.

In October, 1944, there were only 10 deaths, but the total rose progressively each month to 334 in March—or more than 10 a day.

The fate of Allied PWs in the Kuching area alone is believed to be: Dead, 2808; missing (probably dead), 382; alive 1387. It is estimated that altogether there were from 4590 to 4670 PWs in NE Borneo.

Three death marches were ordered by the Japanese. Only 230 PWs out of 553 survived the first and 183 out of 566 the second.

This grim account, which covered the period from August, 1943, to August, 1945, was prepared by the Ninth Division intelligence officers from information obtained from Japanese figures and other sources.

The first prisoners arrived at Sandakan in August, 1942, and during the following months the number was increased by arrivals from Singapore and Jesselton until it reached an estimated total of 2700. Then, in August, 1943, 150, mainly officers, were moved to Kuching. Of the remaining 2550, only 6 are known to be alive.

Until September, 1944, only 20 deaths are reported to have occurred amongst the Sandakan prisoners, but from that time on the mortality rate gained appalling momentum. In October there were 10 deaths. In November 23, in December 50 and in January this year 83.

It was in January that 453 were sent out on the first of 3 death marches through the rugged Borneo mountains to Ranau, about 100 miles to the west of Sandakan. Of these, 230 reached Ranau, while 223 died on the way.

Amongst the remainder, the mortality rate continued its sickening rise. During February, the toll was 177. In March 334. April 250 and May 201.

Then another death march to Ranau was organised. This time 536 set out but only 183 survived.

Between June and August this year 212 died and the remaining 20 are recorded as killed trying to escape. Of the 413 who survived the death marches to Ranau 7 were killed attempting to escape and the remaining 406 died.

Hurricane, Huge Fires Hit Florida

WASHINGTON, Sunday.—A tropical hurricane, with screaming 143mph winds, struck southern Florida yesterday afternoon, sending 50,000 people to emergency shelters.

In the midst of the hurricane, huge fires broke out in some areas.

Miami fire department reported that all 33 hangars at the Florida blimp base, the largest hangars in the world, were on fire. All available fire fighting equipment was sent to the scene.

Miami and Miami Beach reported 89 mph winds which smashed plate-glass windows, carried away beach cabins and lifted roofs off houses.

Police halted all traffic over the 3 causeways connecting Miami and Miami Beach where hundreds were drowned in the 1926 hurricane.

The storm was last reported over Keylargo in the Florida Keys section and still headed north.

Jap Escape Bid At Shanghai

SHANGHAI, Sun.—A Japanese gunboat loaded with passengers tried to escape from Shanghai yesterday. It was captured and brought back to port.

It was suspected to be carrying important Japanese who were anxious to reach Tokio.

The boat was carrying 190, 3 times its normal complement. Allied investigating officers questioned the crew and took photographs of certain people on board for a check in connection with the list of wanted Japanese.

ME FOR 8th ['s] AT SYDNEY

ian PWs released from Jap camps at terday afternoon. The men travelled in rised 128 members of the Eighth Division survivors from HMAS Perth.

Claims Jap Peace Reply Was Lost

NEW YORK, Sun. — Columnist Walter Winchell claims that VP-Day was held up for 24 hours because the Jap reply to President Truman was lost in the State Department. A careless employee tossed it into a desk basket from which a girl picked it up and wrongly filed it. There was pandemonium in the department until the Navy Department sent over a copy which it had eavesdropped from the Japs' radioed message.

Back To Nanking

CHUNGKING, Sun.—Removal of the functions of the capital of China from Chungking back to Nanking, the pre-war capital, is now under way.

It is estimated that it will take 80 days, but it will be a race against time as the waters of the Yangtse recede towards the end of September, hampering traffic. There are 160,000 civil servants and their families to be moved.

■US Troops To Leave Morotai, Biak

TOKIO. Sun.—Gen. MacArthur has ordered the evacuation of US troops from Morotai and Biak. US troops will also be withdrawn from 8 stations in the Philippines.

ALLEGEDLY CAUSED LOSS OF BRITISH BATTLESHIPS

LONDON, Sun.—A man, who the British Secret Service believes was responsible for the sinking of the Prince of Wales and Repulse off the coast of Malaya in 1942, has been arrested, says the Daily Express correspondent in Singapore.

He is Johnek Kemperly, 40, described as of mixed European blood. It is alleged that he was one of Japan's master spies in the Far East and that he radioed information which resulted in the tracking down and sinking of the 2 battleships.

Radio Pacific when I was invited to be interviewed for two hours on a talk-back session. The incoming phone calls relating to this were numerous. Family members of deceased 'Z' operatives were most appreciative to learn just how and where they were lost, for this was the first knowledge they had obtained in 45-odd years.

As the last remaining member of 'Z' Special Unit (NZ) with a complete knowledge of the unit's involvement, I feel that which is now recorded is enough for my fellow friends and companions to be remembered in the years to come. It will happen. I am fully convinced of that! Our line is growing smaller: 2 operatives, 1 Base Radio Operator and 2 Diesel Mechanics in 1999.

The following report relates to Operation Semut I in the Limbang area

TOP SECRET
PATROL REPORT
MELINAU – LIMBANG AREA
BY LIEUTENANT P.V. MIDDLETON

6 October 1945.

Dates in this report are approximate as all count of time was completely lost. At one stage of the patrol we found ourselves 2 days out regarding dates. Facts however are authentic and correct.

ORDERS: Patrol orders were 'To follow the Jap Forces and report the position of same'.

A patrol left Melinau river on 2 Sept. 45 and consisted of Corporals Smith and McLean with 3 scouts. Their orders were to move out for three days and then camp on or near the Jap track and send back one scout to guide the main party, carrying rations to the hideout. Main party consisted of Lieutenant Middleton, Sergeant Gilman, Corporal Graham and eleven native soldiers. This party left one day after the scouting party and joined same on the third day. Two scouts were sent along the Jap track for 1 day but did not make contact.

The track back to base camp at Malinau river was too rough for further ration parties to follow, so Corporal Smith and two scouts set out to find a new route over which rations could be carried. Four days later they returned with rations and 12 carriers.

After Corporal Smith left, a party of 6 natives were sent along the Jap track with the intentions of finding out if the Japs had occupied a longhouse at reference 201504 (this is the place where Corporal Smith was ambushed 3 weeks later). That area was clear and as the scouts had run out of rations they tried to shoot some game.

The firing produced a patrol from Captain Edmeades who sent a note with one scout and kept the remainder with him. Altogether this patrol was out for 10 days, and the return of the scout coincided with the return of the rations party. On the 19 Sept. the party of 5 whites and 20 natives set off for Kuala Madalam. Corporal Smith had been returned sick and his place taken by Private Elder. That evening we camped on the Sungei Mentawai where a perahu from Captain Edmeades was waiting.

At 2230 hours 20 Sept. we arrived at Rumah Badak on the Kuala Madalam. Occupants of this place were 'Standing To' as the Japs had tried to cross the Limbang at this place the previous night. Along the entire route over the watershed and down to Rumah Badak the only dead seen were 4 who had been left to die along the track and 2 who had been hung.

I sent 7 carriers and 2 scouts back to Melinau river as they were no longer required. Contacted Sergeant Sanderson at Rumah Kadu and at his suggestion split my force. Corporals Graham and McLean with 4 soldiers were left at Rumah Badak and the remainder moved upstream to Rumah Kadu where the wireless was.

Sergeant Sanderson was in command of this area so I took over from him and signalled Flight Lieutenant Bartram to that effect. A holding force at Rumah Bilong 20 minutes upstream from Kadu was reinforced by Sergeant Gilman and 1 native soldier.

The two whites who had been in this area for six weeks **'Had not been supplied with rations, clothing or ammunition'. On or about 19 Sept. BBCAU had sent in supplies to be free dropped, but approximately 60% of the stores were lost owing to breakages etc.**

On 22 Sept. a drop of 1 wireless, a small supply of rations and trade stores came in. Frequent signals from me to Labuan failed to produce further stores. We existed on native food and supplies sent to us by Div. troops at Ukong. Ammo supply was almost exhausted and could not be replenished.

During 24 September a message was received from Flt/Lieut. Bartrum suggesting that my party were lost and giving all the news that I had previously sent him. Apparently some people do **NOT** read inward signals but concentrate on sending useless and long-winded signals. During the same 'Sked' Bartrum notified us that the carrying party sent by him to Sergeant Sanderson and carrying 30 rifles, 5 SMG's and 3 tins of First Aid had been ambushed at Madihit and everything lost.

Trying to supply Sergeant Sanderson from Belawit, right through the Japanese lines, is in my opinion, contrary to the most elementary principles of warfare.

The impression I gained was that the force in the Limbang had been

,SULUHAN'

PERKHABARAN PERANG UNTOK SARAWAK BRUNEI DAN BORNEO.

PADA 18 HARI BULAN 7, TAHUN 1945.

SARAWAK DAN BRUNEI. Tentara2 Australia yang telah menangkap kembali kota Brunei sekarang sudah maju masok ka Inggeris Borneo. Perhubongan jalan kereta api lari Beaufort itu bahkan sekarang telah bebas dari Jepun, dan serdadu2 Australia memakai jalan kereta api itu memukul maju ka-Jesselton.

BALIKPAPAN DI AMBIL. Bala tentara kami yang sudah mendarat di Balikpapan pada 1 hari bulan 7, ini sekarang sudah mengambil kota-nya, dan padang kapal terbang Sepinggan dan Manggar. Bahkan Balikpapan kota-nya terlalu perlu di-dalam Borneo Belanda. Dialah tempat minyak yang besar baik dan juga pengkalan-nya bagus.

PELURU2 DAN BOM2 MENGHANCHOR-KAN NEGERI JEPUN. Pada 14, dan 15, hari bulan kapal2 perang Amerika untok mula2 sekali menembak dalam negeri Jepun. Pada 14, hari bulan 7 asap chuma 5 batu saja dari daratan, kapal2 perang itu mengirimkan 1,000 tan peluru masok menghanchorkan kota Kamaishi, yang perlu sekali gudang2 waja itu habis terbongkar, dan kawasan pengkalan-nya sudah hanchor luloh.

Lain hari-nya kapal2 perang Amerika melakukan serangan-nya seperti yang tersebut dikota Muroran, di pulau Hokaido, sabelah Utara dan pulau Jepun sendiri.

Bersamaan juga waktu-nya lebih seribu kapal terbang Serikat dari kapal penangkutnya membom dilain2 tempat dalam negeri Jepun.

Empat hari duluan dari itu, pada 10, hari bulan 7, 2,000 dari kapal terbang kami nembom padang2 kapal terbang dan gudang2 hampir Tokio. 1,000 dari pada kapal penyingkut-nya, dan berhubongan membom kelainan hari-nya. Lain 1,000 itu datang dari pada rupa2 pulau dekat negeri Jepun yang sudah di rampas oleh kekuatan Amerika. Waktu dua hari ini ta'ada satu kapal perang atau kapal terbang Jepun datang menyerang kapal kami atau pun kapal terbang kami. Dendaman ini ampat hari sudah di tunjokan kepada orang2 Jepun tentang kematian dan kerusakan apabila hari-nya itu datang untok kekuatan Serikat akan naik ka negeri Jepun, baik pun kekuatan laut atau pun kekuatan udara akan senang menewasi dia.

KEKUATAN LAUT INGGERIS MENYERANG PULAU NICOBAR DAN SUMATRA. 5 hari lama-nya kekuatan udara dan laut Inggeris membom dan menembak padang2 kapal terbang Jepun, gudang2 dan kapal2 di pulau Nicobar dan Barat laut Sumatra duduk-nya sabelah Barat di ujung Utara dari Selat Melaka. Waktu lima hari itu chuma kelihatan dua kapal terbang Jepun. Ta'ada di dalam negeri-nya dan ta'ada dalam negeri yang di juduki-nya Jepun ada tinggal chukup untok melindongkan dia-nya sendiri.

APABILA TUAN SUDAH BACHA INI SURAT, HARAP JUGA BERIKAN KEPADA KETUA

KAMPOUNG YANG DI LAIN KAMPONG.

BAHASA NIPPON

No. 22.   Bulan 2, 2604.

ニッポンゴ

オヨメサン

昭和十九年二月

灘部隊宣傳部 行發

PENGANTEN PREMPUAN.

"Si-Yosiko punya kakak sudah berkawen kemarin." "Oh, tidak mendengar berita-nya. Dimana dia sudah pergi?" "Pergi ka-Tokyo. Penganten laki2 itu satu engineer dalam kompeni kapal terbang." "Ada-kah penganten laki-laki datang?" "Ya, kami orang semua ada pergi menghantar penganten prempuan ka-stasen."

Usotuki = Membuat bohong. Ame = Hujan. Ame no hu-ra-nai hi = Hari yang tidak hujan. Iku-niti mo iku-niti mo = Beberapa lama, Hari2. Tuzu-ku = Bersambong. Hut-te ki masita = Hujan sudah turun. Suru-to = Dari itu. Taihen da = Menjadi susah. Kit-to = Mesti, Tentu. Mura-zyuu = Semua Kampong. Naga-reru = Hanyut. Naga-sareru = Terkena banyut. Bikkuri-suru = Terkejut. Bikkuri-sa-seru = Membuat terkejut. Tonari-mura = Seblah Kampong. It-te-simau = Berpindah. Tugi-no hi = Besok hari. Zibun no uti = Rumah diri.

BAHASA NIPPON

Bulan 2, 2604.

ベンキヤウ

BELAJAR.

"Si-Amin, engkau tidak ada bermain2 sekarang. Apa-kah engkau buat?" "Saya belajar bahasa Nippon dari bulan dulu." "Ada-kah engkau belajar, selain dari yang di-ajar di-sekolah?" "Ya, saya belajar satu jam satu hari dari Tuan Yamada, yang tinggal di-rumah seblah kami." "Oh, itu bagus." "Saya hendak pergi ka-Nippon dengan Tuan Yamada."

Tuki = Bulan. Yoru = Malam. Tuki no nai yoru = Bulan kelam. De-ru = Timbol. De-nai = Tidak timbol. Hare-ru = Chuacha yang baik. Tokubetu-ni = Lebeh, Lebehan. Hosi = Bintang. Miru-koto ga deki-ru = Dapat melihat. Hika-ru = Berkilat. Amari = Tidak berapa. Kou-sita = Bagitu. Hotondo = Aga2 semua. Zenbu = Semua, Sama sekali. Ugo-ku = Bergoyang. Ugo-kazu ni (Ugo-ka nai de) = Tidak bergoyang. Itu mo = Biasa, Selalu. Onazi tokoro = Tetap di-tempat. Toki-doki = Kadang2. Basyo = Tempat. Kawa-ru = Ubah, Berubah. Naze de syou ka = Apa kena-kah menjadi bagitu?

239

criminally neglected, left to fend for themselves, and expected to do almost impossible things. No white man in that area had been supplied with money, but the powers given to one native Sergeant were, to say the least, a trifle exaggerated. This native had a letter signed 'Rajah' over a signature that looked like Harrisson's and according to it he almost had the powers of a dictator. He was the most unco-operative native I've ever met and as a result I took him into 'protective custody' and re-issued his weapons, etc. The most unsatisfactory feature was the fact that this letter stated that Sergeant Boland was not to take orders from anyone at all, and could at any time act on his own accord.

Actions

During the night 21/22 September movement was heard across the river from Rumah Badak. Extra guards were placed out until daylight but nothing happened.

September 22. Sergeant Sanderson went 3 hours upstream to Rumah Guni to recce that area. Previously this house had been used as a sort of staging camp for the Japs. Investigations showed that a party of approximately 40 had crossed the Limbang river, and according to native reports were making towards Rumah Kadu (previously Jap forces had not crossed the river). They would take 3 days to reach Kadu.

September 25. Sergeant Wigzell and myself went down stream to bring Corporal Graham back to reinforce the HQ at Rumah Kadu. Outside Rumah Lasong which is between Kadu and Badak, the natives informed us there were 30 Japs on the opposite bank. These appeared to be completing the encirclement of Kadu. Shots were exchanged after which the Japs withdrew.

After picking up Corporal Graham we were moving upstream when the Japs opened fire again. At this point, the perahu was in shallow water so we got out and on to a small island and engaged the enemy. This time they were using grenades from cup dischargers. After the action I saw that Corporal Graham had been hit on the hand.

Further upstream we were attacked again making it 3 times in one day. We reasonably suspected that we had killed 5 enemy.

26 September. Patrolling the entire area failed to locate any Japs, but warm fires showed where they had been. One prisoner was caught by 3 women and from his information we gathered that the whole force had moved on. This information later proved incorrect as Corporal Smith ran into a party at ref. 201504 as previously mentioned.

27 September. Taking our POW and one day's rations my party started to return to Marudi, as instructed by Major Wilson. We contacted Lieutenant Holland and a Jap envoy and handed over our

Left: Oxygen apparatus worn by operative in Sleeping Beauty.

Above and Below: Sleeping Beauty on surface and submerging.

POW. 20 Brigade 9 Div. gave us all assistance possible in the way of rations and transport for the return trip.

Signed. P.V. Middleton Lt.

Top: One-man midget submarine – The Welman.

Middle: Four-man Welfreighter under way off Garden Island.

Bottom: Welman on trolley at Careening Bay Camp, Garden Island.

Careening Bay Camp (CBC) Special Boat School and Midget Submarines

Careening Bay Camp situated at the SE end of Garden Island, 5 km off the coast of Rockingham, Fremantle WA was a hive of activity during the war years. It housed our Special Boat School which included advanced folboat training. Students had to be exceedingly proficient in the handling of folboats prior to being instructed in the Motorised Submersible Canoe (MSC), Sleeping Beauty or SB as we called it, plus the one-man Welman submarine and the four-man Welfreighter submarine. The following is an identification and short description of the above craft.

Folboats (British and Australian built). Extensive training on these at Fraser Commando School. Were reliable, 5 metres in length, two-man rubberised canvas canoes, propelled by paddles, single or double, some with well behind the rear set for small outboard, others with improvised outriggers for added stability. These canoes are similar to our modern-day kayaks.

Motorised Submersible Canoe (MSC) (British): the Sleeping Beauty or SB is a one-man submersible steel canoe, just under 4 m in length, operator wearing Davis Escape Apparatus (DSEA) or Salvus oxygen gear, operates from a sitting position, with only his head above water, submerges to about ten metres, battery operated. Speed 3–4 knots on surface, underwater approximately 1½ knots. Transported on the deck of a PT, snake boat or submarine to a position relatively close to intended target. Operator motors in silently, porpoising, attaches magnetic limpet mines (each just under 3 kilos of plastic explosive, similar to that which sunk the *Rainbow Warrior* in Auckland Harbour, NZ, years later) to the hull of the intended target. Each SB could carry nine charges sufficient to sink two ships of 10,000 tonnage. On occasions the performance of the SBs was unpredictable especially underwater. (Fifteen SBs were included in the strike force for the raid on Singapore Harbour in the unsuccessful Operation Rimau, and dumped at sea to prevent their being captured by the enemy.)

Welman (British). One-man midget submarine, operator fully enclosed, designed to detach 250kg of explosive warhead under/near bottom of target. Lieutenant Marris RN was the expert on these. They were certainly hard to handle – Australian engineers designed and attached an effective periscope.

Welfreighter (British). Four-man midget submarine, mainly used for inserting two operatives or stores onto occupied coastlines. They seemed so big and roomy compared with the Welman, and teamwork was the main essential of the crew.

(Japanese two-man submarines were apparently efficient, length 27m, speed 16 knots, two small torpedoes. They rode piggy-back on a mother sub, three entered Sydney Harbour night 31 May/1 June 1942. Five were used in the infamous attack on Pearl Harbour, Hawaii – four were lost and one captured).

It is worth noting that British Chariots and 'X' Craft were operated by the Royal Navy and not by SOE or SRD (Aust). Chariots, manned by two 'charioteers' in self-contained diving suits, sitting astride a human torpedo, were submersible machines and the forerunner of the 'X' craft.

'X' Craft. 4-man midget submarines, length 15m, 39 tons, speed 6 knots on surface, 4 below, carrying two charges each of two tons amatol. Used successfully in fjords of Norway (including immobilising the German battleship *Tirpitz*), Mediterranean and Singapore. The Japanese heavy cruiser *Takao* at dock in Johore Strait was also demobilised during Operation Struggle.

Top secret wartime operations of 'Z' miniature submarine training at Garden Island have been shrouded in secret, or forgotten in the mists of time for the fifty-plus years since the end of the Second World War. With its isolation and tranquil waters, the area was an excellent training ground for clandestine operations against the Japanese in the SWPA.

Apart from numerous army gun positions sprinkled along the western side of the island facing the Indian Ocean as part of the Port of Fremantle's defences, the only other inhabitants were the numerous tammar wallabies, carpet and tiger snakes, along with the other varieties of fauna and bird life. On the open sandy shores of the bay were located two jetties, various workshops, mess and Nissen storage huts which housed the Welman midget submarines and the motor submersible canoes, better known as 'MSCs and Sleeping Beauties'.

A sturdy timber wharf, with a steel gantry erected, was for the purpose of allowing the submersibles to be raised from, or lowered into the ocean for training operations into Careening Bay waters from the shoreline.

Today the Services Reconnaissance Department memorial occupies a proud position on a raised slope overlooking the 'Fleet Base West'. In the latter stages of the Second World War it is estimated that there were eight Welman one-man midget submarines, two four-man Welfreighter transporter submersibles and twelve Motor submersible canoes being used at Garden Island. The rarely seen and virtually unknown British-built craft had been shipped to Australia from England and were unloaded from large packing cases at Fremantle before being taken down to Garden Island.

Welman and Welfreighters were seen at Darwin Harbour in mid-1945 at the Lugger Maintainance Depot, the cover name for 'Z' Special Unit's Darwin Base, which pre-war had been a quarantine station. These craft were preparing for operations against the Japanese in Sumatra when the war finished. The fate of these vessels and their existence has generally been unknown to many other than the SBs.

It is ironic that these secret submarines trained in the very waters in which Australia's future underwater vessels would be based and operated from.

Submarine Operations from Fremantle

CBC and Fremantle were also the starting points for many SRD operations. The following are some of those which were undertaken – 167 submarines (125 American – 31 British – 11 Dutch) operated from this area during the Second World War, making it the biggest submarine base in the Southern Hemisphere.

Operation Python 1. Departed Fremantle in US Submarine *Kingfish* in September 1943. Party leader Major Gort Chester OBE (GB), former resident of BNB, and five operatives were successfully landed on the east coast of BNB. In January 1944, Operation Python II under leader Major Bill Jinkins and five operatives reinforced Chester from USS *Tinosa*. In March 1944, Jinkins and two operatives were evacuated in USS *Narwhal*. In June 1944, Jinkins returned with another operative on USS *Harder* which successfully evacuated Python party of six. Three had been captured and later executed as spies.

Operation Rimau. Departed Fremantle in HM Submarine *Porpoise* in September 1944. Party leader (GB) Lieutenant Colonel Ivan Lyon MBE, DSO and twenty-one operatives, with fifteen one-man SBs departed on this ill-fated mission. Lyon planned to return to Singapore Harbour and repeat the successful Operation Jaywick raid which he led in September 1943, when 39,000 tons of enemy shipping was sunk by magnetic mines (limpets) placed from three folboats. (Four members plus Lyon were on the first Jaywick raid). The Rimau operation was to attach the limpets by SBs, RV nearby, scuttle the SBs, transfer to folboats, RV at Merapas Island where the Rimau party was to be picked up by HM Submarine *Tantalous*. All operatives were lost. Eleven stood trial by Court Martial in Singapore and were executed just prior to the surrender of the Japanese. (Translations of this court martial are recorded in this book.)

Operation Carpenter I. Departed Fremantle in HM Submarine *Telemachus* in September 1944, three days after the Rimau party had departed. Requested by SOE Force 136 – Cello – to insert mainly SOE party into Johore, Malaya to join Chinese guerrillas.

Operation Starfish. Departed Fremantle in USS *Rock* in March 1945. Party leader (Aust) Lawrie Black and three operatives were to recce and demolish the enemy active coastal guns covering the Lombok Strait, between Bali and Lombok Islands. Two were killed. In May, Black and Hoffie were evacuated by SRD ferry party of three, in a Catalina flying-boat.

Operation Robin I (Platypus I). Departed Fremantle in USS *Perch* in March 1945. Party leader NZer Major Don Stott DSO and Bar, and party of eleven operatives were inserted into Balikpapan oil fields area, SE Borneo. The first part of the operation with two folboats, one got to the shore DZ, but the other containing Stott and McMillan were never sighted and were presumed drowned, lost at sea. The second party all landed safely but were continually harassed by the enemy. Four members were lost. The remainder managed to escape to sea and were picked up by a PBY Catalina.

Operation Optician. Undertook two patrols from Fremantle in English submarines in early 1945. Party leader (GB) Captain Noel 'Trapper' Kennard and Sergeant Jim Edwards doing the first in HM/S *Telemachus* and WO2 Jerry Sparke and Sergeant Harry Browne the second operation. The objectives of Optician were similar to Politician with the former operating from British submarines.

Submarine – Folboat Attacking Pairs

This series of operations was carried out by special task personnel of SRD operating by folboat in parties of two, from American and British submarines based at Fremantle. The operatives allowed the submarines' striking power to be increased, enabling attacks on targets in positions inaccessible to submarines (shallow water behind reefs etc.); demolition of beached vessels; reconnaissance and raids ashore; assistance in rescue of downed airmen; evacuation of persons from enemy-held territory and destruction of lines of communications.

Following Jinkins' successful extraction of six Python members aboard USS *Harder*, his submission to the US Admiral to use SRD personnel on American submarines was approved. This project was given the code name of Politician. Later the Royal Navy agreed to similar operations from British submarines and this was given the code name Optician.

Politician Patrols

The following is a brief account of each Politician patrol from Fremantle. (Each patrol is a full story in itself and only the operatives can relate each one as it was.) Only two operatives were aboard each submarine. Operatives were treated by the US Commander and crew as full members of the craft, each stood watch and performed normal duties as officers of the submarine. Major Rowan Waddy (Aust) the supplier of the submarine information in this book, and a member of Politician states: 'For security reasons I was not made aware of any details of these patrols. In fact, I did not even meet some of my fellow Politician–Optician operatives.'

1st Patrol.

Jinkins/Dodds aboard USS *Harder* in May/June 1944. Extracted six Python personnel from British North Borneo (BNB) now Sabah on 8 June 1944. Three operatives were killed.

2nd Patrol.

Jinkins/Barnes aboard USS *Redfin* in Aug/Oct 1944. Native craft boarded in South China Sea. In conjunction with Allied Intelligence Bureau (AIB) Lieutenant Commander 'Chick' Parsons USNR and guerrillas evacuated seventeen persons (including eight survivors of USS *Flier*) near Palawan Islands, Philippines. Finished patrol in Flores Seas.

3rd Patrol.

Jinkins/Chew aboard USS *Redfin* in Oct/Jan 1945 One ship sunk, Makassar Strait, Java and Flores seas.

4th Patrol.

Sachs/Hawkins aboard USS *Bream* in Dec/Feb 1945. Native craft boarded in South China Sea. Recce of oil installations on Itu Aba Island.

5th Patrol.

Dodds/Anderson aboard USS *Bluegill* in Dec/Feb 1945. Native craft boarded, refused permission to raid Itu Aba Island installations.

6th Patrol.

Jinkins/Chew aboard USS *Flounder* in Jan/Feb 1945. Operatives transferred to USS *Pargo* SS264 for recce on Woody Island in Paracel Group to establish enemy location – island shelled. Transfer back to *Flounder*, three days later *Flounder* rammed by another submerged submarine, went to Subic Bay for repairs.

7th Patrol.

Hawkins/Abdul Madjio (Javanese native) aboard USS *Gurnard* in March

1945. Operatives transferred to USS *Brill* in Flores Sea, landed and successfully evacuated five natives (Secret Intelligence Australia, SIA), agents from Sakala Island in Java Sea.

8th Patrol.

Sachs/Perske aboard USS *Bream* in Mar/April 1945. Both operatives were lost during this patrol whilst attempting a limpet mine attack on a freighter from canoes near Masulambo Island, *Bream* was heavily depth-charged (details below).

9th Patrol.

Anderson/Owens aboard USS *Bluegill* in Mar/April 1945. Planned to attack anchored vessels in Pontianak Roads but ships had just moved. Raided railway on French Indo-China coast. Limpet-mined beached ship, torpedoed by USS *Bluegill* near Hondoi Island.

10th Patrol.

Chaffey/Campbell aboard USS *Boarfish* in Mar/April 1945. Sabotaged railway near Tourane and Tamquan Bays in French Indo-China, now Vietnam.

11th. Patrol.

Anderson/Owens again aboard USS *Bluegill* in May/June 1945. Recce to Pretes Island, SE of Hong Kong, followed by landing party.

12th Patrol.

Chaffey/Campbell again aboard USS *Boarfish* out of Subic Bay, Philippines in May/June 1945. Native craft boarded, returned to Fremantle.

When these patrols ceased, US Admiral James Fife, Commander Submarines, Task Force 71, sent the following message to SRD:

> I trust that Major Jinkins, Sgt Dodds and others who served so meritoriously in the US submarines on our war patrols and special missions will understand that, regardless of your eligibility to participate in some of the awards made to the vessels in which you served, we of the submarine service recognise and applaud your achievements. The very nature of your missions were a history in themselves.

Politician 8th. Patrol USS *BREAM* (Sachs and Perske)

This war patrol resulted in the cancellation of US submarines based at Fremantle being used by SRD personnel for special missions.

On 11 March 1945, Sachs and Perske departed from Fremantle aboard the USS *Bream* SS243 on its fifth war patrol. As most submarines did, *Bream* refuelled at Onslow (code-named Potshot), Exmouth Gulf, Western Australia, where they were joined by USS *Rock*. Black and party (4) were aboard *Rock* for operation Starfish and they mingled with Sachs and Perske, finally saying their farewells and wishing each other 'good luck'. Only two of these six operatives survived.

Bream proceeded north, through the Lombok Strait towards their patrol area. Near Masulambo Island in the Java Sea, *Bream* attacked a Japanese convoy en route to Surabaya. One ship was sunk and that evening the convoy and escorts anchored in shallow water off the SE tip of Great Masulambo. Sachs planned to attack the ships with magnetic limpet mines on the night of 15 March. Conditions were good, a dark night, rainy with little wind and just before midnight, they set out to paddle the 4,000 metres to the target area. After attaching their limpets on the ships (with suitable time-delay fuses) they were to paddle NE and rendezvous with *Bream* some 5,500 metres from the target.

Bream's Captain and Sachs were unaware that this convoy had also been attacked by a British submarine at 1700 hrs on the same day. Their torpedoes had missed and it must be assumed that all the enemy ship's crews would have been 'on edge' and very alert.

After proceeding some 2,200 metres, the radar showed that the folboat was an alarming 1,800 metres east of their planned course, probably due to the strong tide. Unfortunately, after departure from the submarine, they were not in radio contact as, when tested, it would not operate. Nothing more was seen or heard and later, *Bream* was unable to make contact at the alternate RV – nothing. *Bream* continued looking for Sachs and Perske by covering as much of the sea north and east of the Island as possible. The submarine's presence was well known and they were harassed by enemy destroyers, but *Bream* continued searching until the night of 17 March.

At 0256 hrs, radio contact was established on the correct frequency. *Bream's* Captain commented:

> **was entirely convinced by this time that the station was phoney, but the voice was definitely Australian and like Lt. Perske. Decided that the Japs had captured Lts. Sachs and Perske and were forcing them to talk on their own frequency, in the hopes of getting information from us, or of trapping us.**

During the heavy depth-charging received whilst *Bream* was attempting to make contact and pick up Sachs and Perske, the submarine was seriously damaged and slowly returned to Fremantle. The names of Sachs and Perske were later found scrawled on a prison wall in Surabaya and we understand that they were beheaded by the Japanese. A member of the fateful Rimau party, Pte D.R. Warne (AIF), was also in Surabaya and died there. (It was later established that many of SRD members of Operation Rimau were beheaded as spies – the majority in Singapore, July 1945, only a few weeks before the end of the war – see court martial translations of documents in this book relating to this).

'Z' Special Unit's Last 'Sleeping Beauty' Finds a Home

They were the elite of underwater stealth in the Second World War, but so Top Secret that the Australian-based Commando Unit which penetrated enemy lines in the so-called 'Sleeping Beauties' of the sea, destroyed those very diving machines in the name of Allied security.

All except one, it seems, which made its public debut at the opening of a small Perth museum dedicated to the world of diving.

Frogmen in the secret commando group 'Z' Special Unit, endured up to six hours at depths of 20 metres in the submersibles, using experimental breathing equipment (Davis) which recycled oxygen to avoid the release of telltale bubbles. But it is gruesome and glorious wartime tales of the elite unit's missions, climaxing with the beheading of operatives caught who were intending to bomb Japanese ships in Singapore Harbour (1944), in which the SBs were to make their most dramatic mark in history.

The surviving steel and alloy canoe-shaped SB now in the Perth museum was found crumpled beyond recognition in a British scrap metal yard. 'We heard it was there,' a former member of 'Z' Special Unit stated, and thus we recovered it.

After restoration the one-time secret weapon lay in a lounge room somewhere in England before being returned to Western Australia, which was the home of the SBs during the war.

Carrying four limpet mines, the SBs were shipped undercover from Garden Island off the west coast off Australia before being lowered into the water near enemy naval holding bays in the North Sea and Singapore harbour. The activity of 'Z' Special Unit has since been credited with saving thousands of Allied lives by assisting in the turning of the Japanese advance backwards.

These SBs seemed to be infallible until one mission code named Rimau went horribly wrong. Following the success of Operation Jaywick in 1943 when seven Japanese ships were sunk in Singapore

Harbour, the men were sent back (volunteered) to take out more of the vessels. The mission arrived off Singapore's coast in a submarine and raided a passing junk. The crew were kidnapped and transported by the submarine back to Western Australia and held in captivity until after the war.

The junk was sailed into a harbour and all stores and equipment were unloaded from the submarine onto it, plus the folboats and SBs. A Japanese motor patrol boat noticed an odd vessel in the bay and came to investigate. The operatives opened fire on the vessel, killing all the crew except one, who managed to swim ashore in a wounded state and gave the alarm. The mission was now aborted, so the junk was sailed out to sea and the top secret SBs were sunk with the vessel to protect their security from the enemy.

The operatives went in all directions using their folboats (kayaks). Many were killed in sharp actions. Ten were captured and found guilty by a Japanese Court Martial of clandestine activities. They were beheaded three weeks before the war ended.

At the end of the war others were dumped off Western Australia near Rottnest Island and in the Cockburn Sound, and have never been recovered including the Singapore Mission 'Sleeping Beauties'. The survivor situated at Perth museum looks to the untrained eye, as nothing more than a worn-out old canoe.

Appendix I

Operational Orders from Major Tom Harrisson OC Semut I for Lieutenant Jeff Westley AIF on his arrival in Borneo to join the party.

W. 2 (J. Westley code #)   **3.6.45.**

ORDERS FOR BAHAU RIVER AND TANJONG SELOR AREA.

At his moment all rice from the TANJONG SELOR area is being sent by perahu to 'BROUGINE' on the BAHU RIVER, rice from MACASSER is also arriving at BROUGINE BY STEAMER and a distribution to Japanese forces is being made from there.

1 YOU WILL STOP THE WHOLE OF THE RICE TRAFFIC IN THAT AREA. You will take all possible precautions against hostile natives as there are many of them in that area.

2 You will make a census of all villages called at whether hostile or otherwise, this will assist the Government in times of peace as most of the country you will be travelling in has not been visited by white men.

3 You will have all tracks you travel over improved by the natives as a voluntary village service. Be firm on this point.

4 You will keep a diary of your movements as well as a track log and times of travel from place to place, detailed maps will be made of these and sent back to Head Quarters periodically.

5 You will go to LONG POENDJOEGAN and <u>KILL</u> all remaining Japanese there. Number there at the moment unknown, maybe 20 odd.

6 You will kill or capture the Government Official 'KIAI HERON'. If able to capture bring back to Head Quarters.

7 You will go to LONG BERINI on the BAHU RIVER and KILL the 'GOORU' there, he is a strong Jap sympathiser and is assisting them whole-heartedly.

8 No food will be sent to you as we have none to spare; you must live off the land. You will find it hard, as reports indicate that the Japs have conscripted all foods for themselves.

9 Do not molest the women and pay full attention to Native goodwill as

our lives in this country depend on it; no shooting up of hostile kampongs except as a last resort, or unless PROGRESS IS HALTED.

10 Route will be Loemboedeat – Pa Kurid – Pa Ibung – then jungle Long Toea – Long Berini – Long Poendjoegan, approximately a fifteen day trip. On arrival at Long Toea you will be in unknown territory, and it is up to you from then on.

11 You will prepare a system of runners so that a message of progress can be sent back every five days, AND SEE THAT THEY DO GET BACK. Your maps, reports and intelligence is of the utmost importance to Corps H.Q. AND THE OUTSIDE WORLD.

12 Bring back all documents taken from the Japanese – bring back all collaborators and informers, capture and bring back all Malays.

13 Propaganda all villages encountered, and bring back all likely guerrilla recruits.

14 On the way back, go to PUN on the RIVER PUN and find out who killed TUAN HUDDIN. Capture and bring back the 'KAPALA'; be particularly careful – one hundred percent hostile kampong.

15 Look out for likely Dropping Zones, both for live drops and store drops. Find also a place where a Catalina can land and take off, preferably on the KAYAN or BAHU RIVERS.

16 You will take ten guerrillas only, comprising five Malays and five Dyaks. One Bren gun ... six grenades ... three sub machine guns ... six .303 Rifles and plenty of ammunition.

17 If all goes well you should be back here one month from now. If you are in trouble do not, repeat do not send for help as all personnel will be occupied elsewhere. If upon your return here you find we have been killed, captured or driven out, you must get out the best way you can, preferably to TARAKAN as there are huge Jap forces to the North of us, the South of us, and to the East of us, but as far as we can ascertain not nearly as many to the West of us, except on and around TARAKAN.

This constitutes your orders. They are very brief but most important. Yours is a most difficult and dangerous assignment, and not one moment, day or night (if you hope to survive) must you forget vigilance. Remember you are in two enemy territories, Japs and natives both.

DO NOT repeat DO NOT get yourself killed as there are too few of us here as it is.

GOOD HUNTING GOOD LUCK AND GOODBYE.

A.1 (Major Harrisson's code #)

[THIS DOCUMENT IS PRINTED IN ITS ORIGINAL FORM]

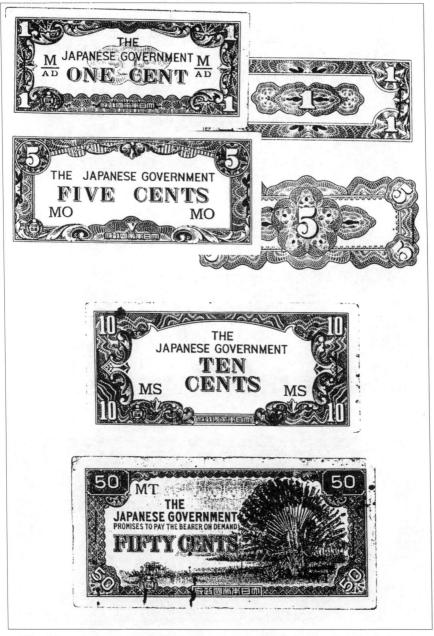

Worthless Japanese occupation currency, printed for use by the Japanese forces in Borneo and Malaya. The natives realised it was valueless, and gave us handfuls as souvenirs. (Note the absence of serial numbers, name of country.)

Japanese occupation currency – higher denominations, but still no serial numbers.

The more adventurous fishermen, crossing to the Philippines island of
Mindanao, and risking being shot if caught by the Japanese, brought back
this currency printed by the Japanese for the occupation.
(Note – no serial numbers)

Genuine currency of the Netherlands East Indies, used in the Dutch Island of Morotai, in the Halmahera group.

Other examples of 'legitimate' currency in circulation in North Borneo
before and during the occupation.

The British North Borneo Company banknote in circulation at the time of the Japanese Occupation. Most of this was confiscated by the Japanese. But a few such as these survived by being well hidden. They were 'exchanged' for the currency we took with us.

The currency taken into British North Borneo by our units, used to pay
the 'troops' we trained, and to buy food from the natives.

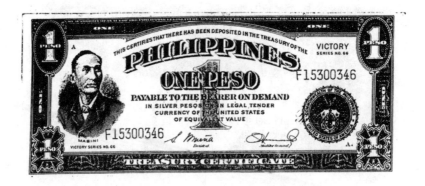

Genuine currency of the Philippines.

Appendix II

THE MAKING OF A BLOOD BROTHER OF THE HEADHUNTING TAGAL TRIBE OF BRITISH NORTH BORNEO

This relates to Lieutenant Jeff Westley (AIF) of the first reinforcement to Operation SEMUT I in his letter dated 20/6/89 to the author Frank Wigzell (NZ)

You mentioned how well you and Sandy got on with the Dayaks and Ibans. I can understand that as I spent time with every Tribe in Borneo, including the treacherous Tagals of British North Borneo, and with them you could expect a dart in the back at any time, day or night. Boy, did I lose some sleep, until one day I heard a story from a wizened-up old senile warrior. He told me that in the old days it was possible to be made a blood brother of a tribe under certain circumstances, and that if one were accepted, he would never be betrayed. This is just what I wanted, and I asked him if he could arrange it. He said that he would talk to the reigning elders, and stated that gifts would have to be exchanged. He also enquired if I had anything to offer. I replied Gold. [Sovereigns minted in 1942 were to pay our guerrillas, as paper money was not acceptable after the Japanese occupational currency.]

Three days later it was arranged. I had to go to a small longhouse half a day's walk away. I was allowed no weapons, including my six grenades. Five 'Kiais', or learned tribespeople of the area, were seated in a circle facing inwards, surrounded by a circle of about 30 decorated braves, standing and facing inwards also. No weapons were in sight. On the mat in the centre of the ring was a knife and a parang pouch – a cup made from two-thirds of a coconut shell. It looked ancient. Room was made for me in the inner circle. Nervously I looked outside to make sure that I was visible to my guerrillas stationed there, for they had their orders.

The elder of the Kiais took charge, picked up the knife and nicked his wrist, and pressed his thumb on the cut. The others did the same. I picked up the knife, looked at the Kiai and then my wrist. He nodded so I followed the pattern. On picking up the coconut shell he placed it in front of me then held his wrist to mine for about half a minute. A small amount of both our blood oozed out and dropped into the shell cup. The other Kiais followed the same ritual. We now got to our feet with one Kiai still holding the coconut shell cup. Next, the head Kiai nicked my ear lobe and held the shell under it, blood spurting into it. The same was done to all the standing warriors. The shell cup was now taken over to a huge jar, and a gourd full of its contents transferred into it (Arak, I believe). It was then handed to me with the sign to drink. I drank. The Kiais drank, then the warriors. Everyone began talking excitedly, and I never understood a word.

My guerrillas were called into the longhouse, and everyone began a session of Borak and Arak. Food was also provided. I was presented with some beautiful bead-work at least a century old, three panels in all. This was a covering from a ceremonial babies-carrying basket worn by the proud father on his back, made from tiny trade beads, and each one threaded on rattan and tied separately They were red, white and black in the form of a rampant dragon. I have never seen anything to equal this in Borneo during the rest of my travels. Will show you one day when next over in this locality. In return I presented each of the Kiais with a gold sovereign, and to make a big deal of it, carved SEMUT I on the King's head with their still bloody knife. It went over real big. From then on I had no further trouble with the Tagals. The moment we entered one of their villages I had it spread around that I was a blood brother of their tribe, telling them in detail of the grisly ceremony and knowing the natives as you do, Frank, you can imagine some of the stories that circulated. One thing that I learned – never, never, hit a Tagal. Kill him, yes, but hit him, you have an enemy for life. One day he will get you – you can depend on it, brother or not.

Jeff

Appendix III

ORDERS TO Lt. FRANK LECKIE (L.I)
FROM Mjr. T. HARRISSON (A.I)

1 You will leave Bawang HQ Aug 17. You will take guide from Malinau, 24 Berang soldiers (for repatriation) and will be accompanied by Tuan Aris, whom you will help in every way to reach Tarakan.

2 Your actions will be governed by the new ORDERS for Armistice Transition, appended.

3 You will see that the copy for LOEMBIS sector is sent by fast runner from Berang. You will see that Kiai there is fully acquainted with the contents.

4 You will see STERELNY is also supplied with a copy and understands it fully. You will be responsible for dispatch of runners from Berang to Loembis.

5 From Berang you will return me a full written report of your trip and the news you hear there, and especially reference PENSIANGAN area Japs.

6 On arrival there you will take over from STERELNY.

7 STERELNY will give you FULL local picture. Your policy will continue logically from this.

8 You will be i/c Admin. and order there. You will of course assist N.I.C.A. in every way. If the Dutch take over your area, you will explain your situation and stay there till you hear from me. You WILL help them in every way possible, with all tact.

9 STERELNY is then to proceed on his patrol **exactly** as previously ordered, except that his attitude to the enemy is altered by the new orders (Copy for him). He will **R.V.** at BAHAU-KAYAN in some way and if not met, will report to **LONG TOEA**. He will not deviate from route or dates or intelligence role. He will not be clearing it himself. That's all. **A.I (Mjr. T. Harrisson)**

Appendix IV

(THIS DOCUMENT RELATES TO THE ARRIVAL OF THE FUJINO TAI NEAR BASE HEADQUARTERS OF SEMUT I, THE BAWANG VALLEY IN OCTOBER 1945, THE SAME FORCE ENCOUNTERED IN THE LIMBANG BY THE AUTHOR IN AUGUST–SEPTEMBER 1945.)

PA KELALAN AREA – ORDERS TO Lt. LECKIE (L.I)

The following information is required:

(1) **ENEMY.**

    (a)   How many Japs in Long Beluyu?

    (b)   Where the rest of the Japs are?

(2) **OWN TROOPS.**

    (a)   Dispositions, with rough sketch.

    (b)   Distribution of amn. at present 15 rds. per man.

        (Suggest remove 5 rds. each man for Brens, and 5 rds. as a reserve at Pa Kelalan.)

    (c)   Grenades. To be withdrawn to Pa Kelalan. Only to be given 1 or 2

        soldiers who really know how to handle them.

    (d)   Keep in touch with **PUNAN TRUSAN** party.

(3) **PADAS FOODS**

    Find out whether it has been removed.

(4) **COMMAND**

    You will take charge of the area.

(5) **COMMUNICATIONS.**

    Daily **SITREP** to be sent to HQ. Special runners to be used for urgent messages.

Signed. P. Bartrum F/Lt.

i/c HQ. 19/10/45.

Appendix V

LETTER TO Lieutenant JEFF WESTLEY (AIF # W.I) FROM Lieutenant FRANK LECKIE (NZEF # L.I)

HQ. BIF.
(Borneo Interior Force)
Bawang 12/11/45.

Dear Jeff,

Still doing business at the old stand, as you can see by the address. Made a leisurely trip back after leaving you and arrived to find the place deserted, except for Paul [Bartrum] and Ray Bennett, who were leaving next day. So I tagged along as well, but only got as far as Ba Kelalan when Sualong and his soldiers told us there were about 400 Nips at Long Beluyu, and they were not too friendly towards the natives. This was the mob that Sandi [Sanderson and Wigzell] had a go at on the Limbang and did over 55 of them.

They fired at the natives at Long Beluyu but got rather the worst of the argument. So we promptly headed for the Bawang again till we could get some news where they intended to go next. Nothing doing for a few days so I went back to Long Kelalan. The next day news came that they were coming our way, so we prepared for a bit of fun. The natives all shot through when the Nips left Long Beluyu but I managed to rally them a bit, and then Paul arrived to have a look at things. We organised a nice little ambush for them and they stopped at Pa Pala that day. Next day Paul, who was itching to get into some Japs after so much admin work, sent me to get the evacuation of Belawit underway. The Nips duly arrived that day and very obligingly walked into the ambush. Sualong did good work on the Bren, as we found out later 20–30 were killed. They retired in rather a hurry to think things over. Then they sprung a surprise attack and attacked at night. Paul had to leave in rather a rush then came back here also, as the soldiers left very smartly for home and mother. Fortunately the Nips had another spell at Ba Kelalan so we had plenty of time to get Belawit cleared out.

In the meantime the Boss (A.I) had left Lawas with 2 Jap Envoys to contact the Japs and try and make them surrender. They had a hell of a trip due to floods and it was only our delaying the Japs a couple of days that allowed them to catch up. Anyway the Envoys went in and after being threatened by the Commander, Fujino, the 2 I/C Kamimura, persuaded him to give it his best. Thank the Lord for that, as I had visions of chasing round Borneo again for a few more months, as a guerrilla once more. The Japs had left Marudi on the 1st. July and had had four months jungle-bashing as they had missed the track across to here.

Their main worry was salt, and they weren't even bothering to kill pigs or cattle, as they couldn't go it without salt. Funny thing to win a fight, but the lack of salt plus being fired upon when they had no idea there were Whites or armed natives in the vicinity, turned the tide. They started off 578 strong and finished up 358 including 5 women and 1 child. Plenty of medical stores, 2 Doctors, 1 Chinese nurse and all the arms in the world, mortars, grenades (mostly Aussie ones), Jugis, pistols, swords (60) and over 200 rifles. So altogether it was a lucky break for us that they turned it in. We lost 2 killed and 2 wounded. Not bad for over 30 Japs. What with Sandi and Frank's 55 in the Limbang, SRD had its fair share of the party.

The AIF 9 Div. did exactly ... towards it. I've included an extract from the 'Table Tops' in case you did not see it. Did pretty well for souvenirs out of it and now have a good sword, pistol and a couple of flags. Dickie Thomas arrived with the Boss as, of all things, Signals Officer. Wouldn't it! He also did very well out of it, getting the same as I plus a good pair of binoculars.

While clearing the Boss's gear out of Belawit I came across the enclosed letter of yours, so I thought I'd send it even if you happen to arrive home before it.

It looks very much as though I'll be lucky to reach Australia before Xmas now, as I'm leaving tomorrow to go out via Long Berang and Melinau. Have to pay off all those soldiers and coolies of yours in the area. The Boss went horribly crook at SRD for clearing all personnel out before he had a chance to arrange things such as payment for soldiers etc. So I've a nice jaunt out to Tarakan as a result. But I'll have a couple of nice days rest at Long Berang before moving on. See if Mama can spoil me as she spoilt you there.

So I'll say cheerio for now, Jeff, and hope to run across you one of these days. All the best for Xmas and New Year, and I hope you arrive home for it. Wish me luck too will you?

Frank.

(N.B. My Friends – I sincerely miss them)
Frank Leckie departed this world April 1975, Christchurch, NZ.
Jeff Westley died at Berri, South Australia, 1995.
'Our lines grow shorter every day'

Appendix VI

THIS MEMOIR WAS RECORDED BY Lieutenant FRANK LECKIE VNZ 66570, AK256, CHRISTCHURCH

Operation 'Stallion V' – Weston – Sipitang – Brunei Bay – Borneo – June 8/11 1945

It was in January 1945 when we heard we were going into Borneo, that very much unknown place whose only claim to fame, as far as we knew, rested in its oil deposits and having the only White Rajah in the world – 'Brooke'. The only other small piece of knowledge we had was of the Dayak pirates who once roamed the coasts, and the question as to whether there was such an animal as the 'Wild man of Borneo'.

However, we settled down to training on the different special courses, the most interesting the classes in Malay language. Even now, reading the Malay greeting of 'Tabeh Tuan' in a book, brings back our first grappling with the language. But, strangely enough, it was not like trying to learn Latin or French because, within a couple of weeks we could string a sentence together. We grew more confident and started up conversations with the Malay boys in the camp. This certainly helped us, but equally provided them with a lot of amusement. But all good things must come to an end, and after eight weeks we passed out (of our course) with, we thought, a reasonable knowledge of most of the subjects including Malay. As it turned out later, this belief was not unfounded as we knew just enough to get by on, until we were out with a party of Malays and Dayaks with no interpreter around. Then we learned fast, but more of that later.

After Commando and para-training we travelled by air to the new forward base in the SWPA area – Morotai in the Halmaheras group of islands, one of the stepping stones South of the Philippines. It was here that we prepared for our entry into Borneo. Organising, equipping and training the party to gain confidence in each other came next. This first party, a rather mixed bag of operatives, consisted of three NZer's, one AIF and one Malay (Marouf), originally a schoolteacher in Kuala Lumpur, plus a guide from the area into which we were going.

We flew a few reconnaissance flights over Borneo to have a look around, with an overnight stop at Tarakan Island, off the North East Coast, where a landing had been made a few days before by the Australians. This Island, formerly a rather important centre for the Royal-Shell interests in the N.E.I., had received considerable attention by the RAAF and US Airforces prior to the Allied landings. It was interesting to see the results in the shattered storage tank areas. The Padre from the AIF HQ, kindly offered to show us over the area in the few hours available, and under his rather inappropriate escort, we jeeped over the island as far as the front line, if such a thing can exist in the jungle.

To an interested layman's eye, very little damage, if any, had been done on the pipe lines or wells. Whether this was by luck or good management we did not discover. It should have been very helpful to those who had to re-organise this field for reproduction at the end of hostilities.

A fortnight later we were on our way, on board a PBY 'Catalina' for the ten hour flight (Morotai/Brunei Bay, Borneo), with the thought 'Well this is the start. Wonder how it will end?' Time droned on. We dozed, we talked, and relieved the crew in the blisters. Suddenly we sighted Mt. Kinabalu in North-western Sabah, the mighty twin peaked monarch of 13,400 feet. The afternoon was almost gone, and we were scheduled to alight on our DZ just after nightfall. Our training was soon put to the test. Gear was assembled and prepared for when the 'Cat' settled herself on the calm waters of the Bay. We quickly dumped ourselves, equipment, arms and outboard motor in the now inflated rubber boat. Within ten minutes we were away.

'Mission Stallion V' was now in progress.

Above:
VNZ 271459 Sgt W.J.
Butt AKS 174 (R)

VNZ 66570 Lt F.J.
Leckie AK 256 (M)

WO.2 Roy Haley AIF
SM. Fraser Island (Aust)

Left:
VNZ 66570 Lt. F.J.
Leckie AK 256.
At Trentham Military
Camp 1940

Appendix VII

From: 9th. Div. AIF Ukong.   **August 1 1945**

2/17 Battalion.

To: Limbang 'Z' Operatives.

CO has visited here. He instructs as follows:

We are under a qualified cease fire order, and he will not send men or ammunition. I am sending you the last of your ammunition – we have an ample supply here. Asked that you keep us posted with facts as to Jap movements and to any reports as to his apparent intentions. When you draw conclusions from anything you see, could you support them with details of your observation? At the moment we are not to take active steps to stop the Jap, and all efforts are being made to produce proof of surrender. So we suggest that you, rather than taking active action against him, maintain close watch on his movements and keep us well posted. You will see it is preferred that the Japs be kept in his large body, rather than broken up into small groups.

This aspect may be hard to explain to the natives – it is their food which is being pilfered, but there it is.

If you or your force are seriously threatened, you should withdraw in this direction. Keep in mind the object required – this is to closely observe the enemy's movement and keep us well informed. Dayaks report that there has been more war between you and the Japs. Hope it is not too serious.

HQ. 2/17 AIF

Appendix VIII

06–2656308 W

06–2655192 Fax

06–2867244

Headquarters Special Forces

G–I–16

Russell Offices
Canberra ACT 2600
AUSTRALIA
1 November 1996

Mr F.A. Wigzell
1/28 Jellicoe Road
Murrays Bay
Auckland 1310
NEW ZEALAND.

Dear Sir,

I am a Major in the Australian Army and am planning (with another colleague, Bruce O'Connor) to walk through Borneo at the end of this year. Our aim is to follow (as many as possible) routes used by WW II Operation SEMUT operatives. I obtained your address from other former operatives. As you are aware, SEMUT conducted guerrilla warfare in conjunction with the allied amphibious landings. It is important for us to be as historically accurate as possible, as we wish to produce a 'Battlefield Bushwalking Guide' so that future generations (of Bruneians, Malaysians, Indonesians and Australians) can do both an adventurous trek, as well as a walk of historical importance. There were four separate SEMUT parties. SEMUT I worked in Kalimantan, Sabah and Sarawak (Limbang, Trusan and Padas Rivers), SEMUT II worked along the Baram, Tutoh and Tinjar Rivers, SEMUT III worked along the Rejang River, SEMUT IV worked around Bintulu and along the Kemena River. We are planning on two major treks in the period 11 Dec 96 to 23 Feb 97.

TREK ONE. Travel up either the Limbang or Tutoh Rivers to Ba Kelalan. From there we will go to Belaga via Long Lellang, Long Akah and Long Lobang. From there we will travel to Sibu. We will then get transport to Bintulu (probably with a small diversion to Mukuh) and travel up the Kemena river to Tubau, before returning to Brunei for a rest. This should take about four weeks.

TREK TWO. Travel from Menggalong to Mendelong, to Ulu Bole, to Eburu, Long Miau, Long Pa Sia, Semado, Pa Pala to Ba Kelalan. The next section I am still unsure of, but the aim is to get to Long Nawang, some 120 map miles to the south and just inside Kalimantan. One option is to cross into Kalimantan at Long Bawan and head down via Pa Kabak, Pa Oepan, Long Toea, Long Berini, Long Komoet, Long Dejali and Nahakramo to Long Nawang. The other option is to head south from Bareo inside the Sarawak border to Long Banga and cross into Kalimantan there. Either way, from Long Nawang we plan to head back to Malinau. There are a few options from here to get to Pensiangan in Sabah. One is to head north to Loembis via Long Boeloeh and Long Semeloemong. The other is to head west then north via Long Berang, Pa Silau, Long Malada, Wai Agoeng, Long Kama, Long Nuat, Long Apan and Long Selor to Loembis. From Pensiangan we would head to Sapong (location of 37th Japanese Army) before returning to Brunei. This will take a month. We are very keen to record your perspective of SEMUT, particularly the names of any guerrillas that you may be able to recall or are possibly still in contact with.

Yours sincerely,

Signed
Jim Truscott

JIM TRUSCOTT.

> Special Air Services Regiment
> Campbell Barracks
> Swanbourne Perth 6010.
> Australia.
> 13 October 1997.

Dear Frank,

As most of you know, I have been writing the enclosed Monograph for the last six months, since returning from Exercise Semut Retrace in Borneo. It is now all but finished, and I would appreciate your comments and advice before I submit it to Army's Doctrine Centre in Sydney for publication. Would you please correct any inaccuracies in the manuscript, and add additional comments and information where you think appropriate. Some aspects are sensitive as you will appreciate, and I specifically seek your advice in these areas. I have tried hard to provide a balanced view in all areas, but again seek your comments on areas which may need additional work.

I would certainly appreciate if you can check the addresses of known surviving operatives.

I also ask that if any of you have any additional photographs that I can include in the Pictorial section, that you may send them to me as soon as possible so that they can be scanned into the next text.

Yours Sincerely

Signed. *Jim Truscott*
Major Jim Truscott

NB: The Monograph on the above is yet to be published. This is part of same. ' As I walked through the mountainous interior of Borneo in late 1996 and early 1997, I was able to meet over 60 former guerrillas and put Semut's achievements into some sort of South West Pacific Theatre and Australian national perspective.' Really a Historical Manuscript.

Major Don Stott and Captain Bob Morton, Cairo – NZ Forces Club.

Major Don Stott, Captain Bob Morton, Lieutenant W. Wordley.

Appendix IX

In April 1941 Greece was invaded by German troops, having previously overrun Yugoslavia and Bulgaria. The Allies were quick to despatch a force of approximately 60,000 to assist the Greek Army against the onslaught of the German war machine. The 6th Australian Division fought gallantly in this campaign and resisted until ordered to evacuate the area. Main German units used in this theatre of operations were the hardened Paratroop divisions, who sustained heavy losses. Substantial numbers of Allied soldiers were evacuated by sea before the surrender. Many escaped into the hills and eventually joined the ELAS or EDES guerrilla forces.

On Crete, Don Stott, whilst serving with an Artillery Unit of the 2 NZEF, was wounded and became a POW. He was interned behind the wire at a camp on the outskirts of Athens. Transferred to the Kokinia POW Camp, he met up with another NZer, Gunner Bob Morton. After recovering from their wounds, both joined the local POW athletic club. Pole vaulting was their forte. With a low surrounding security barbed-wire fence of approximately two metres holding and containing the prisoners within its confines, so was born the plan for one of our most daring POW escapes during the Second World War. The plan was duly approved by the local escape committee, but with a little reservation relating to its success. When both members of the escape team had cleared the height factor of a little over two metres, and during an athletic meeting attended by all the guards of the area, Stott and Morton were to show off their skills. Instead of approaching the bar for a take-off, they instead ran directly at the perimeter fence, where members in the know of the attempted breakout had dug a pole trap and were partly covering it with their bodies. Both escapees made contact with the trap and cleared the wire obstacle, rolled on contact with the ground, recovered uninjured and headed for the secondary undergrowth nearby.

The watching German camp guards were so utterly amazed and astounded at encountering this situation, that not a single shot was fired before the escapees vanished into the protection of the undergrowth. Here the Kiwis soon encountered a group of Greek police who came to their immediate assistance on this occasion, by discharging their pistols in the air, and indicating to the prisoners a direction for flight from the area. Shouting and shooting off their hardware at random, the Greek police proceeded in the opposite direction to deceive the Germans. Jack Hinton, the NZ VC holder who was also a POW in this camp, witnessed the whole escape. With the help of the local inhabitants the pair survived for several months on little food. The loyal Greeks finally supplied them with a small fishing boat, and on their third attempt they managed to cross the Mediterranean Sea and return to 2 NZEF Divisional HQ at Alexandria in Egypt. SOE were soon advised of their escapade and requested that they be seconded to that unit. Both volunteered to re-enter into Greece with the proposed British Military Mission. After instruction in SOE methods and procedures, they undertook a couple of missions in the desert and were lucky to survive these operations. The DZ area which they were to chute into and report from, was totally occupied by the enemy, and the aircraft delivering them just narrowly avoided being shot down whilst on a low approach run.

On being parachuted back into Greece, Major Stott's main objective with the British Military Mission there was to destroy the Asopos Viaduct, and deny the entry into Athens of heavy rail traffic by the Germans. This was the major supply route for Rommel's Africa Corps.

All previous reconnaissances had failed to locate a safe approach to the target. The Asopos Viaduct was situated in the eastern Roumeli, on high Mt Vardoussia, 200 metres in length and a vital link in the chain of supply lines between Solonika and Athens. The viaduct joined two mountain tunnels over a precipitous chasm 100 metres deep through which a raging torrent of water flowed. The location was heavily guarded with machine-gun emplacements and swept with searchlights during darkness. The river approach had never been accepted by the Germans as an area requiring special guarding against the enemy saboteurs. Stott and his party on their third reconnaissance encountered a severe obstruction which required specialist climbing equipment, to enable them to continue with the operation. They now returned to base, and contacted SOE Cairo by W/T, to forward their requirements urgently. A week later the climbing gear of ladders, ropes, spikes etc. duly arrived by air. Operation Washing was now ready to go back into the field.

Retracing their approach through the steep walls and rocky terrain of the river bed, the last obstacle was conquered with the help of the newly arrived equipment. Proceeding a further 100 metres up the gorge, the advance section rounded a corner, and there, directly in front of them was their objective, the Asopos Viaduct spanning the mighty ravine. During the night of 19 June the party advanced towards the viaduct with all the necessary explosives to complete their mission. A reconnaissance around the immediate area of the viaduct disclosed a German sentry on a high observation point. He was quickly and silently disposed of and eliminated with a stiletto, then pushed over a cliff. This action was not observed by the German patrols on the viaduct. Dodging the spotlights, the operatives planted the demolition charges on the main support piers, setting time fuses for 0130 hrs 20th. They then, after completion and not being detected, retraced their steps to the last obstacle encountered and anxiously awaited the termination of the detonator time settings on the fuses. 0130 hrs came and went. Nothing eventuated.

The operatives asked themselves, had they correctly set the charges? Finally at 0205 hrs it happened. Mission members nervously awaited the early dawn to observe their handiwork. With great relief all sighted that the centre span of the viaduct had completely disappeared into the gorge. Operation Washing was now completed, and the party returned to base without any casualties.

For this action Major Don Stott was recommended for the VC by Brigadier Miles of the British Military Mission in Greece. As not a shot was fired during this successful mission, GHQ Middle East was only prepared to issue a DSO award. A bar to his DSO was approved at a later date for his peace overtures to the Germans in that area also.

In 1993 the Local RSA Club on the North Shore of Auckland, approved the naming of their new wing as the 'DON STOTT MEMORIAL RESTAURANT', in honour of their decorated DSO & Bar former resident. Dedication took place in June of that year.

Lieutenant Bob Tapper (AK 253, 'Z' SOA NZ.) who represented the War Graves Commission in the Balikpapan Theatre of Operations SOA, investigated the disappearance of Major D. Stott and Captain L. McMillan. He interrogated numerous personnel of the Japanese Occupational Force at Balikpapan and Coastal Defences, but failed to obtain any information about their landing on the shores, or whether any bodies were recovered in this designated area. If there had been any landings and prisoners taken, the natives would have been the first to know, for such is their 'bush telegraphy' in this country. A Court of Enquiry at the end of hostilities gave the verdict that Major D. Stott and Captain L. McMillan were 'Lost at Sea, Presumed Drowned'.

Bibliography

Amar, Myriam S. (1990), 'List of Special Operations, Australia and personnel involved during 1942–1945', Canberra, Australia: Archives and Historical Studies Section, Department of Defence.

Courtney, G.B. MBE MC (1993), *Silent Fleet – The History of 'Z' Special Unit Operations 1942–1945*, Australia: McPherson's Printing Group.

Griffiths-Marsh, Roland (1990), *The Six Penny Soldier*, Australia: North Ryde.

Harrisson, Major Tom (1959), *World Within, A Borneo Story*, London: Cresset Press.

Horton, D.C. (1983), *Ring of Fire*, UK: Biddles Ltd.

Long, Bob (1989), *'Z' Special Unit's Secret War – Operation Semut I*, Hornsby, NSW: Transpareon Press.

McDonald, Gabrielle (1991), *New Zealand's Secret Heroes – SOE & SOA*, Reed Publishers.

McKie, Ronald (1960), *The Heroes*, Sydney: Angus & Robinson.

Powell, Prof Alan (1996), *War by Stealth – Australians and the Allied Intelligence Bureau 1942–1945*, Melbourne: Melbourne University Press.

Ramsay Silver, Lynette (1991), *The Heroes of Rimau*, London.

Sutlive, Vincent H. Jr (1992), *Tun Jugah of Sarawak*, Malaysia: Sarawak Literary Society.

Waddy, Rowan (1995), *On Operations with 'Z' Special Unit*, Part Three, New South Wales: Fifth Edition.

Wigzell, Frank (1995), 'New Zealand Army Involvement Special Operations Australia, AIB', Auckland.

Glossary of Terms

AGAS	SANDFLY (CODE NAME OF OPERATIONS BNB)
AGH	ARMY GENERAL HOSPITAL
AIB	ALLIED INTELLIGENCE BUREAU
AIF	AUSTRALIAN IMPERIAL FORCE
AMF	AUSTRALIAN MILITARY FORCE
ARAK	RICE ALCOHOL DISTILLED FROM BORAK
ATIS	AUSTRALIAN TRANSLATION & INTERPRETATION SERVICE.
AUSTER	LIGHT SINGLE-ENGINED AIRCRAFT
BBCAU	BRITISH BORNEO CIVIL ADMINISTRATION UNIT
BEAUFIGHTER	CONVERTED BEAUFORT BOMBER
BETTY	JAPANESE LIGHT BOMBER USED FOR STORES DROPPING
BIF	BORNEO INTERIOR FORCE (HQ SEMUT I)
BORAK	FERMENTED DRINK MADE FROM RICE OR TAPIOCA ROOT
BOSTON	WIRELESS TRANSCEIVER OPERATED BY HAND GENERATOR
BUKIT	HILL
CATALINA	TWIN-ENGINED RECONNAISSANCE SEAPLANE (PBY US.)
COMPO	COMPOSITE RATION PACK IN 5 GAL. SEALED TINS, ARMY 03 ISSUE
DC3	AMERICAN TWIN-ENGINED TRANSPORT AIRCRAFT
DZ	DROPPING ZONE
DI-SANA	THERE
EUREKA REBECCA	GROUND TO AIR SIGNAL BEACON
FELO	FAR EASTERN LIAISON OFFICE
F/LT	FLIGHT LIEUTENANT
200 FLIGHT	B-24 LIBERATORS RAAF ADAPTED FOR PARACHUTING & STORPEDO DROPS
F/O	FLYING OFFICER
FUJINO TAI	JAPANESE IN THE LIMBANG WHO WOULD NOT SURRENDER, COMMANDED BY CAPT. FUJINO
GANTANG	RICE MEASURE
GURU	TEACHER

HARBURY	'Z' SPECIAL HQ MELBOURNE, AUSTRALIA
HUTAN	JUNGLE
JAMBAN	TOILET
JAYWICK	SUCCESSFUL RAID ON SINGAPORE HARBOUR BY FOL-BOATS 1943
KALIMANTAN	DUTCH BORNEO, NOW INDONESIAN BORNEO
KAMPONG	VILLAGE
KAPALA	HEAD MAN OF SMALL VILLAGE
KAPAL TERBANG	AEROPLANE
KEPALA	HEAD
KEMPEI TAI	JAPANESE SECRET POLICE
KIAI	TEACHER RELIGIOUS OR SCHOLAR
KIJANG	DEER SAMBA-SEKA ETC.
KUALA	RIVER MOUTH OR ESTUARY
LEKAS	HURRY QUICKLY
MCR I	SMALL BATTERY HAND-HELD RECIEVER
MSC	MOTOR SUBMERSIBLE CANOE
PARANG	NATIVE SWORD GENERAL PURPOSE ALSO
PENGHULU	HEADMAN OF A SMALL DISTRICT
PISANG GORENG	FRIED BANANA
PUKUL	TO STRIKE TO BEAT (RADIO OPERATOR)
RSM	REGIMENTAL SERGEANT MAJOR
RUMAH	HOUSE BESAR = BIG HOUSE
RV	RENDEZVOUS
SAKIT PERUT	STOMACH ACHE
SAKIT KEPALA	HEADACHE
SAMSU	DISTILLED SPIRIT MADE FROM BANANAS
SB	SLEEPING BEAUTY
SELAMAT TINGGAL	GREETINGS TO ONE LEFT BEHIND
SEMUT	ANT (CODE NAME FOR BORNEO OPS.)
SITREP	SITUATION REPORT
SMG	SUB-MACHINE GUN
SRD	SERVICES RECONNAISSANCE DEPARTMENT
STORPEDOS	CYLINDRICAL CONTAINERS FOR DROPPING STORES
SULAP	SMALL HUT OR SHELTER BUILT ON THE GROUND
SUMPITAN	DEADLY BLOWPIPE WITH POISONED DARTS
SUNGEI	RIVER

TABEK	GREETINGS
TEMPAT BUNOH	PLACE OF AMBUSH
UBI KAYU	EDIBLE ROOT OF CASSAVA/TAPIOCA PLANT
ULU	THE INTERIOR UNKNOWN
US	UNSERVICEABLE
WELROD	SILENT SINGLE-SHOT PISTOL

Sungei Limbang

Rumah Bilong

Original longhouse on the southern side of the Limbang river. Easily accessible to the retreating and marauding Japanese. Temporary-type *sulap* dwelling erected on the protected northern side of the river to accommodate the five families of Kepala Bilong's area.

Rumah Kadu

The main longhouse on the northern side of the river housing 35/40 families. Penghulu Kadu's residence – perched about ten feet above the surface of the ground for coolness.

Rumah Badak

Situated downriver from Kadu, on the northern bank. Kapala Badak was one of the first Ibans to walk into the *ulu*, Belawit, and offer his services in that area to 'Z' HQ. About twenty families resided there.

The Ibans and Dayaks from these longhouses were of the Tabon tribe. Great fighters and personal servants and bodyguards to the ruling 'Brooke' Regime of Sarawak before the war.

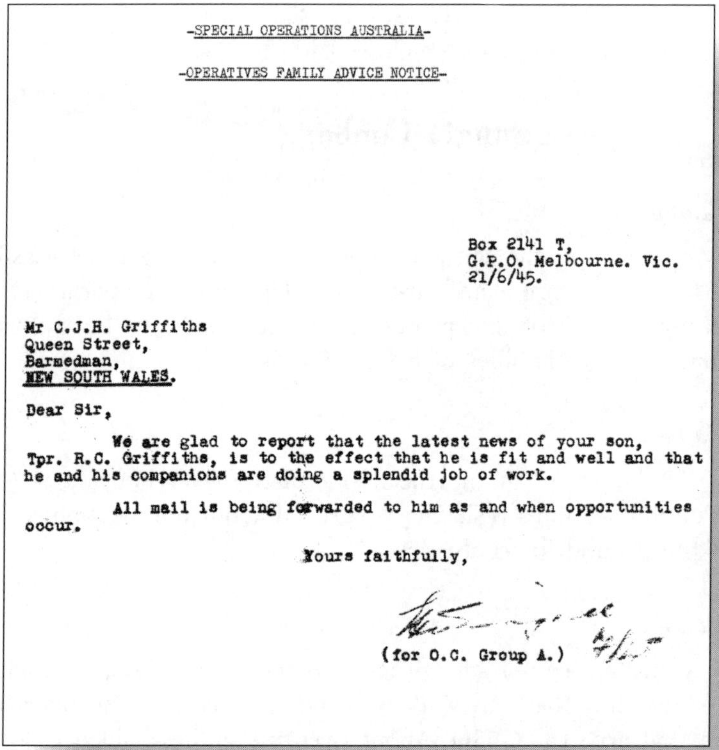

-SPECIAL OPERATIONS AUSTRALIA-

-OPERATIVES FAMILY ADVICE NOTICE-

Box 2141 T,
G.P.O. Melbourne. Vic.
21/6/45.

Mr C.J.H. Griffiths
Queen Street,
Barmedman,
NEW SOUTH WALES.

Dear Sir,

    We are glad to report that the latest news of your son,
Tpr. R.C. Griffiths, is to the effect that he is fit and well and that
he and his companions are doing a splendid job of work.

    All mail is being forwarded to him as and when opportunities
occur.

    Yours faithfully,

(for O.C. Group A.)

The Australians of 'Z' Special Unit had the above notice forwarded to their
'Next of Kin', advising them that their operative family member, whilst on
a mission, was fit and well. We could not forward mail from inside
Japanese-occupied areas. New Zelanders were given the information that
the above would also apply to them. This never eventuated for many of us,
causing much concern in family circles.

All correspondence should be addressed:
Chief of Defence Force
HQ New Zealand Defence Force
Private Bag, Wellington, NZ

Telephone: 4960-999

NEW ZEALAND
DEFENCE
FORCE

In reply please quote:

1325/1

22 August 1990

Mr C. Bennett
Television New Zealand
PO Box 3819
AUCKLAND

Dear Mr Bennett,

Captain Bassett forwarded your facsimile message of 10 August 1990 concerning New Zealand involvement in the Z Special Force during World War II to me for action.

It has been public knowledge for many years that members of the New Zealand Armed Forces served with Z Special Force, which at that time was generally known by its cover name, the Services Reconnaissance Department. Four members of the Second New Zealand Expeditionary Force died while serving with Z Special Force. At least one New Zealander was involved in Z Special Force operations in Borneo during 1944. We have recently been in touch with this man, and if you would like to contact him you should send a letter to us, which we will then forward to him. It is necessary to follow this procedure in order to protect the privacy of the individual concerned.

To the best of my knowledge New Zealand personnel serving with Z Special Force were treated in exactly the same way as other members of the New Zealand Armed Forces with respect to honours, awards and decorations.

Two works which contain much useful information about Z Special Force are, T. Harrison's World Within: A Borneo Story, (published London, 1959) and D.C. Horton's Ring of Fire: Australian Guerrilla Operations Against the Japanese in World War II, (published London, 1983).

Yours sincerely,

J.A.B. CRAWFORD
for Chief of Defence Force

GJB/KB

AUSTRALIAN ARMY

Telephone

CENTRAL ARMY RECORDS OFFICE
356 St. Kilda Road
MELBOURNE VIC 3004

326 5655

In reply please quote

Info Svc/R755-2-5

18 September 1989

Mr F.A. Wigzell
28 Jellicoe Road
MURRAYS BAY 10   AUCKLAND
NEW ZEALAND

Dear Mr Wigzell,

1.   I refer to your enquiry received at this office on
13 June 1989, our acknowledgement card number 12539/89.

2.   The records held by this office are of a personal nature
of former Australian Army servicemen only. This office does not hold
any records of your service whilst attached to the Australian Army.

3.   The Australian War Memorial in Canberra holds war diaries
for many World War II units in which you may have received mention.

4.   I regret our inability to assist you.

Yours sincerely,

S.W. WILSON
Warrant Officer
for Commanding Officer

All correspondence should be addressed:
Chief of Defence Force
HQ New Zealand Defence Force
Private Bag, Wellington, NZ

Telephone: 4960-999

NEW ZEALAND
DEFENCE
FORCE

In reply please quote:

1325/1

27 November 1990

Mr F.A. Wigzell
28 Jellicoe Road
Murrays Bay 10
AUCKLAND

Dear Mr Wigzell,

Thank you for your letter of 20 November 1990 concerning
New Zealanders who served with 'Z' Special Unit. I found the
information in your letter most interesting. I had not realized
that the New Zealand Armed Forces had provided so many men for this
unit.

Yours sincerely,

J.A.B. CRAWFORD
for Chief of Defence Force

28 Jellicoe Road
Murrays Bay
Auckland 1310

FAW/86-94/01

14th July 1994.
Phone:- 09-4794176.

Internal Affairs Dept.,
Historical Branch
Private Bag
Wellington.

Attention Mr. Ian McGibbon.

Dear Sir,

Re New Zealand involvement 'Z' Special Unit-SOA-AIB-WW.11.

I have recently read with interest your statement in the 'New Zealand Herald', that your historical branch is working on the histories of New Zealand's involvement in J Force and the Korean, Malaysian and Vietnam conflicts. It would be a serious loss to this country if these were not recorded, and unavailable for reference in the years 2000 plus.

Enclosed you will find parts of my latest manuscript relating to a group of New Zealand Army personnel seconded to 'Z' Special Unit Australia in 1944. To date, the NZDF and Government have never released any information relating to the above named group, although clearance was given in the late 80's withdrawing the 'Official Secret's' restrictions placed on all operatives involved.

Recently I have recorded the involvement of the eleven 'Signals Personnel' in the group seconded to 'Z' from 2NZEF, for inclusion of the NZ Signals Corps History which is just being completed. Brigadier A.T.Mortiboy has acknowledged receipt of the document. As the first Para Commando group from NZ to have members chuted into enemy occupied territory in the SWPA, it must have some importance in military history as being the forerunner of our SAS, who operated in Malaysia during the 50's.

As the only extant member of the group capable of relating the group's experience at this point in time, I sincerely hope that my research which is now complete, will finally be accepted and recorded in the 'Official WW11 History' where it really belongs. My operative friends will then be known within their own country.

Photographs and other material in my possession are available if you wish to sight same.

Yours faithfully,

F.A.Wigzell. AKS.173.

Historical Branch, Department of Internal Affairs

Te Puna Korero Tuku Iho A Te Tari Taiwhenua

21 July 1994

Mr F.A. Wigzell,
28 Jellicoe Rd,
Murrays Bay,
AUckland 1310.

Dear Mr Wigzell,

Thank you very much for your letter of 14 July, enclosing a copy of your manuscript about New Zealand involvement in the Z Special Unit.

The activities of this unit deserve to be carefully recorded, and you have performed a service in bringing together the material. Your manuscript certainly adds to the history of New Zealand's participation in the Second World War, and will be most useful to researchers in future.

I am afraid that there is no way in which we can directly publish it so as to ensure a wider circulation. We do, however, have a scheme whereby we provide monetary grants to encourage publishers to produce books that will have a limited market. Your first step, if publication is what you seek, would be to find a publisher, who would then submit an application for a grant. I have enclosed a brochure which sets out the scheme in more detail.

Thanks again for taking the trouble to contact me about this matter. I am returning your manuscript with this letter. In the event that you are unable to find a publisher, I would strongly recommend that you deposit a copy in the Defence Library in Wellington.

Yours sincerely,

Ian McGibbon
Senior Historian

State Insurance Tower, Waring Taylor Street, PO Box 805, Wellington, New Zealand. Phone (04) 495 7200, Fax (04) 495 7212